ACHTUNG BABY

The German Art of Raising
Self-Reliant Children

Sara Zaske

piatkus

PIATKUS

First published in the US in 2018 by Picador
First published in Great Britain in 2018 by Piatkus

1 3 5 7 9 10 8 6 4 2

A CIP catalogue record for this book
is available from the British Library.

ISBN 978-0-349-41855-1

Printed and bound in Great Britain by
Clays Ltd, St Ives plc

Papers used by Piatkus are from well-managed forests
and other responsible sources.

FSC
www.fsc.org

MIX
Paper from
responsible sources
FSC® C104740

Piatkus
An imprint of
Little, Brown Book Group
Carmelite House
50 Victoria Embankment
London EC4Y 0DZ

An Hachette UK Company
www.hachette.co.uk

www.improvementzone.co.uk

To Zac, Sophia, and Ozzie

About the Author

SARA ZASKE is an American writer who lived in Berlin for six and a half years. Her articles on her family's experiences in Germany have appeared on Time.com, in the *New York Times* and in Germany's largest Sunday paper, *Bild am Sontag*. She now lives in Idaho with her husband and two children.

Contents

ACHTUNG BABY

Modern Germany

Few people smile on the trains in Berlin. By some unwritten rule, everyone sits silent and straight-faced on the S-Bahns and U-Bahns that run above and below the city. If you see people who are smiling, chances are they're tourists. If they're talking and laughing loudly, chances are they're American.

One gray day in Berlin, my daughter, Sophia, and I were talking and laughing loudly on an S-Bahn full of quiet German passengers. Sophia was two and a half and super chatty. We had recently arrived in Berlin, and everything was new to her. I wasn't about to shush her as she commented on the things passing by her window: the trees, the stations, another train, the cars on the road. She saw a bus, which was her cue to launch into her favorite song, "Wheels on the Bus," at top volume. The wheels really go *round* in Sophia's version. I glanced at the old woman across from us, trying to remember the proper way to phrase an apology, when the most amazing thing happened: she smiled.

Finally, I thought, *someone appreciates how adorable my daughter is.*

Then, the woman opened her purse and pulled out a small piece of candy. She didn't even look at me. She handed it directly to Sophia.

I panicked. I hadn't yet taught Sophia not to trust strangers with candy! In America, people just don't offer candy to children. I battled conflicting impulses: grab Sophia and storm off? Or be polite to the first stranger who had made a friendly gesture?

Sophia turned and held the candy up to me, a huge smile on her face. I let politeness, and logic, prevail: this German grandmother was clearly not trying to kidnap my child, and there was no chance a razor blade could fit in a piece of candy that small. I took it from Sophia, unwrapped it, tried not to be too obvious about examining it, and handed it back to my daughter. She popped it into her mouth—and, amazingly, didn't die.

This experience taught me two things: first, Berliners didn't know about "stranger danger," and second, my assumption that Germans were unsmiling, unfriendly people who were harsh with children might not be entirely true.

As I would learn over the next six and a half years in Berlin, much of what I thought I knew about Germans was wrong—especially the way they approach raising children. The parents I met were almost the polar opposite of the stereotype of the overbearing, strict German parent. In fact, compared to today's American parents who constantly supervise their children, they were positively relaxed.

When my daughter turned three, we invited a family we had met in our neighborhood to a picnic at a local park. It was a sunny spring day, and the park was beautiful with long stretches of green lawn bordered by tall trees. We chose a spot close to an enclosed playground, which had a tall stone wall in front of it. Shortly after arriving, our friends' two children asked if they could go to the playground.

"Sure," their mother said.

"Can I go too?" Sophia asked. I agreed, and all three of them went running off, two three-year-old girls and a five-year-old boy. They disappeared behind the wall, out of sight. No one else moved. Their mother started arranging plates on the picnic blanket. Her husband was talking with mine as he set up the barbecue. Feeling like I was missing something, I got up. "Um . . . I'll go," I said.

"Oh!" the other mother said. "They'll be fine. They play here all the time."

"It's just that—Sophia might need help," I said and followed the kids.

I remember thinking how strange it was that this couple didn't watch their children on the playground. Then I noticed all the other unsupervised kids running around the park. Some parents were watching over babies and toddlers, but most of the adults were at picnic tables or sitting on blankets talking with each other while their children came and went.

This was normal behavior in Berlin. Parents didn't hover over their children on playgrounds, many of which feature large structures like giant wooden boats and towering pyramids made of rope and metal—way more dangerous than the typical American playground of plastic and padded foam. In Berlin, school-age kids also walk to school, parks, and stores alone, or with only their peers as company. Adults rarely interfere in their children's play, not even their fights, preferring to let them work it out themselves.

It's part of the cultural value of *selbständigkeit*, or self-reliance. In America, we might call this "free range" parenting, but in Germany, it's normal parenting. German parents believe that independence is good for children, that handling risk is a necessary part of growing up. This means they trust their children with more tasks as they grow older and supervise them less. Children are also assumed to be capable of making some decisions for themselves even at a young age, including whether or not to take a piece of candy from a nice lady on a train.

Beyond the Stereotype

Whenever I tell my American friends and family about how much freedom German parents give their children, they react with surprise and disbelief. I usually end up reminding them how long it has been since the end of World War II. Because it is true that German parents were strict and authoritarian—in the 1940s. They have changed quite a bit since then.

Many Americans' idea of Germany is still fixed at World War II. The conflict has become somewhat of an obsession in the United States, judging by the sheer volume of books and movies we've produced around the war and the Holocaust. Some historians have even argued that there has been an "Americanization" of German history, which oversimplifies the Nazi years and culturally appropriates the Holocaust. *New York Times* columnist Roger Cohen wrote in 1999 about this tendency, recounting how American tourists were disappointed to find out there weren't gas chambers at the Buchenwald concentration camp. "Before, people did not want to see the truth," said Volkhard Knigge, director of the Buchenwald memorial. "Now they want to see what they expect to see, and we have to disappoint them and show how rich and complicated history is."

Another persistent, oversimplified American idea is that our country was the lone rescuing hero of Europe during World War II, even though historical facts don't support this interpretation. We conveniently forget that it was the Soviet Army, not American forces, that took Berlin and forced Hitler from power. According to the National World War II Museum in New Orleans, more than 8.8 million Soviet soldiers lost their lives fighting in World War II, a number that dwarfs American and British military casualties, which numbered closer to 400,000 each. This fact should not diminish the sacrifice of our soldiers; rather, we should expand our concept of victory to include the significant contributions of our allies at the time.

Blame it on poor history education, exaggerated patriotism, or inaccurate Hollywood movies, but some Americans can't be swayed from this heroic vision even when presented with evidence to the contrary. A friend of mine who works as a tour guide in Berlin told me that the American tourists she takes to World War II monuments and museums remain convinced that it was the United States that won the war. British and Russian tourists, of course, have other opinions.

America as the hero of World War II is so entrenched in our culture that perhaps it is hard to let the other side of that equation, the enemy, Nazi Germany, become a thing of the past. To change our idea of modern Germans, we might also have to change our idea of ourselves.

A Short Historical Update

Most Germans alive today were not born by the time World War II ended. That's not to say they haven't been affected by it—quite the opposite. Learning about the country's role in the war and the Holocaust is part of every German's education. As a result, the culture at large has undergone a major transformation, which was highlighted by the German response to the recent refugee crisis in Europe.

In 2015, while other European countries tried to block the influx of immigrants fleeing conflicts in places such as Syria and Iraq, Germany welcomed them. Average citizens came out in droves to greet the incoming refugees at train stations. They donated money, food, and clothing—so much that police in Munich had to ask them to stop. Some people even opened their homes to refugee families.

At the start of the crisis, Chancellor Angela Merkel said that any Syrian entering the country would be granted asylum. "Germany is a strong country," she said in August 2015. "We have already accomplished so much. We can do it!"

That year Germany took in nearly 1 million refugees alone, more than 1 percent of the country's population of 82 million. To compare, if the United States with its population of roughly 319 million had done the same, we would have taken in more than 3 million refugees. Instead President Obama offered to raise the limit of Syrian refugees admitted to the United States to 10,000, and even that amount was met with opposition.

The newly elected President Trump went even further and tried to stop all incoming refugees by implementing a contested immigration ban his first week in office.

In Germany, assimilating such a large refugee group has not gone smoothly, and the influx stoked fears of terrorism and helped fuel the rise of an anti-immigrant political party, the AfD (Alternative for Germany). However, the initial German response to the refugee crisis was remarkable and, many thought, uncharacteristic. Germany has also so far resisted the wave of right-wing populism that caused the United Kingdom to exit the European Union and propelled Donald Trump into power in the United States. Some have even called Germany the last defender of liberal democracy and its chancellor the new leader of the free world—in a stunning twist of history. Yet Germany's relative openness to refugees and resistance to right-wing demagoguery shouldn't be all that surprising— if we had paid much attention to the changes in German culture post– World War II.

At the end of the war, an estimated 14 million Germans were refugees themselves. Many were expelled from eastern parts of Europe or fled the advance of the Soviet army. Postwar Germany was divided up and occupied by foreign powers, one of which didn't leave for more than forty years. East Germans continued to flee to the West long after the war had ended: an estimated 1.65 million had left the East by the time the Berlin Wall was built in 1961. All this means that a sizable portion of modern Germans remember being refugees themselves or heard about the experience from older friends and relatives.

The "economic miracle" that followed World War II in the 1950s re-built the West German economy and the country's optimism, shaped in no small part by America's financial and political influence. Historian Hagen Schulze notes that in 1957, the Christian Democrat Party (the fore-runner of the CDU party that Merkel now leads) successfully campaigned with a slogan that meant "Affluence for everybody," based on a belief that anyone who worked hard should be able to succeed—a sentiment that should sound familiar to American ears. This period also marked the beginning of the "de-Nazification" of Germany, an effort that was not con-sidered completely successful by many of the generation that followed. The new government also established an agency for civic education, now called the *Bundeszentrale für politische Bildung* (BPB), which is specifically de-signed to "educate the German people about democratic principles and prevent any moves to re-establish a totalitarian regime."

The youth movement of the 1960s sought to make a more dramatic break with the Nazi past. Like their peers in the United States, West German students took to the streets to protest the Vietnam War, but their rebellion against their parents' generation went even further. The German youth saw their elders as responsible for the atrocities of World War II and the Holocaust. They rejected almost everything their parents represented: their authority, their government, and their values, including how they raised their children.

In the meantime, East Germans were dealing with an oppressive Soviet-controlled government that spied on its own people, restricted their movements, and limited their choices. The power plays between the United States and Soviet Union ultimately freed East Germany, but as Schulze points out, it was the East Germans themselves whose protests in 1989 tipped the balance and brought down the Berlin Wall. While Germany has been reunified for more than twenty-five years, many of today's influential modern Germans grew up in the East, including Chancellor Merkel, and they took the lessons from that time to heart.

All these political and cultural events have affected how Germans raise their children.

The youth protest movement of the 1960s brought anti-authoritarian ideas to child care. In Frankfurt, Monika Seifert started *kinderläden*, day care centers, which emphasized "repression-free" education, a philosophy that deliberately set itself against the old "German virtues of obedience, diligence, modesty, and cleanliness." Seifert's anti-authoritarian theory basically held that children should rule themselves—or run wild, depending on your perspective.

The anti-authoritarian kinderläden movement had its share of critics, and today, the parenting norm has moved more to the middle. Regardless, super strict, authoritarian parenting is widely rejected in today's Germany. For example, in 2000, Germany outlawed corporal punishment of children entirely: spanking a child is considered a crime, whether in school or at home. In the United States, the practice is still allowed at home in all fifty states, and nineteen still allow corporal punishment in schools.

In Germany, the legal and cultural shift has made corporal punishment all but a thing of the past. In a 2009 Allensbach Institute poll, only 7 percent of young Germans, ages sixteen to twenty-nine, reported being spanked by their parents. In contrast, a 2013 Harris Poll found that 87 percent of Americans were spanked as children, and 67 percent of current parents said they have spanked their own children—even though extensive research shows that corporal punishment not only doesn't work to get children to comply with their parents' rules but is also linked to a range of long-term problems, including increased aggression, anti-social behavior, and mental-health and cognitive problems. This is according to an analysis of fifty years of research on the subject, which experts from the University of Texas and the University of Michigan published in the *Journal of Family Psychology* in 2016. So despite the lingering "strict" stereotype, today's German parents take a gentler approach to raising their children than their American peers do.

The current German approach to parenting is by no means uniform, and it is complicated by regional differences, especially between the East and West. While under communist rule, East German educators and parents emphasized the values of relatedness, group conformity, and responsibility to their community, as opposed to parents in the West who prized developing children's autonomy, according to a comparison study of child-rearing goals published in the *International Journal of Adolescence and Youth* in 2012.

Germany's reunification in 1989 brought the values of the whole country closer to the West's model, but many attitudes from the East still persist, creating a culture that stresses both independence and responsibility to others. Nowhere was this parenting mix more apparent than in the once-divided city of Berlin, and my little family unwittingly landed right in the heart of it.

I knew precious little about German history before we arrived in Berlin. I mistakenly thought that this country, as part of the developed Western world, would have a similar parenting culture to my own. To be honest, I didn't have much self-awareness of my own cultural norms when it comes to being a parent.

Like many modern American mothers, I was constantly searching for that elusive balance between work and family. I wanted to have children but hoped to continue a writing career. I had also internalized the impossible cultural expectations of the ideal, self-sacrificing mom who places her children above all else.

I wanted to raise my children to be strong, independent, free individuals—all very American values. Yet I tended to use paradoxical parenting practices: constantly correcting my children, overemphasizing their academic achievement, and closely supervising them to ensure their safety. Moving to Germany made me realize how American these practices were—and how misguided.

I remember a moment when I was running through the streets of Berlin, chasing after my two kids, who were both on bikes and going much too fast for my liking. I shouted at them. "*Achtung*, kids!" Which I intended to mean "Be careful!" My children eventually stopped, looking more worried about my reaction than what they had been doing. As I struggled to catch my breath and detail my rules around bikes and speed, I realized how awfully hard I was trying to control them. I had rarely heard a German parent or teacher shout "Achtung" at children, a term usually reserved for strong danger. They have greater trust in their children's ability to look out for themselves. In the face of this difference, I started to question my need for constant vigilance. What was I so worried about? Why was I so anxious when they were not?

The Culture of Control

I had always considered myself a relaxed parent, but living in Berlin showed me how much I had absorbed of the modern American parenting style. Many U.S. adults who were born before 1980 grew up with a great deal more freedom than children do today. We walked to school alone and played outside until it got dark. We had hours of free time and could roam our neighborhoods with only peers for company.

Things have changed drastically in the past few decades, and many Americans believe that primary-school-age children need constant supervision. Some call this "overparenting" or "helicopter parenting," but these terms only touch on the larger nature of the problem. What Americans are doing to our children is much more dangerous and pervasive.

We've created a culture of control. In the name of safety and academic achievement, we have stripped kids of fundamental rights and freedoms: the freedom to move, to be alone for even a few minutes, to take risks, to play, to think for themselves—and it's not just parents who are doing this. It's culture-wide. It's the schools, which have cut or minimized recess or free play and control children's time even at home by assigning hours of homework. It's the intense sports teams and extracurricular activities that fill up children's evenings and weekends. It's our exaggerated media that makes it seem like a child can be abducted by a stranger at any time—when in reality such kidnappings are extremely rare.

Mostly the culture of control is created by average people: our neighbors, friends, relatives, and even complete strangers who feel compelled to shame parents or even call the police if a child is left alone for a few minutes. These actions go way beyond "helicoptering." The helicopters have landed. The army is on the ground, and our children are surrounded by people trying to control them.

Our current parenting culture goes against everything we Americans supposedly believe in as the "home of the free and the brave." Instead we are instilling the opposite in our children: subjugation and fear. We are inhibiting their ability to grow up. There's increasing evidence that our young adults are having trouble separating from their parents and that their mental and emotional problems have increased.

It doesn't have to be this way. Ironically, Germany, the land once known for authoritarianism, today provides a compelling example for how we might do things differently.

Why German Parenting Matters

It is not easy to ignore what happens in Germany. I've heard American critics often dismiss successful policies and practices of European countries—for example, universal health care in Denmark or the great education system in Finland—because they have small and relatively uniform populations. You can't say the same about Germany, a country geographically the size of the state of Montana with more than 82 million people crowded into it. (That's more people than the population of California, Texas, and New York put together). Germany is also increasingly diverse: 16.4 million people, more than 20 percent of the population, come from an immigrant background.

Germany is also a world leader—economically and politically—and regularly appears at the top of lists of the most admired countries in the world, even beating the United States. This is an incredible rebound from the country that suffered a crushing defeat in World War II and was universally reviled for the crimes of the Holocaust. Germans have grappled with their Nazi past and actively looked for ways to ensure it never happens again, including changing how they raise and educate their children. If today's Germans feel it is important to promote their children's independence, then we Americans might do well to take a hard look at reasons why we do not.

I don't intend to hold the entire country up as a uniform model. Germany has a range of regional and cultural differences, and just like people everywhere, German parents have a variety of opinions and parenting styles. However, during the six years I lived in Berlin, I did discover some interesting attitudes and practices that should be useful for American parents.

A good portion of this book will focus on the city of Berlin, not just because the majority of my experiences occurred in that city, but also because the capital city holds a unique position within Germany and, arguably, the world at large. As the epicenter of a reunified country, it represents the melding of the cultures from the former communist-controlled East with the more capitalist, U.S.-aligned West.

Berlin is not Paris. It is not a fancy place—in some places it's downright gritty—and half of it seems to be under construction most of the time. As the city's former mayor Klaus Wowereit once famously quipped: Berlin is "poor but sexy." Young people, artists, and tech innovators are drawn to the city's low rents and open culture. Berlin also attracts many families. It is a city in the process of being reborn culturally and literally:

while Germany has a low birthrate overall, Berlin is in the midst of a baby boom.

While some of the attitudes I highlight in this book are specific to Berlin, many of the parenting practices are common throughout the country, such as encouraging young children to walk to school and talking to them honestly about the past. Whether in Berlin or in Munich, in the countryside or in the city, most Germans place a high priority on fostering self-reliance, independence, and responsibility in children. The parents and educators I've met backed up those values with real actions, letting children play and learn without constant supervision and correction, trusting them with simple tasks and choices, and giving them plenty of physical and intellectual room to grow into healthy, whole individuals.

I used to assume that America was the best, most free place to bring up my children, but living in Berlin shattered that notion, and I saw how far we had strayed in our parenting from our values of personal responsibility, self-reliance, and most of all, individual freedom.

Many American parents believe freedom means we are "free" to raise our children as we see fit, a nice sentiment on the surface, but too often this attitude means depriving children of their freedom. Today it is American parents, not Germans, who are more authoritarian: we constantly supervise our children, and direct their choices in education, activities, and future careers. This parenting style robs children of the ability to develop the attributes we supposedly hold most dear: personal responsibility and self-reliance.

At first I was surprised to find better ways to raise children to be free, responsible individuals in Germany. In retrospect, it makes a lot of sense. Germans, after all, know something about the dangers of a culture of control. German parents worry too, but they refuse to let fear drive their interactions with their kids. They treat their children as capable beings worthy of trust, and, most important, they respect their children's rights: to move freely, think for themselves, and ultimately as they grow older, to run their own lives.

My experiences in Germany made me question whether the many things that pass today in America as parenting "truths" are cultural, not universal. If they are cultural, that means we have the power to change them. I now believe that we Americans should value our children's rights more highly, not just for the sake of their childhoods but for our future as a democratic society. We cannot claim to value freedom if we raise children who never have a chance to experience it.

1

Leaving America

I never planned on raising my children in a foreign country, and surely not in Germany, a place my ancestors fled many years ago. I always assumed they left for a good reason, and returning to the proverbial fatherland simply was not on my list of things that would help my kids get a good start in life. Looking back, I now see that moving to Germany was one of the best things my husband and I ever did for our kids, even if it was by accident.

Almost every American has an immigration story. Some are even true. My mostly true immigration story stars a German merchant marine from Prussia named Gustav Zaske. Gustav reportedly walked off his ship in Nova Scotia, Canada, at the end of the nineteenth century. No one knows exactly why he jumped ship, but legend has it that Gustav planned to walk from Nova Scotia all the way to Milwaukee, Wisconsin, where one of his relatives lived.

Something happened on the way: he took a wrong turn and ended up near Zilwaukee, Michigan. There he met a five-foot-tall, red-haired beauty named Anna Schulz, also a German immigrant. He fell in love and married her, and they had a son, who became my great-grandfather. Gustav never did make it to Milwaukee.

The moral of this story, I had always assumed, is that you don't always end up where you planned to go. But another good lesson might be that love will take one look at your plans and laugh and laugh.

My Milwaukee was San Francisco. I had wanted to run away to California ever since I was a ten-year-old girl growing up in the deep snows near Buffalo, New York. After attending college at the University of Michigan (also super cold), I finally took off for California, driving across the entire country.

I found a job in a bookstore in Oakland because I imagined that working with books would somehow inspire me. I also figured it would be an easy job, leaving me plenty of time and energy to write. Working a real retail job killed that dreamy notion quick.

I started to avoid the constantly ringing phone and the customers who had less of a clue about how to find what they wanted than a German immigrant walking across Canada. I spent more and more time in the warehouse, talking with a handsome Hispanic stock boy named Zac, who made me laugh. Zac wasn't working in a bookstore for inspiration. He was trying to figure out how to make a living in the expensive Bay Area with only a high school degree. He'd taken a few community college classes, which he had paid for himself, and I remember telling him one fateful day, "You know you should just do it: take out loans and go to school full-time. Get your degree."

And he listened to me! Which, I must say, was an extremely attractive thing to do, and I eventually married him for this and his many other attractive qualities. However, some ten years later, Zac had not one degree but two and was about to get his third, a PhD. He had also scored an interview for his first job as a full scientist—in Germany. The position was at a research institute in the northeast of the country, ironically also in the area once known as Prussia that my ancestor Gustav had fled so many years before.

When Zac landed in Germany for his interview, he sent me an email. "Everyone here looks like your dad!" he wrote.

It was funny and true, but this wasn't part of my plan! Even if northern Germans resembled my relatives, I didn't have any special attachment to the country. Like many German Americans, our family had been disconnected from their homeland for a long time.

German Americans are the "silent minority," as *The Economist* once called us. We are also the largest. (This is true if you don't lump all Americans descended from Spanish-speaking immigrants into one Hispanic category.) Still, at 45.5 million, according to 2015 census estimates, Americans who claim German ancestry outnumber all other groups, even the sizable number of Americans who have English or Irish heritage.

While Germans were here from the founding of colonial America, the real boom came later. My ancestors were part of the more than 5.6 million Germans who arrived between 1820 and 1924, according to U.S. immigration figures. These German immigrants have been credited for introducing America to everything from beer to the Christmas tree to kindergarten.

But the American public turned against German Americans at the start of World War I. Hundreds were tried and convicted on trumped-up charges, others were tarred and feathered, and some were killed outright by mobs—and this was before the Second World War, an event which only increased suspicion toward German Americans.

Given this climate, it is not surprising that many people stopped identifying as German. They abandoned outward signs of their culture and stopped speaking the language—I know Gustav's son, my great-grandfather, did. By the time I was growing up, the only signs left that my family was German were small things—a dish of red cabbage at big family meals and the older folks who said *gesundheit* when someone sneezed. So the fact that the grandparents of my grandparents came from Germany would not help me at all if I went back to my ancestral homeland some 160 years later.

The German institute offered Zac the job and included some funds to help us move. We waited to discuss this big decision until he came back to the States. I definitely wasn't all set to pack up our life and go.

At that time, we were living in a college town in Oregon, where we had moved primarily for Zac's studies but also so we could afford to start a family. In California, I had finally found work writing, as a journalist. I even made it to a big daily paper in San Francisco, but it was a job more impressive in name than in salary. In Oregon, I found a solid job writing for a nonprofit. With my salary, Zac's graduate stipend, and the lower cost of living, we had managed to buy a small house. We also now had a little girl, Sophia.

After Sophia was born, we started juggling family and work like so many American parents. I stayed home with the baby for the three months of maternity leave I was allowed, and Zac took off as much time from his studies as he could. Still, at four months, we had to put Sophia into part-time child care. I'd then use my lunch hour to pick her up, bring her home, nurse her, and get some form of lunch into my own mouth before rushing back to work. Either Zac or my mother, who had moved nearby, took care of Sophia in the afternoons.

For Zac, it wasn't much easier. On the afternoons that he had Sophia, he would wake up before five a.m. so he could get in some hours at the lab before rushing home to meet us at noon. More than once, he had to bring Sophia to a meeting. In the evenings, he would be up late studying and writing at home. It was a tough routine, but we made it work.

I couldn't see how we were going to make it work in another country though. We discussed the move at length in conversations that went something like this:

"This is our last chance to go somewhere before we finally settle down and become boring," Zac said.

"Who's boring? I'm not bored," I said.

"You're too busy to be bored."

"I'm too tired to be bored," I said. "But I don't want to live in Germany for such a long time."

"It's a three-year contract," Zac said.

"Three years is a long time," I said. "I'll be old when we get back. Germany will steal the last of my youth."

"New experiences will keep us young," he said. "We'll be learning a new culture, a new language!"

"Gesundheit," I said. Zac looked at me oddly. "That's all I know how to say in German."

"How about *Sprechen Sie Englisch*?" Zac said.

"I think I'll be saying that a lot."

"But think of Sophia. She'll be bilingual!" Zac said.

"Don't tell that to my mom," I said. My mother was a retired French teacher, who had her grandchildren all call her *Grandmère*. She would be firmly against Sophia learning German instead of French—and, most of all, against us taking her granddaughter so far away.

"How about the city? Is it nice?" I asked Zac.

"Well, the institute is in a small town."

"How small?"

"Six thousand people, but I could commute. We could live in Berlin," he said.

"Berlin?" I didn't know much about the capital of Germany other than a smattering of information from my high school history classes. I knew it was where JFK had declared himself a Berliner, and that the Wall had existed there and had been torn down. I was somewhat intrigued.

"You'll be able to take some time off," Zac said. "We could have another baby. You could stay home, have time to write like you always wanted."

He had my attention now. "Could we afford that?"

"More than if I took a postdoc in the United States," he said. "Berlin is an exciting place. It will be an adventure. Really, when are we going to have another opportunity like this?"

I had to admit he had a point. I could see that Germany offered some real opportunities for our family and our careers, and wasn't it me who had told Zac all those many years ago to chase his dreams? If we stayed, I knew we'd both be settling, not even giving our dreams a chance. So this time I listened to Zac. We were moving to Germany.

A Cold Arrival

We landed in Berlin in January, not exactly the best month of the year to be in northern Germany. The holidays were just past, and because of the high latitude, the sun only appeared for six or seven hours each day. Still it had snowed and everything, including the tall city buildings, looked enchanted, coated in glistening white. We stayed in a hotel near Mitte— the center of Berlin—that bordered a huge park. The first chance we got, we bundled Sophia up and took our two-year-old for a fun walk through the snowy woods. It felt almost like a fairy tale. Here we were in this huge metropolis, and yet somehow we found ourselves in a forested winter wonderland.

The next day, we left to stay in a guesthouse near Zac's work, in a small town about forty-five minutes east of Berlin. Here, it was a snowy wonder-land too but minus the city buildings. A few days later, Zac started work, and I was a stay-at-home mom for the first time in my life. Outside of those first three months of maternity leave, I'd never had so much time with my young daughter all by myself. Sophia and I had a whole stretch of eight hours together every day—in a foreign country, in a small town with no car, and a bus that ran only once an hour. While the snow fell, it was easy. We built snowmen and forts. We had snowball fights and took sled rides (me pulling while she sat, sang songs, and ate snow). I made her hot cocoa and elaborate lunches.

When the snow melted, so did the fairy tale. Everything turned muddy, and entertaining a two-year-old mostly inside for long stretches of the day was a challenge. It started to feel less and less like we were playing together, and more like work—often boring work. We were also isolated. I had no friends to call on or mom groups to join. Most of the other people in the guesthouse were single without children and away at work during the day. As much as I loved my little daughter, she literally had the conversational skills of a toddler. I began to look forward to the time Zac came home, so I could finally have another adult to talk to.

Nadine, the woman who ran the guesthouse, must have noticed my daily struggles with my daughter. After we had been there about a month, she suggested we try to see if we could find a spot for Sophia at the local child-care center.

"But I'm not working," I said, confused.

"She will have other children to play with! And they have a playground and more toys," she said. "I think it will be more fun for her, no?"

This was the first time I encountered the positive attitude many Germans in the East have toward child care, and she made some good points on how it might be better for both me and Sophia. Still, I waved the suggestion off. Child care, in my American mind, was to benefit working parents, not the children themselves. Besides, this situation was temporary, I told myself. We'd soon be moving to Berlin, where there would be more things for Sophia to do.

We started taking trips to the capital city every weekend to search for an apartment. We finally settled on Friedrichshain (pronounced "freed-ricks-hine"), a relatively affordable, formerly working-class neighborhood with pockets of trendy stores, clubs, and restaurants. The only trouble: we couldn't find a landlord to rent to us. We would show up to apartment viewings and run into a dozen other applicants who had filled out their applications beforehand and spoke fluent German. The landlords appeared friendly to us, and some didn't even mind speaking English.

Still, we were never the first choice as renters, not necessarily because we were American, but because they didn't think we would stay. It was the opposite of what we had experienced in California, where landlords seemed to prefer tenants who would leave after a year, so they could hike up the rent with the next lease. German landlords, on the other hand, valued the security of steady renters, and many Berliners looked at apartments not as short-term residences, but as homes where they would live for ten, even twenty years.

Then we found our dream apartment. It was in an old historic building from around 1910, a rare survivor of the bombs from two world wars. It had high ceilings, wide windows, and wood floors that stretched through spacious rooms. The whole building had been renovated and included an elevator, also a rare find in Berlin.

We wanted this place, badly, so we asked Nadine for help. She agreed to go with us to meet the landlord. She not only made communications easier but also knew how to clinch the deal. She pulled out Zac's work contract, which said, among other things, that he was guaranteed a salary for three years. At the time, most of the Western world was in a recession, and unemployment in Berlin was particularly high. "Look, he's got a good job," Nadine told the landlord, slapping the paper down in front of him. We got the apartment.

Everything in Order

Getting our apartment was one of the first lessons I learned about how things were done in Germany. It was important to have the right piece of paper. Our adventure was going to require a lot of paperwork.

Another key document was the permission for me to work in Germany. I always knew I wasn't cut out to be a stay-at-home mom, and the months in the country had confirmed that. Plus, any extra income I brought in definitely wouldn't hurt. So, early one morning, Sophia and I bravely set off for the *ausländerbehörde,* the immigration office located on the opposite side of Berlin.

Even from the outside, the ausländerbehörde seemed to confirm the negative stereotype of Germany's socialist bureaucracy. The building itself was a massive, intimidating block of gray stone with long lines of people waiting in front of it.

When I finally made it to the front of the line and handed over my documents, I quickly realized I had another big hurdle to face.

"*Frau Tsah-skuh?*"

It took me a moment to realize the woman behind the desk was speaking to me. Her eyes were still on the papers I had handed her. Our family always said our name as "Zask-ee" with a buzzing *z*, a flat *a*, and a Polish-sounding "ski" at the end. I hadn't heard it pronounced correctly in German before.

"*Ja?*" I said, smiling. She didn't smile back. She launched into a rapid string of German.

"Um . . . *Sprechen Sie Englisch*?" I asked.

She looked at me over her glasses. "*Nein.*" Then, slowly: "*Sie sind in Deutschland. Wir sprechen Deutsch hier.*"

I knew enough to understand that I was in trouble. My toddler daughter yanked at my hand impatiently. A long line of people stood behind us. I could feel the weight of their eyes. Like me, they were foreigners from all over the world. Surely, these bureaucrats didn't expect all of them to speak German? But, yes, they did. Even though most Germans know some English, I would soon learn that official business is always conducted *auf Deutsch* at all government offices, even at the agency in charge of immigrants.

I had traveled about an hour by train and foot across Berlin with my two-and-a-half-year-old in tow and waited another half hour in line before I had made it to this point. I didn't know much German yet, but I had to try.

"*Wiederholen Sie bitte?*" I asked, using a phrase I'd learned from a language CD that was supposed to mean "Please say that again?" (I would later learn that Berliners usually say *Wie bitte?* or "How's that please?")

The woman sighed. She repeated what she'd said slowly and loudly. I caught the word for number and room. She gestured behind her and handed my papers back to me. "*Danke,*" I said and backed away from the counter. I wandered down the hall and found a pair of waiting rooms. In each room, people were seated on plastic chairs, staring at a screen displaying different numbers. *This was the DMV,* I thought, *on steroids.* Underneath the screen, I saw a red plastic snail number dispenser like the kind you find at a butcher's counter. I went up to it to take a number only to find there were none left. I checked the next room, same story. I tried asking the guard, who threw up his hands at my accented German. I gave up and went home defeated, but only temporarily.

This was just one of many experiences I had visiting government agencies, or *ämter.* At another office, I sat outside a door for forty-five minutes to get a *kita-gutschein,* a magical document that would allow me to enroll my daughter in child care for a fraction of what I had paid in Oregon. I waited for a long time as other parents went in and out, only to learn upon my turn that I had been waiting outside the door for the wrong part of the alphabet. When I found the right door and handed over my application, the official asked for another document that I did not have with me.

"Next time bring a whole binder," a German friend told me later. "That way they can't come up with something that you don't have ready to hand to them. Plus, you look prepared."

Seeking more help, I joined a mom's expat group, and soon found a new German-speaking friend who was willing to help me at the ausländerbehörde: Taska, an American raised by a German mother, who'd lived in Germany for seven years. She was also eight months pregnant. I didn't bring Sophia that time, but the size of Taska's belly moved us up in line. Still, we didn't get any farther than the waiting room, but I left feeling hopeful because after some negotiations with the woman behind the desk, Taska found a way for me to make an appointment.

In the meantime, I tried to master the task of grocery shopping. Our new apartment, which may have been a classic from 1910, was across the street from a shopping mall that was more of a classic from 1990. In the basement of the mall was a grocery store, which looked pretty much like any grocery store you'd find in the United States, only smaller. It had shopping carts, aisles, and even old American pop music playing over the intercom. *No problem*, I thought. *I know this kind of place.* I plopped Sophia into the cart seat and started down the aisles, singing along to "Maneater" by Hall and Oates. Sophia laughed and helped me pick out fruit and yogurt. Everything was going well until I reached the checkout line.

I stood at the counter as the checkout clerk rang up my purchases. She said something to me. I smiled. She said it again and jabbed her chin in the direction of the piling-up groceries. I noticed there was no packer, so I started to fill my own bags. The clerk looked at me like I'd lost my mind. She said something that sounded angry and made a sweeping gesture with her arm. I turned and saw how the other customers were quickly refilling their carts with unpacked groceries then pushing them over to the side where they packed their bags out of the way. Rushed and embarrassed, I threw my groceries back into the cart, while my daughter did her best to "help" by picking up items off the counter and randomly dropping them again.

I paid and pushed my cart off to the side to pack my bags. It felt crazy, but after several trips to stores, I realized that I never waited more than a few minutes in line because everyone moved out of the way and packed their bags themselves.

When my appointment came again for the ausländerbehörde, Zac went with me. We left early, but we had a difficult trip. It was snowing, and the trains were delayed. The sidewalks were icy, making it hard to rush without slipping. By the time we got to the office, our assigned bureaucrat was already meeting with someone else.

"*Es ist vorbei,*" he said, waving us away. The appointment has passed!

Zac looked at his phone. "It's only fifteen minutes after."

The official repeated that the appointment had passed, more loudly.

"We can wait," Zac said.

"*Nein.*"

"But the snow—" I stammered. "The trains—" It was no use. He sent us home. Late was late, which apparently was unforgivable in Germany. I soon learned this was true for almost any appointment, even social ones. Germans show up at the time a party starts, not ten minutes late as most Americans tend to do.

I was starting to get the message about how things were done in Germany: Show up on time. Pack your own bags. Get your paperwork in order. Be prepared. In short, be responsible.

Life in Germany was not a never-ending bureaucratic nightmare, even though when we were slogging back home through the snow from that trip to the ausländerbehörde, it felt that way. The German system will reward those who are organized—and persistent.

For instance, I followed my friend's advice and went back to the kita-gutschein office with a binder. A few weeks later, I received the gutschein for Sophia in the mail. I wrote several letters with copies of documents and soon we were also receiving *kindergeld* as well, a monthly benefit the German government pays to families with children, and I made another appointment at the ausländerbehörde. I showed up on time with a binder full of documents and left victorious with a new page in my passport, permitting me to work in Germany.

It wasn't my victory alone. I had help. Another thing I learned from these experiences was that despite first impressions, many Germans are friendly in a meaningful way. They may not smile and chat with strangers as Americans do, but once you get to know a German, they will often do whatever they can to help you. Throughout our early days in Berlin, we were never short of German friends and colleagues who volunteered to help us get settled in their country, navigate their formidable bureaucracy, and even move furniture that didn't fit in our small elevator up several flights of stairs—a true test of any friendship.

We had a lot to move because our beautiful apartment was also completely empty. New tenants in Berlin bring everything with them including the kitchen sink—quite literally. There was no sink in our kitchen—nor was there a stove, a refrigerator, or cupboards. The ceilings had no lights, only holes with wires hanging down. We started acquiring all these necessary things slowly, one at a time, and our apartment started to look like a real home.

When a German wants to know if everything is all right with you, they say, "*Alles in Ordnung?*" meaning literally "Everything in order?" After a few months in Germany, I could say our life was finally getting in order. Our apartment was close to a train station, and Zac arranged to get a monthly card so he could commute to work—and take us all around the city for free on weekends. With the gutschein, I would soon be able to enroll Sophia in child care and have a few uninterrupted hours to work every day. A new bakery opened downstairs in our building, sending up warm smells of bread and pastries. Every morning, I'd go downstairs to buy fresh rolls. We started exploring Berlin, which in the spring was transforming from a cold, dark place into a green city full of open-air cafés and tree-filled parks.

Just as I'd hoped, there was a lot more for Sophia to do in Berlin. We were delighted to discover that our own *kiez* ("neighborhood") had several excellent playgrounds within walking distance of our apartment. We gave them names according to their inventive play structures: "spider park," which had a circular web-like swing made of rope for groups of kids to swing in; "shady park," which had nothing but trees, some wooden huts, and a sand pit (Zac also called it "boring park," but Sophia liked it); and "tire park," which had a large circle of tire swings. Sophia enjoyed all these playgrounds, but they were nothing compared to "Dragon Park."

Sandwiched between blocks of apartment houses, Dragon Park featured a huge green wooden dragon about twenty feet high with big teeth and a gullet made of rope mesh that kids could sit in. Two giant slides extended off its side. In front of the dragon, wooden poles were driven into the sand with ropes slung between them about six feet off the ground, which children used to walk precariously between the poles. Some of the other structures were obviously meant for smaller children, like an easy obstacle course that snaked around the dragon's feet. It ended in a long dark tunnel made of wood, too small for parents to crawl into with their kids.

Children were almost always swarming over this park. On one of our early visits, some older kids had climbed onto the top of the dragon's head, and one boy had gone to the edge of the dragon's jaw and started dangling from it with both hands. It was a long drop to the sand below. "Achtung!" I called out to him. He didn't even glance in my direction. I looked around wildly. Where were his parents? Aside from a few parents playing with toddlers in the sand, all the adults were hanging out on the edges of the park, sitting on benches and drinking coffee. No one seemed bothered by the dangling boy but me.

By the time I looked back, he had dropped to the ground and run off. In the meantime, my own daughter was taking off toward the tunnel. Sophia crouched down, peered into the dim interior for a moment, then crawled through. I stood outside, wondering what I would do if she suddenly freaked out and started crying in the middle. I needn't have worried because she popped out the other end and ran across a wooden bridge and slid down the short slide at the end.

I did go with Sophia up the back of the dragon, though. Once at the top, she wouldn't go down the slide or sit in the dragon's mouth. It was too scary. However, after climbing down its back, she went up again, this time with her father—then she came down again. It was like she was working up her courage to face the rest of the dragon.

Watching Sophia run around the Dragon Park, I felt a mixture of worry and pride—along with a twinge of jealousy. The playgrounds of my childhood had all followed the same formula: slide, swing, teeter-totter, sandbox. They were nothing like this. This was real fun.

It also wasn't immediately clear to me how this freewheeling, slightly dangerous playground fit into a society that requires you to have all your forms in order, insists you show up on time, and expects you to pack your own bags. But it makes an odd sort of sense when viewed as part of the value Germans place on responsibility. Each child at the playground was expected to judge for herself what she could or could not do. Parents did not run around after their children telling them this slide was too fast or that climbing structure was too high. The children learned to manage the risk on their own and prepared themselves for each new challenge, like Sophia was starting to do with the dragon.

When Zac and I walked back to our apartment from Dragon Park that day with our tired and happy three-year-old between us, it seemed as if we almost belonged. We were less like foreign tourists and more like residents. Yet, I couldn't ignore the feeling in my gut that told me everything would soon be out of *"ordnung."* Actually, it was more of a nauseous feeling. I was pregnant.

2

Berlin Babies

Berlin did make staying home with Sophia easier. We now had a huge number of playgrounds and play cafés especially designed for young children to visit, not to mention a host of museums and child-oriented activities. During the week, we had most of these places to ourselves. Aside from parents with small babies, there were no toddlers or other young children running about. They weren't in the stores running errands with their parents either.

It soon became clear that the vast majority of young children in our Berlin neighborhood were in child care during the day. I was living in a place where being a stay-at-home mother with a three-year-old daughter was an anomaly. In fact, across Germany, more than 92 percent of three-year-olds are in some form of early childhood education, according to the Organization for Economic Cooperation and Development (OECD).

Our apartment building overlooked a green, triangular city park with a small playground at the center. On one side of the triangle was a restaurant and an ice cream place, and on the other side were two *kitas* or child-care centers. I could always tell when most parents picked up their children from kita, usually around three or four p.m., because the playground would suddenly be full, and a huge line would form outside of the ice cream shop.

Despite the wide use of child care in Germany, or perhaps because of it, I still had a difficult time finding a child-care spot for Sophia. I had the all-important gutschein, but the two kitas across the street from us had no available space. I then tried every kita in our immediate neighborhood and was met with the same answer: "*kein platz.*" No place. They told me to call back in August.

My timing was off. Berlin kitas normally only enroll once a year in late summer. Still, after nearly six months at home together, I was ready to work and I could also see the wisdom of Nadine's advice: Sophia needed other children. With some help and persistence, we found a spot for Sophia at a bilingual kita in the Treptow district directly to the south of our neighborhood that was willing to enroll her a few months early.

When I took Sophia for her first day at kita, we were greeted with chaos. More than a dozen small children were running around squealing. A pair of boys had opened a chest on the side of the room and were hurling objects behind them in an effort to find a particular toy. Children as young as two were climbing up and down the stairs to a high loft space built above us; one kid dropped a stuffed animal over the side to watch it fall.

When Friedrich Fröbel first invented kindergarten in 1840, he envisioned early childhood education as taking place in a type of Eden where children would be nurtured like plants. He also felt strongly that play was the way that children learned best, but I doubt that Fröbel had imagined the pandemonium of play that I saw at my daughter's kita.

Kita is short for *kindertagesstätte,* or child-care center. It is a hybrid institution that often includes care for nursery-age children (ages zero to three), as well as children in what we in America would consider the preschool and kindergarten years. While kindergarten is an academic class in the United States, kitas and kindergartens in Germany are separated from schools by their physical location and their focus. At kita, academic learning is not as important as play.

In fact, at Sophia's new kita, it seemed like all the kids did was play—loudly and with wild abandon. I wasn't the only American who felt that way. Nicole, a fellow American expat who lived on the west side of Berlin, described her daughter's kita day to me this way: "I drop her off. She goes screaming and running around, takes a nap, and then goes screaming and running around again."

Sophia had been in child care in the United States since she was four months old. Before we left, she'd been going half days to a child-care center with several teachers watching over a group of eighteen toddlers. (It got loud there sometimes too, but I'd never seen it as wild as the German kitas she went to.)

Located on the bottom floor of an apartment building, this kita was organized into three rooms: one for infants and toddlers, a middle room for three- and four-year-olds, and a small room for the older kids in their last year or two of kita before starting school. When the principal first showed us around, that room was empty. "The older kids go out on a field trip almost every day," she explained.

Sophia would be in the middle room, which was the largest, but with all the kids running around, the space seemed awfully small to me. In the midst of the mayhem, a young man came over to greet us. He crouched down to introduce himself to Sophia and shake her hand. She had never had a male teacher before, but within a few minutes, he had charmed her. In fact, he was a favorite of all the kids.

I was asked to stay the first few days to help her settle in there, but Sophia was off and playing almost the instant we arrived. I sat in the corner of the room, and she barely noticed me. After a couple days, the teachers told me I didn't need to stay anymore.

In addition to the main room, the children also had a "garden" to play in, a small area in front of the building that was filled with sand and toys. I heard other parents say they didn't like that the garden was so small, but the kita tried to make up for that fact by taking the kids out as often as possible. Sophia's group didn't make as many field trips as the older kids, but they often visited the playground or the woods in the massive 216-acre Treptower Park across the street. They had a yoga class once a week in a separate studio space. On one trip, they went to a spa to try out the sauna.

Although this kita was supposedly bilingual, only two other children understood English well. There was one native-English-speaking teacher, who rotated among the three rooms of different-age children, and Sophia's main kita teacher spoke English as well, but it was less than perfect. After the first few days, he pulled me aside to ask why Sophia kept saying she needed "to go party," then run from the room. Trying not to laugh, I found myself explaining the meaning of the word *potty* to the embarrassed young German.

I was one of only two parents who picked up their child midday. I soon saw that this was unusual, but I didn't think about it too much at the time. I was still sticking to the American idea that any child-care experience, even preschool, should be limited, that the ideal situation was for the child to be at home with me. The timing was sometimes difficult, especially as the long stroller walk through the park sometimes lulled Sophia into a nap that she woke up from minutes after getting home, but all in all, I felt tremendously lucky. Sophia loved playing at kita, and I loved the ability to have some time to write—and more frequently, as I got bigger, to take a nap.

Where Midwives Rule

Having Sophia at kita also helped me solve another pressing problem. I needed to find a midwife. In Germany, midwives, or "*hebammen*," not doctors, are the primary caregivers during the birth process. They handle prenatal care and the delivery itself, whether in the hospital or at home, as well as postnatal care. Doctors usually only come into the picture when there are problems that require major medical intervention.

After some research, I found a midwife, Anjet, who was willing to talk with me in English. (My German-language CD set was a little short on the subject of pregnancy.) The only problem was that her office was located in the Berlin district of Kreuzberg. Although close to our own district of Friedrichshain, Kreuzberg had once been on the other side of the Wall, so that meant there were no direct train connections. To get to Anjet's office, I had to take a U-Bahn (the Berlin subway), then a tram, and then a second ancient U-Bahn that traveled on top of the historic redbrick Oberbaum Bridge over the Spree River into Kreuzberg.

On the day of my first appointment, I dropped Sophia off at kita and headed out extra early. Kreuzberg is known for its good restaurants and large Turkish population. I planned to grab a quick lunch there: a two-euro falafel *im brot*. It was excellent but left me incredibly thirsty, and I drank a whole bottle of water in a few minutes.

Still early for my appointment, I walked calmly down the street and looked for the address. I couldn't find it. I crossed the street and looked again. I passed it three times before I realized the office was in the *hinterhaus*, the back portion of the building. It took me another few minutes to discover that the office was above a yoga studio and, like many buildings in Berlin, the only way up was the stairs. At this point I was late, and with all the walking and being pregnant, I now had to pee.

Anjet waited patiently for me. (She was probably used to her patients having to use the restroom immediately on arrival.) She acknowledged my profuse apologies about my lateness with a slight nod of her head.

"Still we must end at the same time," she said. "I have another appointment coming."

"OK. Sorry," I said and fumbled with my notes. I'd brought a list of questions I wanted to ask her.

Anjet was a tall, smart, young German woman. Younger than me. This set me back a bit. Before I started my quest for a midwife, I'd decided I wasn't going to have one who hadn't had children herself. And I could tell what the answer was going to be before I even asked that slightly rude question: "Do you have kids?"

"No," she said. "Though I hope to someday." Anjet then told me about her training—three years at a specialized school for midwives—and the many years she'd been in practice, as well as about all the services she provided.

I swallowed, knowing I was being unreasonable. Of course, she was a professional. For Sophia's birth in the United States, I had also hired a midwife, though in America this was considered an unusual decision. Doctors control most of the birth and labor process in the United States. At the time, I wasn't thrilled with the hospital culture that treated birth like an illness. My midwife in the States had twenty years of experience and five kids herself, all of whom had been born at home. I had a lot of confidence in her, and she had given me great care.

Yet despite my best efforts, Sophia had been born in the hospital—after thirty-two hours of labor I needed a little "go juice," or pitocin, a drug that strengthens contractions. I have few complaints because Sophia arrived healthy and happy. (With my midwife advocating for me at the hospital, I'd also managed to avoid having a cesarean, which the doctor had initially suggested.) Yet the whole hospital birth experience had been infused with so much unnecessary stress and antagonism that I did not want to repeat it, especially at a hospital in a foreign country in a language I hadn't mastered yet. So once again, I found myself trying to have a home birth, only this time with a German midwife.

Since my first interview with Anjet was only fifteen minutes, I tried to tell her everything that had happened with Sophia's birth, what I hoped for my second child, and how nervous I was about going to a German hospital all at once. I was speaking so fast Anjet had to ask me several times to repeat information. Her English was excellent, but I was testing the speed limit. I took a breath and slowed down.

Finally, I came to my most important question: "So if I have to go to the hospital, will you come with me?"

"If that happens, I won't be able to deliver the baby. There will be another midwife in charge at the hospital," Anjet said. She assured me that chances were good that I could have the baby at home, since second births were usually easier. She also told me that midwives in Germany were allowed to administer some drugs at home, including a drug like pitocin. I blinked at her. That little difference might have saved me a harrowing trip to the hospital the first time around. Still I wanted reassurance.

"But you'll come with me?" I insisted. "If nothing else works, you will go with me to the hospital?" I was a little terrified about going to a German hospital—even the word for it, *krankenhaus*, didn't sound like any place I wanted to be. If the ausländerbehörde was like an American DMV on ste-roids, I shuddered to think what a German hospital might be like.

"Yes, I will come," Anjet said.

I smiled and shook her hand. I had my midwife.

My first visit to a German hospital came well before my son was born. I had to fill out some forms. In Berlin, pregnant women who intend to give birth at home or at an outside clinic register at an area hospital ahead of time in case they need to be admitted during the birth. This seemed an improvement to my experience in the United States, when I'd shown up in the emergency room only to be faced with a nurse wielding a clipboard full of insurance forms she wanted me to fill out while I labored through contractions.

Anjet recommended a hospital in Kreuzberg with a good reputation. I liked the idea of registering in principle, but I went to that krankenhaus prepared to do battle. After my experiences at the various government offices, I came armed with my binder full of documents, a German dic-tionary, and a notebook filled with pretranslated sentences and questions.

I needn't have bothered. The krankenhaus was nothing like the aus-länderbehörde. The hospital, a long, low building, sat on top of a green hill on the banks of the Spree River. The maternity ward looked like a typical doctor's office with padded chairs and soothing pastel walls. After a short wait, I was met by a nurse who, upon hearing my terrible accent, quickly switched to English. She took me into an office with a round table and patiently explained each form I needed to fill out and sign. She gave me no lectures and made no snide comments about my birth plans.

The only scary form I had to sign was one that said that if I was unable to respond, I agreed to let the doctors do what they thought was necessary to save my life and that of the baby. I filled out blanks, checked boxes, signed, initialed, and signed again. I walked out of the hospital twenty minutes later into the bright riverside park. People were picnicking on the hospital's front lawn as leisure boats floated lazily down the river. This krankenhaus didn't seem like such a bad place to have a baby, if I had to go to a hospital, that is.

The American Disadvantage

Giving birth, even in the hospital with the best of modern medicine at your side, is still a risky thing for women to do. Of course, it's much less risky in developed countries, but the United States, which is supposed to have one of the best medical systems in the world, has terrible maternal and infant mortality rates in relation to its peers.

In fact, by moving to Germany, I had increased the odds in favor of my own and my baby's survival.

According to the Centers for Disease Control and Prevention (CDC), the number of U.S. women who died from pregnancy-related causes was 15.9 per 100,000 live births in 2012. In Germany, it was six per 100,000 live births in 2015, according to the World Health Organization (WHO). Even women in Saudi Arabia and the former war-torn regions of Bosnia and Herzegovina have a better chance of surviving pregnancy than American women. The U.S. numbers are pretty bad, but perhaps even more distressing, the maternal mortality rates in the United States have been getting worse, not better, even while rates in the rest of the world have been improving.

The story for babies is similar. Nearly six infants out of every 1,000 American infants die before they are a year old. In Germany, the infant mortality rate is almost half that: at 3.4 per 1,000 births. Why the disparity? Scientists at the National Bureau of Economic Research (NBER) asked exactly this question in a study titled "Why is infant mortality higher in the U.S. than in Europe?" They compared the U.S. statistics to Finland, which has one of the lowest infant mortality rates in the world at less than three per 1,000 births, and Austria, which has a rate close to the European average (and near Germany's rate).

The study pointed to inequality as a main issue: when looking at subsets of the data, the authors noted that "infants born to white, college-educated, married women in the United States have mortality rates that are essentially indistinguishable from a similar advantaged demographic in Austria and Finland." I fit into that demographic, so perhaps my baby's odds at survival were about even whether in the United States or in Germany. Yet for the millions of women who don't fit perfectly into that privileged realm, they'd be better off in Germany, which does a better job at achieving equality than the United States.

I've often heard the argument that European countries have better health outcomes because their populations are more uniform with fewer people of different races and backgrounds, but that's not entirely true of Germany. More than 20 percent of the population consists of people with a migrant background (this term includes foreigners, as well as naturalized German citizens and citizens whose parents were migrants). One of the largest minorities are people with a Turkish background (about 2.7 million according to 2011 census figures).

Pregnant Turkish women in Berlin used to have poorer perinatal results than their native German peers, but a study by Bielefeld University researchers found that the gap has narrowed considerably over time. From 2003 to 2007, babies born to mothers of Turkish origin had roughly equal outcomes to those born to mothers of German origin in terms of stillbirths, preterm births, and congenital malformations. The study's authors cited two most likely reasons for the improved outcomes: that Turkish women had become more accustomed to German culture and its health system, and, on the other side, that health-care providers had adapted better to serving the diverse communities in Berlin. The government and other agencies also launched a number of initiatives during this period to improve health and access to care. Of course, there are still problems with inequity in Germany. The divide is just a lot greater in America.

In Germany, all the services for prenatal, birth, and postnatal care were available to nearly every woman without regard to race, economic status, education level, or even citizenship. I, for one, took advantage of almost all of it. I went to every prenatal visit with Anjet. I listened to the baby's heartbeat. I heeded advice to watch what I ate and drank. I stood on scales. I had an ultrasound. I peed in a lot of cups that were tested for signs of protein or too much sugar. It all felt similar to what I had done in

America with my earliest pregnancy, except for one critical difference: I had control over my own health records.

One of the first things Anjet did was to give me a *mutterpass* ("mother pass"), a little white notebook that she and other health-care professionals marked up with my test results and handed back to me. I was responsible for bringing that pass with me to any pregnancy-related appointment. I also had all my test results at my fingertips whenever I wanted them. In the United States, most health-care professionals do not let patient records leave the doctor's office. You have to formally request them to be released to anyone, even to yourself. I did this when we left the States since I didn't know who my doctor would be in Germany. To get my own information, I had to fill out a legal form, pay a copying fee, and wait several days before I could pick up my file.

In America, I sometimes felt like my own medical information was being deliberately kept from me. For instance, for my first ultrasound in the United States, a technician did all the measurements of the soon-to-be Sophia but was not allowed to tell us anything other than the sex of the baby. Zac and I left that appointment with the eerie feeling that something might be wrong (there wasn't). Different states and individual medical facilities have varying rules on what an ultrasound technician can and cannot say—ours apparently erred on the side of extreme caution refusing to say anything even though she hadn't noticed any abnormalities. So we had to wait two weeks while a doctor whom we had never met looked over the technician's measurements, then forwarded her report on to our midwife, who then delivered the information to us.

In Germany, for the ultrasound, I made an appointment at a doctor's office, brought my *mutterpass*—and the whole family. The doctor, not a technician, did the ultrasound right there in his office, in 3-D no less. As he measured each feature of our tiny fetus, the doctor told us immediately that the baby was in the normal range. Sophia sat next to us, alternately bored and fascinated—until the doctor announced the fact that the baby was a boy—then she almost cried. She'd wanted a sister. We parents, on the other hand, left the doctor's office delighted that we were having a healthy baby boy. We had the evidence, the doctor's full report, in our own hands.

A Berlin Birth

I grew bigger and slower. It took an extra-long time to get Sophia to her kita in Treptow that summer. She was still enjoying it, for the most part, even if she couldn't understand most of what anyone said to her. The teachers assured us that she would pick up the language just through immersion, mainly by playing with other kids. And she did pick up some things. She learned a few key German words right off: *nein* and *meine* (no and mine), but that was not always enough to get along with children who spoke only German. At three and a half, she was just starting to play with other kids, instead of only side by side as many toddlers do, and she soon gravitated toward the two girls in her class who understood some English. It was funny to watch them play. Sophia would talk to them in English, and the girls, who could understand English but didn't often speak it, would respond in German. Without even intending to, they were slowly teaching Sophia a new language.

Then, early one fall morning in Berlin, a full week before my due date, I knew I couldn't take Sophia to kita at all. I felt a deep pain low in my stomach. I looked at the clock: five a.m. Zac had a big meeting that afternoon. He'd told me the night before, half joking, that I could have the baby any day but that day. Still, there was plenty of time. After all, my first child had taken thirty-two hours to be born.

"Oh!" Another pain. I nudged Zac. "What time did you say your meeting was?"

He sat up. "What? Why? Is the baby coming?"

"Maybe," I said. "But you can probably still make your meeting."

Zac didn't take any chances. He woke my mother, who was staying with us, and who, for some reason, started sweeping the floor. I called Anjet. She asked how often the contractions were coming. I had another contraction while I was talking to her. She said she'd be right over. Sophia got up and started running around the apartment.

While my mother herded Sophia into the kitchen for breakfast, I got into the bathtub and tried to relax. I hoped this wouldn't end again with a visit to the krankenhaus. At least I'd already filled out my paperwork. No matter what happened, everything would be covered by my German insurance. In the United States, I'd paid more than $3,000 out of my own pocket when Sophia was born. Despite being in a foreign country, I had a lot less to worry about. I added some more warm water to the bath.

Anjet showed up and timed my contractions. "They are getting slower, yes? Maybe you are too relaxed. Let's get you out of the bath."

Three hours later, Ozzie was born onto a flowered bed sheet spread on the floor of our Berlin apartment. It wasn't painless, and I'll never say it was easy—but compared to the thirty-two-hour drama of Sophia's birth, it sure was fast. I would like to attribute the speed to that famous German efficiency, but it was probably because second births tend to be easier. I do credit the German culture around birth and its health system with giving me more control and support over the whole birth process than my home country did.

That's not to say Germany does everything around birth perfectly. I've heard plenty of negative stories from other mothers. One friend had a birth that ended with an unwanted suction extraction she felt pressured into. Another who went to a busy hospital in Berlin was told by a stressed-out attending midwife that she wasn't the only woman in the hospital giving birth that day. That birth ended in a *kaiserschnitt*, "an emperor's cut," which is what a cesarean is called in Germany. In fact, it seemed that nearly every pregnant woman I knew who went to the hospital for a birth ended up with a kaiserschnitt.

Germany has a cesarean rate that is nearly as high as the United States, where one in three births end with the surgery. For more than twenty years, the international community has placed the "ideal rates" of cesareans at between 10 and 15 percent, according to the World Health Organization, which cautions that these major surgeries should only be done in emergencies because of the short- and long-term health risks for the mother and child. While most of the mothers I talked to felt they had no other choice than to opt for surgery, a kaiserschnitt rate that high indicates that German as well as American doctors might be in an unnecessary hurry to get out the surgical tools.

Many of the Berlin hospitals are set up for natural birth, and theoretically, having midwives in charge should lessen the need for surgery, since they are trained in allowing the birth process to progress normally, as opposed to doctors who are trained in medical interventions. But unfortunately, many German midwives are leaving the profession following a recent dramatic hike in insurance costs.

Lorna Ather, who works as a "pregnancy concierge" helping mothers-to-be arrange everything they need to prepare to have a baby in Berlin, told me it's getting harder to find midwives. Many no longer handle the delivery part of the process, instead offering only before and after care. "Now women need to find a midwife as soon as they find out they are pregnant. They're really booked out," Lorna said.

I was fortunate enough to have two midwives to help me. Anjet handled my prenatal care and the birth, and her colleague Kristine came over to my house for the postnatal care. This is not just for home births: all women receive follow-up home visits from a midwife. And if the mothers don't already have someone at home to help with cooking, cleaning, or child care for siblings, Germany's public insurance will cover the cost of hiring short term help for that, too.

Good after care is more than a matter of providing some help. Remember that NBER study that found such inequality around infant mortality in America? One of their key recommendations was to increase after-care home visits to new mothers, which are still relatively rare in the United States. The study found that having these visits can result in fewer infant deaths.

My visits with Kristine were great. She not only checked the development of the baby and my recovery but answered my questions and gave me information on infant care in a way that was much more helpful than the condescending lectures I'd received when I had my first child. For instance, instead of telling me not to sleep with the baby in the same bed, as the American nurses did, Kristine gave me all the pros and the cons of co-sleeping—and then she left it for me to decide what to do. It was this way with almost every topic. Her primary purpose was to give me information, not to dictate my behavior.

Our new baby grew strong and healthy for the most part—though he did catch a cold from his big sister a few weeks after being born. We named him Ozzie. *Oz* means "strength" in some languages, but what we didn't realize at the time was that Ozzie also sounded close to the German slang word *Ossi*—a somewhat derogatory term for a person from East Germany. But he essentially was an "Eastie," at least by birth.

Ozzie lived up to his strong name and was holding his head up after ten days, a fact that impressed our pediatrician. By three months, he had managed to learn how to move by rolling around and scooting on his belly, which made my *rückbildung* exercise course a bit difficult. I was pleased to learn I could take this free course, which was specifically designed to help new mothers get back into shape. It was like a gentle Pilates or yoga class that spent extra time on the muscles that had been stretched by pregnancy.

I thought the idea of such a course was fantastic. I could only find space in an all-German class so I learned many new words. For each class, all the mothers showed up with their babies. Some of the exercises even incorporated the child, but the instructor told us that we could also stop to tend to our baby's needs.

So at any given time, some of us were nursing, rocking, or changing our babies. Most often, I had to stop to reposition Ozzie because he would roll halfway across the room if I wasn't careful. Other babies I noticed with some envy were calmer. Some slept through the entire class. I was rarely so lucky because, as I was discovering, one thing Ozzie did not like to do was sleep.

3

Attachment Problems

When I took Ozzie in for his twelve-month checkup, the pediatrician took one look at me and said, "You need help."

I think I agreed with him. I don't remember, because I was in a fog of fatigue that had lasted many months. He took out his pad and wrote me a prescription for a sleep consultant, and that's how I met Cathrin. My prescribed sleep specialist started to visit our apartment on a regular basis. She asked a lot of questions about Ozzie's routines and behavior and spent some time observing as I played with my son. She said she wanted to see what happened when I told Ozzie no.

"Oh, I know what happens," I told her. "He cries and throws himself on the floor." For the most part, my son had a sweet disposition (still does), but as an infant, he had trouble dealing with any kind of disappointment or frustration. During Cathrin's first visit with us, he demonstrated his capacity for drama when he grabbed for my glass of water, and I moved it out of his reach. He cried and flopped facedown on the carpet in an almost cartoon version of a tantrum.

Cathrin raised her eyebrows. She made a note. "The first thing we will work on is getting him to accept no from you during the day, so that you can tell him no at night."

I nodded, but I was confused. I told him no all the time! "No, don't stick your fingers in the electrical sockets! No, you can't eat that piece of jewelry, that plastic toy, that moldy crumb of something you found from heaven knows where." Ozzie didn't pitch a fit every time I said no, but sometimes he did. I couldn't always tell when it would happen, although he did have a knack for doing it at the most inconvenient times, like when we had guests over or in the middle of the grocery store.

Cathrin gave me specific instructions on how to say no. I should say it in a calm voice, never angry, and if he had a tantrum, I should not immediately comfort him, but wait and observe. Only when he was calm again, without getting what he'd wanted, could I then comfort him. I followed her advice, and after a few weeks, his fits of anger grew less and less. It was working. I reported this success to Cathrin, and she said it was time to work on the bigger problem—sleeping through the night. Even with getting him to accept no during the day, my infant son still ruled the night, and I had a sinking feeling that I knew why.

Like many American mothers, I believed in "attachment parenting," as promoted by the books of Dr. William and Martha Sears, which meant I strove to create a bond with my infants through physical closeness and being responsive to their needs. So, I carried my babies as much as possible; I breast-fed, mostly on demand, and attended to their cries day and night.

With my daughter, it had worked well enough, but I hadn't followed everything the Seares advised. Since I had to return to work after three months, I still breast-fed, but the "on-demand" part was impractical, and I weaned Sophia at night at eight months. For a few bad nights, Sophia cried a lot even when Zac held her and rocked her. Soon, however, she accepted that milk wasn't available at night and learned to self-soothe with a pacifier. After that, she woke up only two or three times at night.

Ozzie was a different story. He was not having any of this night weaning stuff. He had no interest in a pacifier or his father's lullabies—or mine for that matter. He would go back to sleep after having one thing, and one thing only: breast milk and not in a bottle—it had to come from the source. During the day, he didn't care so much about nursing. Ozzie was eating solid food early and enthusiastically, but at night, nursing was the only thing guaranteed to make him sleep. Still, he was up on average eight or nine times a night, every night. I know, because Cathrin had me keep a night journal with how many times and how long I got up to help him go back to sleep.

I have many excuses for how this extreme situation came about: he got sick a lot that first year; I couldn't let him cry too long in an apartment; he was keeping Sophia from sleeping well; and then after hours and hours of rocking and singing, for the love of everything good in the world, I just wanted him to go to sleep!

Looking back, I can see that a large part of the problem was my over-devotion to attachment parenting. After reading some of the Seares' books, I was convinced that I would damage my child if I didn't follow their theories of constant closeness and attention to the baby's needs, and I'm not the only one who thought this way. I know American mothers who have given themselves back problems from wearing their babies in slings; others who wouldn't hear of having a babysitter for even a few hours, not even a relative, for fear the separation would somehow hurt their attachment with their babies. There are probably even more mothers who have been so focused on attending to their children's nighttime cries that they go months, even years, without a decent night of sleep.

To be fair, plenty of parents have gone to the other extreme with the so-called cry-it-out method, advocated by parenting "experts" like Richard Ferber. This method calls for instituting strict schedules for feeding and sleeping, and a willingness to let the child cry for long periods of time to train the baby to those schedules. Eventually the baby is supposed to get used to the schedule and fall asleep easily. It may work for some babies, but if you've ever had the experience of listening to a "Ferber" baby who is resistant to the method, it has got to be one of the most painful things in the world to hear.

These two polarized methods have made it to Germany too. The Sears

books have been translated into German, and Ferber's ideas were popular-
ized by the German psychologist and behavioral therapist Annette Kast-
Zahn in her 2008 best-selling book *Jedes Kind Kann Schlafen Lernen* (*Every
Child Can Learn to Sleep*).

Still, I noticed something else also going on in Germany. I met parents who told me their babies went to bed at night without a problem.
One German mother told me her eighteen-month-old put herself to
sleep. She'd play a while in the crib, talk to herself, and then nod off. I
remember not believing her completely, but she did look suspiciously
well rested.

Another time, while having an afternoon coffee with a German friend
at her home, she excused herself to put her baby down for a nap. She
returned five minutes later. I waited for the screaming to start. There was
none. "He's asleep?" I asked, incredulous.

"Not yet," she said. "But he should be in a little while. He's tired."

As we talked, I could hear him gurgling and babbling in the other
room. She got up to visit him a couple of times, but eventually the playing
sounds grew less frequent, and there was silence. He was asleep. *What an
unusual baby,* I thought.

But it wasn't that unusual. In fact, it's part of a tradition in Germany
of parents who actively encourage babies to be comfortable by themselves.
In fact, one survey cited in the journal *Pediatrics* in 2005 found that only
one in five German parents stay in the room with their babies as they fall
asleep.

German Parents and Attachment Theory

I didn't realize the significance of this German attitude toward sleep until
I met Robert LeVine. A Harvard professor emeritus of education and
human development, LeVine has studied parenting practices in cultures
all over the world and continues to write on the topic. He contends that
attachment theory doesn't have the solid basis in scientific evidence that
its proponents claim. Instead it arose out of a "moral campaign" to change
the way children were cared for in the United States and Great Britain.

LeVine said supporters have ignored evidence that casts doubt on attachment theory—including studies of German parents and their infants.

The whole idea that a baby's attachment to her mother is critical to human development didn't originate with the Searses' books. Attachment theory was first conceived in the 1950s by British psychologist and reformer John Bowlby. After working with mentally ill, delinquent, and institutionalized children, Bowlby came up with a theory that babies needed to form a close attachment to their primary caregivers for normal emotional and cognitive development. Infants who did not develop this secure attachment were at high risk of mental illness later in life.

Bowlby's theory gained traction after development psychologist Mary Ainsworth conducted a now-famous study called the "strange situation" in Baltimore in the 1970s. This study is so well-known that today descriptions of it can be found in many popular parenting books. Basically, what Ainsworth did was to have mothers leave their babies alone for a short time, then she observed how the babies reacted to this "strange situation." The infants who cried when their mothers left and were comforted upon their return were deemed "securely attached." Those who responded in different ways, such as ignoring their mother's absence or not being comforted on her return, were regarded as "insecurely attached." Ainsworth's Baltimore studies revealed that the majority of infants, about two-thirds, were securely attached while the remaining third fell into one of the insecurely attached categories. Many subsequent studies in other countries revealed similar results.

Bowlby used Ainsworth's experiment as proof that his theory was universal, but that's a step too far for LeVine. Instead, he argues that the value of strong infant attachment is more a cultural ideology than a universal truth. LeVine said that Bowlby and other proponents tended to dismiss any contrary evidence: in particular, the results of a 1985 study by Karin and Klaus Grossman of mothers and infants from the north German town of Bielefeld. The Grossman study found that the majority of the German infants, a full 49 percent, fell into an insecurely attached category called "anxious avoidant," which meant they avoided or ignored their mother when she was in the room and didn't seem to be bothered when she left.

Along with other categories, a full two-thirds of the German infants were deemed insecurely attached. With such a large majority falling into this supposedly abnormal category, it's apparent that, at least in this culture, insecure attachment wasn't the exception, it was the rule.

"Bowlby wants to argue that attachment is universal and that what Mary Ainsworth found in Baltimore is universal for all humans. But what was found in Bielefeld is grossly different, terribly different," LeVine told me when I met him in Berlin. "So they just ignored it for many years."

And it wasn't only Bielefeld. Another study by Lieselotte Ahnert and Michael E. Lamb in 2000 of East Berlin parents found similar results. LeVine pointed out that if Bowlby's theory that insecure attachment leads to mental illness were true, there would be a huge rash of mental illness in northern Germany, since those babies have now grown up. Likewise, a rather large minority, 35 percent, of American infants who were deemed insecurely attached in these studies would also be prone to mental disorders. Obviously, this is not the case in either culture, and it's a serious flaw in Bowlby's argument for the necessity of secure attachment as defined by his theory.

LeVine proposes that the difference is simply in cultural values. German parents are known for valuing *selbständigkeit*, self-reliance, in their children, and they start instilling this quality early. LeVine is not the first to criticize attachment theory, which has become so central in child development circles, as well as in popular parenting literature. In her 2005 book, *A Perfect Madness: Motherhood in an Age of Anxiety,* Judith Warner detailed how such a demanding parenting style puts women in an impossible position, and the sociologist Sharon Hays called it part of an "ideology of intensive mothering." However, LeVine's argument and other cultural criticisms of attachment theory are particularly pointed because they speak to the heart of what the theory claims: the supposed benefit, or harm, to the baby.

Independent Infants

Promoting independence in babies can easily be found in German parenting literature, even as attachment is discussed. These two ideas are not seen to be in conflict but to work together. "Raising a self-reliant child is a process that begins at birth and continues throughout the child's entire upbringing," writes German pedagogical professor Dieter Spanhel in an article for the *Familienhandbuch* ("family handbook") website. Spanhel goes on to say that a balance must always be found at every stage of development between watching over the child and letting the child become self-sufficient.

Remo Largo, a Swiss pediatrician, once called *"Der Gott der Kindererziehung"* (the god of parenting) by the German newspaper *Frankfurter Allgemeine,* also speaks a lot about this balance. His best-selling book *Babyjahre* ("*Baby Years*") has been a mainstay for many German parents. Largo preaches a calm, nonjudgmental approach to parenting. He does evince some of the baby-wearing, co-sleeping ethos often found in American attachment parenting literature, but he also talks a lot about independence.

For instance, in his chapter on sleeping, Largo criticizes the over-emphasis on attachment: "Many people think that having the closest, tightest possible physical relationship to their parents builds children's psychological well-being and basic sense of trust," he says. "To me, this seems like an overly one-sided idea of how children's self-confidence develops: self-confidence is born not only of security, but of independence as well."

In fact, in Largo's view, helping a baby learn selbständigkeit by learning to sleep alone is essential and is actually a sign that they feel secure. "Once children can fall asleep on their own, they will be less dependent upon their surroundings and will suffer less from fears of abandonment when they wake up at night in a dark room."

So in Largo's view, the ability of the child to fall asleep by herself is evidence that the child feels secure. It really is a shame his books are not available in English. Instead of sentiments like this, I had absorbed passages that demanded I give my older baby more, not less, attention, like this one from *The Baby Book* by the Searses: "Don't be afraid to listen to your baby. You are neither spoiling him or being manipulated . . . you can get right to the heart of the problem and provide nighttime company. Move a mattress or a roll-away bed into your baby's room and lie down next to his crib when he goes to sleep . . ."

The Searses' books do caution against letting yourself as the caregiver become worn out, and they have a whole section on how to set boundaries with all nighttime nursers, which I read many times. Still, this always comes with the admonition to "let the baby be the barometer" of any new nighttime parenting approach. And quite frankly, my second baby was a lousy barometer.

When I was in that tired fog of parenting, I was so caught up in being a sensitive mother that I didn't realize my overresponsiveness might actually be holding Ozzie back from reaching the secure, independent feeling that Largo writes about. And at first, it didn't appear my consultant could find a solution. Cathrin never advocated for letting Ozzie cry it out, though she often told me I should wait a short time before responding to his nighttime cries. She also assured me that one day he would learn to sleep through the night. It was a developmental milestone that all babies reached. I couldn't force it to happen, but I could encourage it.

Cathrin spoke a lot about bonding and reading the baby's cues, but she also talked about setting limits, about acting "clearly"—essentially I should be consistent. After I got Ozzie to accept a no from me during the day without having a major meltdown, Cathrin recommended we move on to saying no during the night: night weaning. I was to play with Ozzie for a long time in the evening and give him one long nursing session before bed—in other words plenty of "Mom time"—but from that point on, when he woke up in the night, I was supposed to tell him a gentle no. Yeah, that didn't work.

He screamed and screamed. I sang so many lullabies my voice grew hoarse. Zac walked with him, rocking the baby in his arms until his muscles were sore. Sometimes, Ozzie would go back to sleep only to be up again forty-five minutes later. Sophia, who shared his room, appeared to sleep through it all, but the bags under her eyes told a different story. The entire family was exhausted.

After a couple of weeks without success, Cathrin suggested I stop nursing altogether. I remember how carefully she said it, as if afraid of offending me. "In my experience, extended breast-feeding can some-times interfere with sleeping through the night." She put two hands out in front of her. "That's just what I've noticed."

I didn't take her advice right away, and when I did, it wasn't an instant cure. He still got up multiple times a night for about two weeks. But then came the night when he slept a whole seven hours in a row for the first time in his young life. He did it the next night and the next. It took me a bit lon-ger. I kept waking up and listening to the silence before going back to sleep. It was marvelous.

Years later, I contacted Cathrin to see if I could get her honest opinion about attachment books like Searses'. She was still cautious about express-ing any blanket judgment. She pointed out that the advice she gives is individual for each family, taking into account a host of factors such as number of children, housing situation, support network, and any financial or health problems, as well as the parents' "core beliefs" about parenting.

Cathrin didn't feel there was any one "dream book" that can address all children's sleep problems. She did say that books like Searses' often sug-gest to mothers that "'if my child doesn't sleep well or cries a lot, I have not done enough, not given enough, not understood enough.' Then the helplessness they feel just continues to grow until they are in com-plete despair."

Looking back, I see I fit that picture quite well, and I wonder how many mothers are doing this now, given the rise of the "natural parenting" movement, which puts its claim to universality front and center in its name: being "natural" implies that other parenting approaches are "un-natural" or wrong. The nonprofit organization that promotes this move-ment, Attachment Parenting International, recently put up an appeal with the headline "Attachment Is Everything." Really, everything? That's cer-tainly a big claim and one that doesn't hold up against cultural critiques like LeVine's. The problem with this high-stakes philosophy is not just the pressure it puts on parents, and on mothers in particular, but also what it can do to the child.

As I experienced, attachment practices can backfire, creating a re-inforcing loop. As Cathrin put it, "Every day, the baby learns that if X happens, Y happens. Over time, the cognitive pattern etches itself into the baby's brain like a highway."

While Cathrin wouldn't advocate for any single sleep prescription that fits everyone, I think there are a few things American parents can learn from the German approach to promote their baby's independence and good sleep habits.

First, we can relax a little on the attachment issue. If we can accept that the attachment theory is a cultural value and not a universal truth, it takes a lot of the heat off: you can put your baby down to play by himself, without fearing he will develop into a psychopath. If you don't breast-feed on demand you are not a terrible mother. We all want a loving bond with our children, but in all the hype around attachment parenting, it's good to remember that detachment is also important—that our job as mothers is to give our babies not only unconditional love but also the space to develop into their individual selves.

Second, set loving boundaries for your baby as he gets older; as I was learning to tell my one-year-old son no without him having a fit, Cathrin emphasized that I was not to comfort him during his tantrum, but only afterward when he had calmed down. Then I could hug him and even praise him for getting his emotions under control, but the no still stood.

Third, set a good pattern for sleep. This is also about establishing boundaries. If you can create a routine for sleeping that involves putting the baby down awake by himself and he learns to fall asleep happily on his own from the start, you can avoid a lot of the bad experiences many parents have. Babies will go through phases, but setting this pattern will make it easier to reestablish. While I still can't advocate for crying it out, there's nothing wrong with waiting a little. When a baby cries, our first impulse is to rush and soothe him, but sometimes waiting a few minutes gives them a chance to figure out how to soothe themselves.

Last but not least, just as you don't wake a sleeping baby, I recommend not interrupting a playing baby. We're told that parental interaction with children is key to their well-being and future success. German parents have heard this, too. Bettina Lamm, a cultural psychologist, told me that German middle-class parents will often engage their babies in dialogue as if they can talk back, even though they can't possibly answer. She also told me that American mothers in one study took this even further and read books to three-month-old babies, who cannot possibly follow along, in a belief that it will help them learn later. (I blushed when she told me this because I've also read books to both my tiny infants.)

Interacting with our babies is fun and good for our relationships, but we could relax a little. Our babies also need time to explore on their own and get involved in their own play without our interference. This space will give them a chance to develop their concentration skills and independence. And for the parents' benefit, a baby who can entertain himself is a much easier baby to care for, and one who is more likely to be able to soothe himself to sleep at night.

I once had a boss who, in another context, advised that it is important to ask yourself not only what you should do, but what you should stop doing. I think this is common advice in the business world, but many mothers could benefit from asking themselves this question too, at different stages of their child's development. Perhaps it's stopping breast-feeding or co-sleeping when it's no longer necessary. Maybe it's giving up the effort to entertain babies constantly or not dropping everything to answer their demands for comfort immediately. Not doing something for your children is perhaps the hardest when children are so small and seem to need so much—and our culture demands that we mothers be the ones to provide it all. That's where the Germans have a few more approaches that might help.

Mother Knows Best?

Germany is not immune from the "mother myth" that has gripped most of Western culture. Traditionally, the domain of German women was relegated to *kinder, küche, kirche* ("children, kitchen, church"), and in West Germany, as more women started to work, they faced being called a *rabenmutter* ("raven mother"), after a bird that is notorious for neglecting its young.

These sentiments should sound familiar because American culture still considers that a mother who is at home full-time is the best situation for children, in spite of the fact that today the majority of mothers work at least part-time, and more than half hold down full-time jobs. In the United States, there's a lot of talk about women "choosing" to stay home or going to work after having children when most often it comes down to a simple matter of economics.

The traditional male breadwinner–female homemaker model doesn't work financially for most American middle-class families. It didn't for us. When my daughter was first born, Zac was earning only a graduate student stipend, so I worked up until the moment I felt contractions, took three months off, and when that was up, I packed my briefcase full of guilt and went back to the office. Many American women have similar situations. Even as more women work, the old expectation for mothers to be constantly available for their children not only persists but has been given new life by the supposed universal benefit of attachment or "natural" parenting.

German women feel these pressures too, but the country has more ways to counteract both the old and new myths around motherhood. For one thing, they have access to consultants like Cathrin, who are trained to work with families as individual cases, each needing unique solutions and not blanket cure-all philosophies (and whose services are covered by health insurance). But many other German social customs and policies actively support a more tempered idea of motherhood than the be-all, end-all caregiver for children. One of my personal favorites I call "men pushing prams."

On any given day in Berlin, I would see an unusual sight: men, young and old, pushing strollers with their infant children, by themselves, without their wives, in the middle of the day. They were also at the *kindercafés* (coffee shops made for parents with children), in the grocery stores, and at the playgrounds: all the places where you might expect to see only mothers. At first I thought it was because they were unemployed, but I soon learned that I was witnessing the effect of a generous paternity leave policy.

In Germany, both parents can take partially paid *elternzeit* ("parent time") for up to three years and still return to their position. A great many parents of both genders take advantage of this. Still, with the attendant old pressures and traditional roles, more women take time off and for longer periods—typically a year—than fathers do. Nationwide, 96 percent of mothers took advantage of the leave policy, while only an average of 34 percent of German fathers took parental leave in 2016—though in one city, Jena, 57 percent of fathers took leave, according to the Federal Statistics Office. Most of the men took just three months. Still, three months of paid leave is exactly three months more than most American fathers get.

The idea behind paternal leave is equity: men should be allowed time to be parents just as women are, and if more men take time off for their children, fewer women of childbearing age will face discrimination in the workplace. It is not a perfect policy by any means. I've heard tales of young women being suspiciously passed over for jobs, and both fathers and mothers can be reluctant to take the time off because of the potential damage it could do to their careers.

However, if used, the policy yields some great benefits for the child. Maternity leave means young infants get more close time with their moms early on, when many women feel that babies need their attention the most. And by encouraging fathers to take some time off, more children get to know their father as a primary caregiver for some period of time. (It's interesting to note how little time is spent in popular attachment literature on the importance of infants bonding with their fathers.)

This leave system gives working families more options for caring for young children. German mothers have some time at home, without the financial stress of losing their income entirely. When mothers are ready to go back to work, they have several choices for caregivers, including the father of their child. Professional child care in many forms is another option and it is heavily subsidized in many places by the government. When I was in Berlin, we paid about €100 (about $112) a month to send my daughter to half-day care; in the United States we'd paid more than $800 a month and could only take a $3,000 tax credit on that total bill for the entire year. Working parents can hire a *tagesmutter* (a "day mother") to help care for a young child in their home. Alternatively, they can join a *kinderladen* (usually a smaller day care run by parents), but one of the most popular choices is a more institutional type of day care like kita.

When I look back on those exhausting first years with my son, I have a lingering sense of failure. Not because I wasn't there for him—I was, constantly. Ironically, it's because I *was* there for him all the time that I failed. I was trying too hard, and I lost perspective. How much easier would it have been if I'd set more gentle boundaries earlier with Ozzie? If I'd put more limits on our nighttime routine, wouldn't we all have slept and felt better? I was tired for nearly two years. I'm sure it affected everything and everyone around me. That's a heavy cost.

Yet motherhood in modern times is doomed to feel like failure. Both traditional ideals and the ones now being pushed by attachment or natural parenting, as well as other rigid philosophies, are not realistically attainable, and, more important, may not be worth striving for in the first place. A strong bond between mother and child is wonderful, but it's not everything, not even close. It's good for mothers to ask for outside help, not just for their own sanity, but for the sake of their children. Because as I learned the hard way, they need more than just one person can possibly give them.

4

Small Children, Small Worries
(Kleine Kinder, Kleine Sorgen)

I was sitting in a chair that was way too small for me, my knees almost to my chest as I tried to hold my squirming little boy in my lap. It was the first day of orientation for Ozzie's "toddler" class at our new international kita. It was a hot summer day, and my son was eager to get down and crawl around the classroom. Self-conscious, I looked at the other parents around me, mostly mothers, whose children all looked older than mine. I was relieved to see at least two other "crawlers."

As we waited for the meeting to start, I tried to strike up a conversation with the British woman next to me who had a beautiful, well-behaved little girl on her lap. "How old is she?" I asked.

"Almost two," she replied. I realized too late the trap I'd laid for myself. "And how old is yours?" she asked.

"Eleven months," I replied.

"He's awfully young, isn't he?" she said.

"My daughter went into child care at four months," I said. She looked shocked. "I'm from the States," I quickly explained. "We only get three months of maternity leave."

"Oh, that's terrible," she said.

I had to agree. Whenever I tell any European that the United States has no paid parental leave, I would get the same reaction. I had taken advantage of our time in Germany and stayed an entire year with my son. After the juggling act I'd done when Sophia was a baby, being home with Ozzie felt almost indulgent. I say almost because with a baby at home and a three-year-old in preschool for a half day, I didn't have much time for anything outside of mothering. I was supposed to be working on my writing, per our original plan, but I was exhausted. I had managed to use the hours spent nursing and rocking a baby back to sleep to imagine a whole novel. As of yet, though, I hadn't had the time to get it out of my head and onto paper. So when Ozzie neared the one-year mark, I was more than ready to put him into kita for a few hours a day.

By luck and persistence, I'd managed to find two spots open at a much-sought-after public "international" kita in the fashionable Berlin neighborhood of Prenzlauer Berg, a few train stops to the north of our own neighborhood. Sophia's first kita in Treptow had been a good place, but she was still having some language troubles. We'd learned she had been trying out her own brand of American foreign diplomacy: first, she would negotiate, in English, with another child about why it was her turn with a particular toy; then when the confused German-speaking child refused to give it up, she would resort to the use of force. It wasn't all the time, but it's never fun to hear that your normally sweet young daughter is hitting other children. We worked with Sophia on the problem, and her behavior improved.

Yet, when an opening came at an international kita that was filled with other children who spoke both German and English, we jumped at the opportunity. At the new kita, they still prescribed only immersion to help her learn German, but there were many more English-speaking children at this kita. Each class had one teacher who spoke only English and another who spoke only German. Luckily, they also had a spot for Ozzie in a toddler room, which was specifically reserved for children ages one to three.

Sophia, who was now four, would be nearby, down the hall, in a group for older kids, hopefully learning how to get along better with others.

Ozzie's future kita teachers explained how the process of "settling in" to the toddler room would work. For a period that could last as long as six weeks, one parent stayed with their child at the kita. So at first, I went to kita with Ozzie and was in the room the whole time he was there; then, a few days later, I would leave the room for a few minutes, then longer and longer, until eventually I would leave him there and not come back until the afternoon. The idea was that he would become more comfortable with the new environment and his caregivers, as well as with the idea of Mama leaving and returning. In effect, we were making Ainsworth's "strange situation" less strange.

Sitting in the toddler playroom for several weeks, I met some of the other parents—mostly mothers. About half were from English-speaking countries and half were German. We all talked about our children, and how well they were adjusting to kita. We also spoke about our own desire to go back to work and have some time to ourselves. In these conversations one thing struck me over and over about the German mothers in particular: they had almost no guilt about putting their young children into child care. "I think it's really good for her to be around the other kids," one mother told me. "She'll learn from them." I heard this sentiment often, especially from parents who had only one child and thought their child really needed more interaction with other kids. In Germany, the single-child family is quite common, but even parents who had more than one child said it would be good for their younger children to play without their older siblings around. One mother pointed out how nice it was for her daughter to have a new space outside of their apartment to explore and make her own.

These comments were vastly different from the attitudes of the mothers I knew in the United States, including myself. If anything, we American moms spoke of putting our babies and young children in child care with regret: it was a necessary evil, something we had to do because we had to work. I learned later that the positive attitude toward child care I heard in Berlin is not found all over Germany, either. It's more common among

Germans who live in the eastern half of the country. A study published in *International Journal of Adolescence and Youth* in 2012, more than two decades after the Berlin Wall fell, found that young Germans who lived in the East still had a more positive view of child care than those in the West. They also favored starting their children earlier and having them stay longer in child care. Heidi Keller, one of the authors of the study, told me that the wider use of child care in the former communist GDR was behind the different attitudes. "In the early day-care system, there's much broader coverage [in the East]," she said. "It's much more familiar for people to bring their children to school early, and it was part of their upbringing in GDR."

The Kindergarten East-West Legacy

The development of kindergarten has had a troubled history in its home country. The way young children were educated was often at the mercy of various political storms that shook Germany, as history professor Ann Taylor Allen pointed out in a chapter for the anthology *Kindergartens and Cultures*. Probably the most obvious disruption was the Nazi party, which rejected Fröbel's kindergarten concept as weak, and instead worked for early education that raised a "hardened generation—strong, reliable, obedient and decent," according to a brochure on how to run a Nazi kindergarten written by Richard Benzing in 1941.

After the war, West Germany pushed a family model similar to the 1950s American family: with the father as the sole breadwinner and the mother at home with the children. This meant there were fewer kindergartens since most children remained home. Then came the 1968 generation, which pushed for change on a number of fronts, including women's ability to work. A group of mothers in West Berlin started their own child-care centers called kinderläden. This model spread and some antiauthoritarian proponents began creating kinderläden with few rules—their philosophy was that children could best raise themselves. These new spaces and feminist activism helped increase the number of kids in child care in the West, but kindergarten enrollment was not near the level in the East.

After the war, the communist East German government rolled out an aggressive expansion of kindergartens, as Allen documents. By 1962, more than half of the young children in East Germany were in kindergartens. By 1988, that number had risen to 81 percent. This corresponded to a high rate of women in the workforce; at that time, a full 91 percent of East German women were employed.

While the GDR kindergartens in the East were run with a clear political agenda, there was an interesting side effect to this aggressive expansion, which I experienced on the east side of Berlin more than twenty years after the fall of the Wall: many Berlin mothers took returning to work and enrolling their child in care as completely normal. Their mothers had done it, and in some cases, so had their grandmothers. If I had entered my children in a kita a few miles to the west in the same city, I might have experienced a different attitude. One fellow American expat, Anna, lived in Charlottenberg, an expensive southwestern district of Berlin, when her children were born, and found herself surrounded by mothers who had abandoned their high-flying careers as lawyers and businesswomen just to stay at home longer with their children. I had a hard time believing her because it didn't sound like the Berlin I knew.

Still, in general, child care is now considered a right in Germany. Since 2013, every German child from ages one to six is guaranteed a spot at a child-care center, and the city of Berlin has been making steady moves toward making it free at every age. Today, about 59 percent of two-year-olds are enrolled in some form of early childhood education, and among older children, preprimary education is nearly universal with children ages three, four, and five enrolled at 92 percent, 96 percent, and 98 percent, respectively, according to the Organization for Economic Cooperation and Development.

Far fewer children in the United States are in any kind of early childhood education, with only 23.4 percent of children under five in formal child care, according to the Center for American Progress. The high cost of care is most likely the main deterrent, but I also think the lingering stigma around child care discourages many parents from enrolling their children if they don't have to. Even if they do, they try to limit the hours, like I did.

In the United States, the entrenched ideal is still the stay-at-home mom. Despite the fact that 71 percent of mothers are now working outside the home, the majority of Americans still think it's best when one parent stays at home full-time, according to a 2014 survey by the Pew Research Center. Given how few of those full-time parents are men (only 16 percent), the pressure remains on mothers to be stay-at-home moms, a term that has notably changed from the *housewife* of the '50s and '60s, increasing the emphasis on motherhood as a woman's highest priority. Whatever it is called, this occupation has declined considerably since 1970, when nearly half of mothers in two-parent families worked only in the home. For both my mother's and grandmothers' generations, the baby boomers and post–World War II generation, women were expected not only to maintain the household but be available for their children until they graduated from high school. In their view, leaving a baby, even a toddler, in the care of anyone else was heartless.

"I just don't know how you can stand to leave this beautiful child!" my otherwise supportive mother exclaimed to me once when Sophia was eighteen months old.

The weight of her judgment was like a body blow. "It's not like I have much choice, Mom," I told her.

But in Germany, I did have a choice. I could have applied for *elterngeld* (money for parental leave) and taken a longer time off to stay home with my second child, but after having a whole year off with Ozzie, I knew that having a few hours to do something other than care for a child would be better for me and, therefore, better for my son. Still, it felt selfish. Hearing the other Berlin mothers express such positive attitudes toward kita helped alleviate some of the guilt. I certainly liked the idea that other kids and the new experiences at kita might be good for Ozzie.

I was also getting the best of both the East and West because I was surrounded by parents and teachers who had the East German perspective of kita as a normal, positive experience for young children and who had also adopted the West's more open curriculum, which rejected political or authoritarian rules in favor of child-centered play and social skills.

When I asked the history professor Allen about the differences she saw in today's American and German systems, she said that Americans see kindergarten as an academic class, while Germans see it primarily as child care. That could explain why Berliners often used the words *kita* and *kindergarten* interchangeably, even though kita often includes children younger than three. For those young kids like Ozzie, kita was essentially child care, but that didn't mean there was no learning going on. It just wasn't academic learning.

Early Kita Skills

Learning at kita for a one-year-old like Ozzie meant mastering "gross motor skills," like walking, or "fine motor skills," like using forks and spoons. None of it was purposely done through training or structured activities. Ozzie learned through play. He also picked up the language this way, without any formal instruction. Like his sister, Ozzie's first German words were the key ones for toddler relations: *meine* and *nein*. On the friendlier side, he also learned to say *hallo* before he could say the English version, hello.

To keep track of what he learned, Ozzie was given a long, bright green binder (Germans, I was starting to notice, love binders). In this binder, the kita teachers collected his drawings, and made observations on his behavior. They often wrote down direct quotations from him, his first words, and, then later, his more chatty thoughts, including his likes and dislikes, such as this gem about nap time: "I like it loud, when I have to go to bed. Then I like to jump around and giggle with my friends in our beds." Apparently, getting Ozzie to sleep was difficult for his kita teachers as well.

The teachers kept track of Ozzie's development, noting developmental milestones. For instance, I received a sheet that described Ozzie's "competencies." For example, "ego competencies" were about things like developing confidence in his ability to make things happen, and "social competencies" looked at his ability to be part of a group and play alongside others. There were also categories for knowledge and learning, but these were accomplishments like "communicating one's own wishes and intentions to others" and "developing the patience to repeat an exercise"—not academic skills. The kita instructors scheduled meetings with the parents to discuss progress and any issues. It was soon clear to me that kita was much more than babysitting.

While the teachers paid close attention to Ozzie's development and sometimes guided him, they resisted interfering. One of my favorite projects was a daylong observation of Ozzie where one kita teacher shadowed him and reported on what he did all day. Here is a sample ("you" refers to Ozzie):

"You see Finn going into the cupboard and closing the door. You run there, peeking into it through a hole. Finn is starting to giggle and so you are sharing a laugh too! Now Finn pushes open the door and then you close it. You are both having fun and repeat this game many times. But when Finn gets too wild and gives the door a real hard push you get a bump on your head. Now you are crying a bit. Fortunately, Paul joins the game and you get distracted. Now the hide-and-seek game continues, but you have learned to be more cautious and you make sure to stand farther away from the cupboard door!"

This passage was typical of the kita's approach to the kids. The kita teacher carefully observed what the children did but didn't hurry to intervene at the first sign of trouble. My impulse would have been to run over the minute I heard crying, but reading the whole story, I can see that doing that would have not only spoiled Ozzie's fun but also interrupted his learning process.

In the United States, most of the child-care workers I came into contact with had little formal training. Educational standards for child care vary from state to state, but most don't require much more than a high school diploma, and some states don't have any education requirements at all for entry-level jobs in the field, according to the Bureau of Labor Statistics. In Germany, on the other hand, all kita teachers are trained professionals: most go through two to four years of specialized education, as well as an internship, before taking a job in a kita. I felt assured my son was in good hands. This education also meant that when the kita teachers brought up an issue Ozzie was having, they had real ideas about how to solve it. Far from being threatened, I found this to be a great help.

Zac and I now had new allies in parenting. As I had already learned from Ozzie's sleep troubles, we didn't always know the right thing to do, not by instinct, not from our experiences with Sophia, not even from reading parenting books. The books didn't talk back, and they did not know my son's individual quirks and his everyday activities, but his kita teachers did. Anyone who has ever tried to live up to the ideal of the parents who are everything for their child knows this quest can be awfully quixotic—and lonely. With kita, we didn't have to be so alone.

It's telling that a language as precise as German doesn't have a word that literally means parenting. The word often used is *erziehung*, which means education or upbringing, and kita educators are called *"erzieher(in)"* (the added "in" is the feminine form) as opposed to *"lehrer(in),"* which means "teacher." This term seems to indicate that the job of raising a child is not limited to the *mutter* ("mother") or even the *eltern* ("parents").

Many German experts back up the idea that raising a child isn't only the job of the mother or the parents. Karl Heinz Brisch is a German psychologist whose research focuses on the importance of early parent-child bonding. He seems to be nearly as pro attachment theory as William and Martha Sears. Brisch even has his own trademarked training program, called SAFE in German and in English, to promote "secure attachment," and he rails against the fears some German parents have of "spoiling" their babies by being too responsive to their cries. Yet Brisch still believes in quality child care. The psychologist told the German newspaper *Die Zeit* that after his lectures people would sometimes approach him to tell him that they agree that "the children belong with their mother!"

"That's not what I am saying," Brisch explained. "Children need emotionally available caregivers with whom they can securely bond. Those caregivers could certainly include day-care staff in addition to the parents."

In contrast to Brisch's attitude, the Searses' books offer this warning within a chapter on "Working and Parenting" in *The Baby Book*: "The most important contributor to a baby's physical, emotional, and intellectual

development is the responsiveness of the mother to the cues of her infant."
The message couldn't be more clear: the Searses believe it is specifically the
mother who must be the most responsive, and if she is not there because
she is working, she is doing damage.

The German parenting icon Remo Largo points out that the idea of the
mother as the sole caregiver is an idea that came about after World War II,
and that babies are actually predisposed to bond with more than one
person. "Although it varies from child to child, children are generally able
to adjust to different caregivers even during their first year of life," Largo
said in an interview with the popular German women's magazine *Brigitte*.
"Nature set it up this way because not every mother is able to care for her
child—in the past, many women died in childbirth."

Instead of focusing on who is doing the caregiving, Largo argues that
the quality of care is really what matters. This is the same point that Brisch
makes as well, and he advocates for improvements in the German nursery
system, including better training and pay for the instructors and a higher
ratio of caregivers to children.

Quality of Care

In the United States, the day-care system has a particularly bad reputation.
Part of the persistent negative perception may be a hangover from the rash
of child-care sex abuse allegations in the 1980s and 1990s. A good number
of the cases relied on the testimony of small children, which today many
believe was unduly influenced or even coerced by parents, police, and psychologists. As the PBS *Frontline* documentary has chronicled, many of the
charges from those cases have since been overturned. Yet the damage had
been done, and those horror stories destroyed a lot of trust in American
child-care institutions. No doubt it also put a chilling effect on a profession already hindered by low pay.

Today, you would be hard-pressed to find many day-care workers in
the United States who are male (only 5.1 percent are men, according to the
Bureau of Labor Statistics). Anti-abuse advocate groups such as Stop It
Now! advise day-care centers to institute a two-adult rule, which means

no adult should be alone with a child at any point. This recommendation is meant to help prevent abuse (or accusations thereof), but as a policy, it seems pretty impractical for any but the most fully staffed day-care facility.

The worry about abuse accusations can also inhibit child-care workers from forming a caring relationship with children. An American colleague once complained to me that the child-care teachers never hugged the children. It seems like it would be awfully hard for small children to bond with caregivers who are afraid to touch them.

Despite all this, most American child-care situations are not, in fact, horrible. According to a landmark 2007 National Institute of Child Health and Development (NICHD) study, most child-care settings in the United States provide "fair" care, with about 10 percent providing very high-quality care. The NICHD defines positive caregiving as a host of activities including having a positive attitude, encouraging children, and listening, talking, and singing to children, as well as having positive physical contact. All of the child care found to be of fair quality did some of these things, some of the time. While far from a rousing endorsement, the NICHD study also found fewer than 10 percent provided very low-quality care. In short, most of it isn't bad.

This same study found the amount of time that children spent in child care had no positive or negative relation to their readiness for school. Instead, by far the most predictive factor of children's success was not whether they were in child care but their family's characteristics, such as their parents' education level or ethnic background.

The developmental psychologists Hiltrud Otto and Heidi Keller go even further in defense of early child care. They point out in a chapter of the book *Contemporary Parenting* that not only the NICHD study but also the European Child Care and Education Study (ECCE) and the German National Study of Education and Care in Germany (NUBBEK) "did not show any negative effect of children's day-care experiences on their development, no matter how early extra-familial day care started, how much time the children spent in care, and what the format of this care was." In fact, if any effects were noticeable, Otto and Keller noted they were positive and children from disadvantaged socioeconomic backgrounds "profited from day care substantially."

I wish I had known this way back at the start, when I first put Sophia in child care in the United States. We were lucky to find good child-care spots for her, and she had bonded well with people other than me: her father, her grandmother, and several good child-care teachers. Still, I felt like a bad mother. Although I dismissed comments like my mother's "How could I leave her?" as overly traditional, they still echoed in my head. I should have felt more confident that leaving her at child care did her no harm, that it might even be good for her. She had quality care and benefited from new people and experiences. She also knew from an early age that I would always come back.

At both the German kitas that Sophia attended, they had a settling-in period for children of all ages. Each time for Sophia, it took only minutes, not hours or days. She was used to adapting to new people and situations.

It took Ozzie much longer to see that kita was a good thing. While he loved the toys and kids, he did not want me to leave the room. We had no extended family in Germany, and because of Zac's commute, he had less time to spend with Ozzie than he'd had with Sophia. One of the first questions Ozzie's kita teachers asked me was whether he had ever had a babysitter. I had to think about it for several minutes before realizing how exclusively I had been with him. Ozzie hadn't been without me for more than an hour or two, for an entire year. Naturally, that made the adjustment to kita all the harder. It took nearly the full six weeks, but he did finally settle in and learned to enjoy kita without me there.

When my mother came to visit us in Berlin, she said she smelled another woman's perfume on her grandson. It was true. I'd noticed it before, but it didn't bother me. "That means someone has been hugging him," I said, giving him a squeeze myself. "You have to admit he is very huggable."

Child-Care Benefits

We don't have all the benefits of the German system in the United States, of course; the cost of such care is still a huge obstacle for many families.

It's clear we need political action to make child care more affordable for everyone, including working- and middle-class families who tend to get squeezed the most. While it's popular to talk about improving access to child care in politics—especially when it's promoted as "universal pre-school" or "early childhood education"—real progress has been slow. The biggest hurdle seems to be the expense, but Germany is proof it can be done without breaking the bank. Still, some individual states have implemented programs, including Oklahoma, Florida, and Georgia. If more parents, on all sides of the political spectrum, started telling their representatives how important the issue is to them and joined national and local advocacy groups like Child Care Aware of America, Children Now in California, or the Campaign for Children in New York City, we could make quality, subsidized care a reality in the United States.

Even without a political change, American mothers can look at the German example and at least lose the guilt. If you can find a quality child-care center with caring, educated staff, your child will have more advantages than a child raised solely at home does, including new experiences and relationships. You will have partners in raising her, and more time and space to become a better parent yourself. Your child will also be taking a big step toward developing more independence.

Within a few months, Ozzie loved going to kita. Not getting ready for it, per se (I have yet to meet a toddler who likes to get dressed to go any-where), but once we walked in the door, he'd be off playing before I would have much chance to say good-bye.

On his second birthday, we proudly arrived with cupcakes for every-one. I knew from other birthdays that most parents didn't stay for the party, but I lingered for a moment to take a picture. I watched as all the tiny toddlers gathered to sing "Happy Birthday" and "*Hoch soll er leben!*" ("High may he live!") Ozzie sat down on a kita teacher's lap. She gave him a hug. He focused on the cupcake with the lit candle, and when he blew it out, he didn't even look up at me. I had a funny feeling, almost like I was an intruder. I took my picture and left, unsettled.

As I walked home, I consoled myself: later that day I would pick him up again, and we would have our own family celebration. Ozzie still spent more time with his family than at kita, and more time with me, his mother, than with anyone else . . . wasn't it a good thing to give him some time away? I did not need to be there for every single moment in his life, not even for every single celebration (I would soon realize that my kids would have several parties every birthday). I was still a little sad about missing this event, but I was also starting to see that the cultural compulsion I felt to be with him all the time might not be the best thing for him—that maybe it was healthier that he should start having some of his own experiences without the constant presence of his parents.

5

The Democratic Kindergarten

In Sophia's new kita classroom, African snails the size of a human head were crawling on the tabletops. My daughter, now four, would be attending this kita group in a room down the hall from Ozzie's toddler room. This would be her second kita in Germany, but I hoped this one would be different from the first and include more preparation for school. When I asked about the giant snails, Annika, the head teacher, told me they were for the class's snail project. I smiled and nodded like a polite American, but I remember thinking what an odd project that was. After all, how much could there be to learn about snails? *Maybe the children were also learning about the letter* s, I thought hopefully.

I thought wrong. Annika wasn't teaching the alphabet in a creative way. She hadn't even picked the project. The children had. I didn't know it at the time, but this kita, like many kitas in Germany, followed what's known as "*situationansatz*," which translates to "situation approach." In practice, it means that the kita teachers observe the situation—what games the children play, scenes they act out, or real events in their lives. Then they

71

look for learning opportunities that arise out of what the children are already interested in.

Sophia was in the last years of kita, nearing the age for kindergarten, yet there were none of the typical things I'd expect to find in a U.S. pre-school or kindergarten: no alphabet letters on the wall, no cork boards displaying sheets of addition problems or practice sentences. The ambitious American parent in me worried a little. I knew that back home kids were learning academic skills earlier and earlier. I'd read scary articles about entrance exams for preschool and about how kindergarten had become the new first grade.

Here I was in the land that invented kindergarten, and it looked like the Germans had gone in the exact opposite direction. I could see through the big windows at the back of the room that all the kids were outside playing. Just like at Sophia's previous kita, most of what the kids did here was play and play some more.

At this point, I wasn't too worried about academics. Sophia was still four. What I cared most about was that she was happy. She'd been a little sad to leave her other kita and anxious about going to a new place. Annika talked with Sophia for a few minutes, then invited two girls inside to meet her, a German Egyptian girl named Mariam and a German Australian girl named Emma who were within a year of Sophia's age and fluent in both German and English.

I watched as the three became friends in the space of five minutes. They showed Sophia around the room, and then asked to show her the "garden," which is what Germans generally call the outside play space at kitas. Before I knew it, Sophia was running away from me with a half a wave of her hand as a good-bye. That was about all the "settling in" she needed.

Despite the dominance of play, I soon saw that the kita had some structure. The children were supposed to be in the room by nine a.m. for *morgenkreis* ("morning circle") when the instructors and children sat on the floor, sang songs, and talked about what was going to happen that day. There was a set time for lunch and snack, a resting time (although no kid was forced to sleep), and a table time for quiet work like coloring or games.

Still, the kids spent the majority of the day in the playroom or the garden, pretty much doing whatever they wanted.

This was intentional. The teachers all expressed that the children learned best by playing with other children, with little emphasis on academic skills.

"I think the most important thing they learn in kita is social and emotional development, to be school-ready," Annika said. "It's not really learning ABC's or numbers or things like that—it's knowing how to communicate, knowing their strengths and weaknesses, knowing how to get help, how to solve problems and conflicts. These are the basics they'll need for when they start school."

When I asked the kita's principal, Ulrike, what the children should know before starting school, she also emphasized similar traits versus cognitive skills. "They should have a lot of competencies, such as being curious," she said. "At the same time, they should learn to accept mistakes—that mistakes are there in order to learn and shouldn't frustrate you but lead you to another idea. It's a really important first step to being willing and motivated to learn." Ulrike also talked about developing "an inner drive," so children would want to find out things for themselves, and about giving the children more responsibility.

When I asked her about academic skills, Ulrike did say that children entering school should know how to at least write their names and how to count from one to twenty, but even these relatively modest goals were mostly taught through hands-on projects—projects that were usually determined by the students themselves.

Faster or Better Learning

We Americans are notorious for wanting to hurry our children's development. The Swiss psychologist Jean Piaget famously called this "the American question"—whether it is possible to speed up children's acquisition of cognitive milestones, a goal which Piaget thought was dubious. In a 1970 interview with *Psychology Today*, he answered this question with another: "Is it a good thing to accelerate the learning of these concepts?"

Good or not, many child experts don't think it's possible to push children to another stage before they are ready. "Development happens," my pediatrician once told me. "You can't force it, and you can't really stop it either." The child expert Remo Largo has a favorite proverb that embodies this idea: "The grass doesn't grow faster if you pull it."

Yet we Americans can't seem to resist pushing and pulling our children to make cognitive achievements earlier and earlier. Piaget first observed this American desire in the 1970s. I can only imagine what he would think about what we are doing now.

The U.S. Common Core academic standards include more than ninety literacy and math skills—for kindergartners. This means five- and six-year-old children are expected to learn things like basic addition and subtraction and to read emergent texts. Common Core proponents argue that these skills are achievable and should be learned through playlike activity rather than using things like worksheets. Robert Pondiscio, a senior fellow with the Thomas Fordham Institute, has pointed out that the standards don't call for turning kindergartens into academic pressure cookers: "Nothing in Common Core—not one blessed thing—precludes schools and teachers from creating safe, warm, nurturing classrooms that are play-based, engaging, and cognitively enriching."

He may be right that it is possible, but the rush to acquire these skills also begs Piaget's question—is it a good thing? Even if the children have the ability, it's hard to believe that every single five-year-old child is ready and willing to learn ninety cognitive skills without heavy-handed teacher intervention and without sacrificing something else.

After years of speculation about what was happening to early childhood education, University of Virginia researchers decided to look into whether American kindergarten had truly become the new first grade. They evaluated data collected from thousands of kindergarten and first-grade teachers between 1998 and 2010. Their report, which came out in early 2016, found that not only were kindergarten teachers spending a greater amount of time teaching math and reading—with an increased use of textbooks and workbooks—but also that less class time was spent on things like music and art. Also, the number of teachers who spent at least one hour a day on child-selected activities dropped as did the likelihood that a classroom had discovery or play areas. "We were surprised to see just how drastic the changes have been over a short period of time," said Daphna Bassok, the lead author of the study. "We expected to see changes on some of these dimensions but not nearly so systematically and not nearly of this magnitude."

The study is proof of what child development experts such as Nancy Carlsson-Paige have been warning for years: that the pressure of high-stakes testing has extended to kindergarten. Carlsson-Paige, a professor emerita of education at Lesley University, said kindergartens and even publicly funded preschools have moved toward more direct drill-and-grill–style teaching as a result of the testing reforms that punish schools and teachers if students perform poorly. It has become "a threatening and punitive climate because teachers feel the pressure to get those scores," she said.

And Carlsson-Paige has witnessed how this pressure gets passed on to the children. "In some classrooms I've visited, I've seen the horrible constraints children are under, and they're completely disinterested," she said. "You can see them turning off when they are five years old."

What's worse, the sacrifice American kindergartens have made is in pursuit of a goal that has questionable value. For example, there has yet to be any significant scientific study that shows learning to read at an early age has any benefit. In fact, a 2010 study done by Sebastian Suggate, a New Zealand native who now works at the University of Regensburg in Germany, showed that children who first learned to read at age five had no advantage over children who had learned to read at age seven. By the time both groups in the study were eleven, the late readers were indistinguishable from the early readers.

Many American kindergartens and preschools used to follow an emergent curriculum, which is similar to the German situationansatz we found at our Berlin kita. That type of curriculum can still be found at private preschools and kindergartens, but as the University of Virginia study showed, public schools have abandoned that play-based, child-centered curriculum in favor of more formal didactic instruction—and the trend was even more pronounced at schools that served predominantly low-income and minority students.

One big thing that American parents can do to help our kids' long-term success is to find a play-based preschool. We can interview our children's prospective kindergarten teachers as well. Many do their best to resist the academic pressure put on kids at these early ages. Parents have the power to take the pressure off at home too. You can politely refuse to have your child do homework.

To help everyone's children, we should advocate to end the push of academics into kindergarten. Defending the Early Years, a nonprofit Carlsson-Paige helps advise, has many tool kits to help parents organize. You can speak with your principal. Write your school board and government representatives. Find ways to join together with other parents. Personal actions are good, but individual parents often find the inertia in many districts hard to fight alone. Be like the Germans and start a *stammtisch*, a regular table, at a coffee shop to meet up with other parents and discuss school issues every week. You can also use organizing groups like Parents Across America to help elevate your voice. You can run for the PTA to make it a more active organization, or better yet, run for school board. It will take a sustained effort of many people and using the elected channels of power to make a real difference.

Somehow German kitas and kindergartens escaped the academic pressures, and they provide a good illustration of what our early childhood education system could be. Like the United States, Germany has fallen prey to what they call "academic shocks"—the sudden fear that their kids are falling behind the rest of the world. Each shock in Germany has been followed by huge political debate over educational reform. Yet there was strong resistance to any effort to push academics into kindergarten, fueled in part by the antiauthoritarian sentiments many Germans still hold.

In the 1970s, the German government commissioned the *Deutsche Jugendinstitut* (German Youth Institute) to develop a "social-learning curriculum" for early education, and this eventually gave rise to the situation approach that was adopted nationwide and can still be found in many public kitas and kindergartens.

The durability of the situation approach is perhaps a testament to its benefits and its basis in solid research. Critics of the Common Core regularly point out that the standards for earlier grades were made without input from early childhood education researchers. Also, as author Paul Tough details in his book *How Children Succeed*, a growing body of research shows that ultimately the children who go on to do well in school and in life are not necessarily the ones who master cognitive tasks but those who develop a "very different set of qualities, a list that includes persistence, self-control, curiosity, conscientiousness, and self-confidence." He points out that people have different names for these qualities: "noncognitive skills," "personality traits," or, more generally, "character." I might call them kita skills, because these are the same qualities our German kita taught my children, and in a most interesting way: by helping the children teach themselves.

Children in Charge

A wonderful thing happens when you let small children decide what they want to learn. They become intensely engaged.

At our kita, learning was almost always directed by the children. Sometimes the teachers would notice a hot topic being discussed by the children. For instance, when the World Cup came around, rather than fight it, the teachers created a project around *fussball* ("soccer"). However, most of the time, the children chose the topic directly. It would start with a morning circle when the kita teachers asked the children for project ideas. Of course, some of the topics the children came up with didn't work well. Some would be too broad like "animals" or too specific to hold the whole group's interest for several weeks. One of the first projects Sophia suggested was "the human heart." Not many of the other children were ready to back her idea, but when the teacher suggested they widen the topic to the human body, suddenly the rest of the kids were on board. They wanted to know how their muscles worked. What did the brain look like? How do the eyes see? The ears listen?

At the start of the project, the children would list all the questions they wanted to answer and state what they already knew about the topic. Over the next weeks, the kids would explore their subject through books, film, and art projects. Sometimes, they would go on field trips to get information, such as to a museum, and other times, they'd invite a guest expert to visit. For the body project, a doctor came in to answer questions from the children.

While my two children were in kita, their classes did projects on outer space, music, underwater life, jungles, and a number of places, including New York City and Egypt. One of my personal favorites was playgrounds, which involved the children visiting all the playgrounds within walking distance of the kita. (The child who suggested this project must have been a budding genius.)

No matter what the project was, the kids were excited and engaged because they had ownership of the subject; it wasn't forced on them by a teacher. The only goals to achieve were the ones they set for themselves. The child who had the original idea had an extra feeling of leadership and pride. I know Sophia did. One day she brought home a full-size picture of herself that had been traced on butcher paper and that she had painted. She proudly pointed out parts of the body and told me what she knew about them.

It was clear that the projects encouraged the children's curiosity. They built self-confidence by giving the children the control, choosing what to learn, and finding out how to answer their own questions. The projects also helped them learn a measure of self-control, learning how to concentrate for extended periods of time. The one thing they did not necessarily teach was good behavior—that was another issue entirely.

Discipline

The garden of our kita was a wild place, especially at the end of the day when there could be thirty or more kids tearing around the play structures.

Our kita approached most rules the same way they approached

projects: with some guidance, they let the students make the rules. I witnessed some of these sessions when the teachers asked the kids, "What should the rules of our room be?"

For the most part, the kids already knew what they should do. "Put the toys away when you are done!" "No hitting!" "Don't stand on the tables!"

"Why?" the teacher asked. "Why not stand on the tables?"

"You could fall off and get hurt!"

"*Und* we don't want stinky *füsse* where we eat!" another child said in mixed German and English. The room erupted in laughter.

"I want to come back to 'no hitting,'" the teacher said. "Why shouldn't you hit?"

Again, the kids had easy answers. "It hurts!" "They might hit you back," and "They won't play with you anymore."

The last answer was perhaps the most powerful. The kita teachers never forced children to play with each other or to "get along" if they didn't. They also never punished them. As I mentioned earlier, Germans have rejected authoritarian ways of handling children. Corporal punishment, spanking, or hitting children whether by teachers or parents is against the law.

Even more, I've rarely even heard a German mother raise her voice at a child, and I've never heard an angry reprimand from a kita teacher—not once, even though they deal with groups of eighteen or more energetic young children every day.

Our kita's philosophy was that the kids themselves were the best ones to enforce their own rules and solve their own conflicts—that they learn best from each other what is socially acceptable behavior. The teachers took an observational approach in this as well. Sometimes they would pull children aside if things got physical or too intense and talk with them, but rarely did they interfere in their everyday arguments.

I can't say that I always agreed with this philosophy, and I wasn't alone. At the international kita, I found common discomfort among many of the other English-speaking parents, who worried about the free-for-all attitude, especially in the kita's yard or garden. "It's totally *Lord of the Flies*!" an Australian mother remarked to me once. I agreed.

Now that she could make herself understood, Sophia had managed to avoid most conflicts at her new kita. We were relieved to know she wasn't a natural hitter. She remained tight friends with Mariam and Emma with only some mild arguments. Mariam, the oldest, was clearly the leader, but she "graduated" the following year, and a new little girl came into the group, a German New Zealander also named Emma. Both the Emmas were the same age, and both were bright, fun girls with strong wills. Sophia soon learned the problem with having two friends like this. When the two Emmas fought, usually over what all three of them would play, Sophia was stuck in the middle and given the impossible task of picking a side or face losing one friend or the other.

My best advice—"Just walk away" or "Don't play with them if they are mean"—was only met with tears. Luckily, the kita teachers had some better strategies. "We guided them, we observed what the problem was, what each of them wanted," Annika told me. "We did a lot of talking, a lot of mirroring with the kids, asking, 'How do you think the other girl feels when this happens?' They looked at the consequences, and then we let them solve the problems. If they said, 'I don't want to play with her,' we needed to accept this. Maybe tomorrow, or ten minutes later, it would change."

Annika's approach wasn't an instant fix by any means. The arguments came and went for months, but Sophia learned from this process so well that by the time she reached elementary school, she was an expert at conflict resolution. At our first parent meeting, her first-grade teacher called Sophia a "sunshine girl" who "spreads peace wherever she goes." As proud as I am of her, I know Sophia did not get that skill from me. I'm a little shorter on patience than I would like to be, and I would give my left arm for Sophia not to inherit that problem. That she doesn't have my temper is part nature—despite a few toddler disputes, Sophia has always tended toward gentleness—but it is also part nurture. Controlling her temper, and dealing with those of others, was a skill she learned from her kita teachers.

It took me a long time to realize that children, even very young ones, need adults other than their parents, that we parents are limited by our own characters and experiences in what we can teach our kids. Of course, these other adults—teachers, relatives, neighbors, and friends—can never take the place of parents, but they can teach our children things that we parents can't. And sometimes, children need to be away from the strong influence of their parents to help establish themselves—even if they are only three or four.

Kita Trips

Before moving to Germany, I would have never considered letting my small children stay somewhere overnight without me. Soon after moving, I learned that from a young age German children try out *übernachten* ("overnights") with grandparents, other friends, and even at their kita.

At Sophia's first kita, just before she turned four, a new, very enthusiastic (and very tattooed) young kita instructor offered to take all the kids to a camp for two nights. Another teacher would come along, as well as a parent chaperone, for fifteen kids. This made me, as well as many of the German parents, nervous. It was a voluntary experience, but nearly all the parents agreed to let the children try it. Sophia was excited to go. After talking it over with another mother, Judith, whose daughter was friends with Sophia, we agreed to the trip. *The two girls would have each other,* we thought. Still, we had our phones ready and mapped out how to get to the camp for what we expected would be a middle-of-the-night phone call to pick up our stressed-out daughters. The phone call never came.

After the second day, I rushed to the kita to pick up Sophia, worried that I would be met with tears. On the walk to the kita through the path in Treptower Park, I saw a lovely sight ahead of me: a string of kids holding hands with their two teachers, singing songs as they walked. Sophia was on the end next to her sleepy friend. When I caught up with them, Sophia babbled to me all about her adventures, which sounded pretty much like any day at kita except longer: "We read books. We played in the garden. We had all these bouncy balls!" Then I took her home, and she fell asleep and slept for twelve hours straight.

At her new international kita, the children had an overnight in the building itself. They played games, took a tour of the neighborhood, and had a disco party. Still no phone call home, but she slept well that time (thanks, I assume, to the disco dancing).

Writing on the parenting site *Mobile-elternmagazine,* German psychologist Gisela Preuschoff calls the first overnight separation for children "a psychological achievement." I particularly like how she describes handling this difficult milestone: ". . . fear also helps us grow, if we learn to overcome it. Letting go and hanging on belong together in life like the ebb and flow of the tides. Again and again, we encounter some situations where we have to hold on, and others where we have to let go."

I felt a lot of that ebb and flow as a parent in Germany. Sophia was the kind of child who would run away to play the instant I left her at kita, only to greet me with a full-barrel run into my arms at the end of the day. She would cower behind my knees at the sound of a loud hand dryer but also climb the highest tree in the park and even the fences—if I let her. More and more, I knew I would have to let her do things that I wasn't comfortable with, and luckily, along with this realization, I had more and more confidence in her ability to handle new challenges.

Teaching Kita Skills in the United States

Even without a German-style preschool or kindergarten, American parents can help emulate some of the lessons taught by kita teachers. We can find opportunities to engage our children's curiosity by having them do projects of their own choosing at home. It is a great activity for vacations. My kids love doing projects to this day. They pick the topic and decide the ways they are going to find the information, such as going to the library, asking experts, or maybe taking a trip to a special place like a museum or zoo.

For better discipline and self-control, we can involve children in making the rules of the house—and win an easier road to better behavior that way. Parents can wait before we get involved in their fights, letting them figure it out for themselves, and when they can't, instead of punishing them, we can ask them questions, as Annika did for Sophia, to help them to see how the other child feels. Young children are naturally self-centered, so this is a good way to help them practice empathy early. Maybe you can't give your children a kita trip, but there are simple ways to let them have an overnight adventure away from their parents: a sleepover at a friend's house or a trip to Grandma's for the weekend.

What might be trickier is leadership and responsibility, since developing those skills requires that children be among a group of mixed-age children, but perhaps an insightful preschool class or a special club can help.

For Sophia, I saw it happen over the course of several years in Germany. Sophia went from being a follower in her group of friends, the girl stuck in the middle, to become a real leader. The difference was apparent in her class "country" project. In keeping with their international mission, the kita held an "international week" every year when each group presented the results of their "country" project. The places chosen were usually countries, states, or cities that had some connection to one of the children in the group. The first year Sophia was in this kita, the country was Egypt, which was part of Mariam's heritage. For the presentation, Sophia dressed as a typical Egyptian kid in a long white shirt. She had a single line to say, and she was excited to participate, telling us facts daily about the pyramids and King Tut. But when it came time to say her line, she became shy, hid behind the teacher, and refused to say anything. The presentation moved on without her.

Sophia's last year at kita, the group chose New York City for their project. This time, Sophia dressed up as the Statue of Liberty. She stood tall and told everyone how the statue was a gift from France and greeted immigrants to the United States. She not only delivered her lines well but helped prompt some of the more nervous kids with their lines. So much had changed in a short space of time. Naturally, Sophia was older, but she had also been training to be a leader.

Sophia's kita group was mixed-age, so children as young as two were together with six-year-olds. The children were expected to take on more responsibility as they got older, with the oldest children considered to be the leaders of the group. This was part of their preparation for elementary school. "The more we give preschool-age children responsibilities, the more they will feel oriented and secure when they enter school," Ulrike said.

For lunch, three tables in the group were set up with different-size chairs. Each year, the children moved up a table, so they all looked forward to the time when they would sit at the "big table." The older children were given tasks like going to the kitchen to get the snack or the lunch. This was considered a privilege and a sign of trust. No adult went with them to supervise, and if there was any misbehavior, the children involved wouldn't be allowed to get the meal the next time.

The older children were also assigned to help a younger child get dressed to go outside. This process taught the older children patience and responsibility for each other—with the side benefit of taking extra pride that they were able to dress themselves alone. For the younger ones, they had a model to look up to who was much closer to their age, someone who had less authority than a parent or teacher, which made getting dressed more fun and less of a power struggle.

Sophia's experience of kindergarten would have been much different for her in the United States, where kindergarten is a single-year class attached to a primary school. If she started that year at age five in America, she would have been among the youngest children in the entire school; instead she had the experience of being the oldest leader of an entire group of younger children.

In Germany, by the time she was six, Sophia had learned how to explore subjects guided by her own curiosity. She had built her social skills, or "character." She knew how to care for others and resolve conflicts. She was independent and had no trouble being somewhere without her parents, and perhaps most important, Sophia had practiced being a leader, building her self-confidence in a safe, nurturing environment before entering the potentially more intimidating atmosphere of elementary school.

Sophia did not know how to read beyond a few words here and there. When I anxiously asked whether I should teach her, Annika advised me to wait: that learning to read was something special all the kids learned together in school. That's not to say that Sophia hadn't learned any academic skills. She knew her ABC's. She could write most of her numbers and letters, which she had learned not only through teaching activities but also by copying her friends at kita—she even wrote a few Egyptian characters that Mariam had taught her. She knew how to count to twenty and had even let go of her favorite made-up number "eleventeen." And somehow, though she'd had no formal language instruction at all, she'd learned how to speak German fluently.

Sophia, her kita teachers assured me, was now ready for school.

6

Starting School

We brought Sophia to her new school on a Saturday. Our local elementary school was a huge tan stucco building with a red-tiled roof—an architecture style somewhere between rustic villa and insane asylum. We entered the school's stone courtyard and walked into a crowd of well-dressed German parents and grandparents. Their children, also dressed in their finest clothes, ran in and around the adults. We waited awkwardly in the crowd, exchanging as much polite conversation as our limited German would allow. A little blond girl wearing a traditional German dirndl dress hid behind her father's legs and stared shyly at my dark-haired Sophia. They didn't know it yet, but they would soon become best friends.

Finally, a bell sounded, and we climbed three flights of stairs to a large cafeteria converted to a theater with chairs facing a small stage. A teacher directed our daughter to the front row where the other new first graders were sitting. I walked Sophia to her seat. Because her kita had not been in our neighborhood, she knew no one at this school.

"Are you OK here by yourself?" I asked. Sophia's eyes were big, but she waved me away. I left to find my seat with Zac and Ozzie among the other parents in the back, none of us knowing quite what to expect.

We hadn't planned on this: on being in Germany long enough for our daughter to start first grade. What was supposed to be a three-year contract for Zac had become a permanent position, and luckily too. It was the height of the recession, and American universities had precious few open positions for scientists. Our house in Oregon still hadn't sold, and we were on a seemingly endless cycle of bad renters and urgent repairs. I had started using my journalism skills to supplement our income with copyediting and article writing, but for all intents and purposes, we were stuck in Germany.

There was one big consolation: Our children were thriving. Ozzie was fully bilingual and finding his way at the international kita, and Sophia was excited to go through one of the biggest events in every German's life—*einschulung*, the start of school.

When I was a child, the first day of school meant some new clothes and a backpack. My mother took my picture, and she cried. Then I walked into the school. I knew it was a big occasion, but it was nothing compared to the German einschulung.

In my effort to learn German, I had found a *sprachpartner*, or "language partner": Kordula, who was everything and nothing you might expect of a modern native of East Berlin. She was a tall, beautiful blonde who grew up in the GDR and never moved far from home yet had traveled all over the world. Kordula wanted to improve her English to help with her travels, and in turn, she helped me learn such necessary words as *schweinehund*, literally "pig-dog," and apparently if you have a large one, you are very lazy. (I've seen saltier translations for schweinehund, but I'm sticking with "pig-dog.") Kordula was also one of my key resources for cultural questions. When I told her that Sophia was starting school, she asked me what I was doing to prepare for the big party.

"Party?" I asked.

"Come on!" she said. "Starting school is a big deal! It isn't in America?"

"Kind of, but there usually isn't a party. We celebrate graduation—the end of school."

"Only the end?" She looked at me like things must be very sad in America. She held out a thumb and her first two fingers (which is how Germans count). "The three biggest events in your life are einschulung, *jugendfeier,* and getting married." This stunned me because the first two words didn't translate well—and I had to admit I didn't even know what jugendfeier was. Kordula explained it was a special party at age fourteen, when you were considered no longer a child but an adolescent.

Kordula was giving me her East German perspective, because jugend-feier was a secular event promoted by the GDR to replace religious confirmation. While most Germans mark age fourteen as the entry into young adulthood, how they do it depends on their religious and regional backgrounds. Einschulung, on the other hand, has deep roots in both the East and West, and it's celebrated in a similar way at nearly every school nationwide.

I didn't want to have a big schweinehund, so I started researching the custom. In the late spring, I noticed that strange "starting school" items appeared in Berlin stores: giant three-foot cardboard cones and monster backpacks, called *schulmappen.* These hard-shell packs were meant for first graders even though they were wider than a typical six-year-old's back. Schulmappen came in a variety of themes, such as dinosaurs, fairies, or pirates. The best ones had matching items like a pencil case, called a *feder-tasche,* and a snack box, *brotdose.* Sophia chose an underwater-themed schulmappe with a crab on the front. It cost a whopping €120—and it was not the most expensive one. We swallowed our hesitation at spending so much on a backpack and bought it.

We'd already received a supply list from her teacher that was incredibly specific, down to the shade of each color pencil. (Sophia would need exactly one dark green pencil, one medium green, and one light green.) I didn't take Sophia with me to shop for these items as I planned to put some of them in one of those giant cones. I soon found out they were called *zuck-ertüte* because traditionally they were filled with sweets, thus the *zucker* (sugar) in the name.

I investigated the cone tradition on the Internet and by asking friends—because I couldn't imagine any child needed that much candy. I learned that the zuckertüte filling could include school supplies and gifts like stuffed animals. Another common item to give was a watch or an alarm clock, so they could start learning to track their own schedules—and no doubt work on the German value of being *pünktlich* ("punctual").

Thankfully, we were pünktlich for Sophia's einschulung at the school, because the room filled up fast with parents holding up smartphones for pictures. The principal, a white-haired man with a mustache, got up on the stage and spoke at length about the importance of the day. With so many proud relatives crammed together on a summer day, the room grew quite warm. Ozzie squirmed next to me. I couldn't see Sophia. I wondered how she was faring, if she was wilting from the heat or anxiety.

Finally, the principal finished his speech, and a troop of children dressed in a rainbow of colors took over the stage. They began to dance silently. From the imagery, I gathered it was about the passing of the seasons. The dance ended, and the children lined up on one side of the stage. Each picked a sunflower out of a nearby bucket. A teacher started to call the new first graders one by one to the stage. Before I could worry if Sophia would be too shy to get up on the stage, there she was, taking a flower from the second-grade boy who would be her *partner-kind* to help her transition into her mixed grade class.

Then Sophia was gone again—leaving with her new classmates to have a group picture taken. The parents were all directed to the courtyard where we were served champagne in plastic glasses. When Sophia returned to us, we presented her with her zuckertüte. It was nearly as big as she was.

After the school celebration, most of the German kids went home to have big parties with their entire families. Being expats, we had no extended family nearby, and many of our friends were having an einschulung that day as well. Families of new first graders across the entire city of Berlin all celebrated the start of school on the same day. Our little family walked home to have lunch together, a bit stunned by the magnitude of the whole thing.

This event marked a big shift in our time in Germany. Until now, both of our children had been at a bilingual kita, and as American parents, we moved easily through a half-English world. Many of Sophia's friends had chosen the private Berlin Bilingual School to continue their German-English education. After some debate, we had decided against this path in favor of our local public school up the street. It had a great reputation, it was close and free, and most of all, we hoped it would give Sophia a firm grasp of her new language. This school would be all German, all the time.

Even though it was a public school, we were pleased to find that it operated on a Montessori model, where children self-direct a lot of their own learning. In fact, many Berlin primary schools follow this model. Sophia's first three years would be spent in a mixed, first-through-third-grade class. Still, if we hadn't liked the educational program of our local school, we could have applied for a spot in one of the other public schools in the city, which have a range of approaches. Some have a special focus, such as sports or music. My friend Taska chose a public elementary school with a math and science focus when her son turned six.

There were also public international or bilingual schools, including a British school. Many expats covet a spot at the American JFK public school in southwest Berlin, where children are taught a curriculum similar to what they would receive in the States. We could even band together with other parents and start our own, as the parents who'd created Berlin Bilingual School had done. One thing we couldn't choose, however, was to keep Sophia home and teach her ourselves.

Homeschooling is illegal in Germany. When the law was challenged by the Konrad family, several German courts ruled against them, and in 2006, the European Court of Human Rights upheld the German ban on homeschooling. An appeals court in the German state of Baden-Württemberg ruled that "Schools represented society, and it was in the children's interests to become part of that society. The parents' right to provide education did not go so far as to deprive their children of that experience." The homeschool issue aside, this argument is revealing: first it shows that Germans feel children have the right to the company of other children and adults who are not their parents, and second, that by the tender age of six, the government views children as having rights that go beyond their parents' control. So that wonderful einschulung ceremony also meant that a big separation had begun.

Play School

The separation between parents and child marked by the start of school was reinforced a few weeks later when Sophia's entire class went on a week-long trip together. I had gotten used to overnights through the kita experience, but those were one or two nights—this was an entire week, for a six-year-old. I hadn't experienced anything like that as a kid. Yet, in Berlin, this class trip early in the year was a common practice at primary schools.

The purpose was mainly for the children to bond with one another. There would be little formal instruction that week. The children would stay in cabins in a nearby forest, go hiking and swimming, cook, and make crafts—basically play. Of course, Sophia was all for it. She packed her own bag days before the time to leave. As instructed, I gave her a little money for her wallet, so she could buy treats at the camp's kiosk.

When the day came to leave, she went with her new class without so much as a backward glance. Zac and I missed her terribly, and so did Ozzie. We were to expect no phone calls, though the kids all wrote a postcard home. I got hers the day she came back, all tanned, scabby-kneed, and happy.

I tried to pry information out of her about the trip and got little beyond that they "played" and what sort of sweets she did or did not buy at the kiosk. She admitted that the nights were a bit hard, but she hadn't been miserable. I started to hear her talk about more classmates, and soon it became obvious that she had a new best friend, Maya, the little blond girl we'd seen at her einschulung.

After the trip, Sophia's school life was underway in earnest, but that still meant half days of instruction interrupted by several recesses and a lengthy lunch. I studied her schedule, which seemed to have an awful lot of *freiarbeit* on it. This "free work" was first conceived by kindergarten founder Fröbel, and the educator Maria Montessori picked the idea up and expanded on it in her method of teaching.

At our school, there were only a few sessions a week with the classic "sage-on-the-stage" type of instruction, in which a teacher stands up in front of the class and lectures while students sit and listen. In Montessori, children had a small amount of direct instruction and were then left to play with materials designed to help them learn literacy and math concepts. They also had workbooks to fill out and tests, but each child finished these at his or her own pace.

Sophia's class was a mixed-grade class of first through third, so there was some flexibility in when a child had to learn a certain concept. The mixing of ages also helped the children learn from each other. This is not particular to Montessori schools; many elementary schools in Berlin combine at least the first two grades of elementary school.

The length of instruction was also fairly common. While many German elementary schools are moving toward full-day instruction, half-day schools are traditional. Ours was a combination. The school advertised itself as a "reliable half-day school with open-all-day service."

Like the majority of kids in her class, Sophia went to *hort* after formal instruction ended. Hort is after-school care, and it was held in the same school building. Hort occupied several rooms inside where the kids could play, including one for crafts, one devoted entirely to Legos, and a *kuschel-raum*, a cuddly room for quiet reading. After instruction was over, the kids checked into hort in these rooms, but after some time, all of them would go outside to the school's *hof* ("yard"). Sometimes, the instructors would organize special activities, but mostly the children were free to play whatever they liked.

When I came to pick Sophia up, I often had to go searching for her among the variety of playground structures, including swings, slides, trampolines, a large wooden boat, and a three-story tower. On the edge of the yard was a small natural area of trees and large bushes. Here, the kids would play things like chase, hide-and-seek, and other made-up games, mostly out of sight of the hort instructors. It was among this small piece of planned wilderness where I most often found Sophia after school.

Despite the big event of einschulung, I didn't see how first grade was dramatically different than kita for Sophia. While she had some classroom instruction, the majority of her day was still play. Needless to say, this worried her American parents some.

Educational Priorities

We hadn't listened entirely to Sophia's kita teachers. We taught Sophia to read, in English, before school started. Since she was going to a German school, we figured she needed a head start on English. Not being teachers, Zac and I used a cheesy-sounding but effective book called *Teach Your Child to Read in 100 Easy Lessons*. The anxiety American parents have around early learning was clear from the many titles in this category. If you believed all the claims, you could apparently teach your child to do anything at any age. There was even a book that said you could teach your baby to read and do math.

Many Germans are concerned about their children's academic achievement as well. Traditionally, students in Germany are separated by ability in fifth grade, with an upper track for students destined for university, a middle track, and a vocational track. This system has become more flexible with the introduction of new comprehensive schools; however, once placed on a track, especially if it's the lowest track, a child would have a hard time moving up. Those are some high stakes, very young, but even this looming division did not make parents at our school want to push their first graders too hard.

I was struck by this attitude at a meeting for first-grade parents. Sophia's class was large, with twenty-seven kids total, spanning three grades, seven of whom were first graders. So for this meeting, nearly twenty parents met with the teacher, Frau Schneider, and her helper, an *erzieherin* ("instructor") named Frau Müller. I remember Frau Schneider saying that some children might not master reading right away, not even by the end of the first year. "Don't worry," she assured us. "They will all learn to read eventually." To my surprise, most of the parents nodded their heads in agreement.

Despite the apparent lack of intensity at this level, Germany is not a country that takes education lightly. You cannot do a job in Germany without proof of some formal training in that field. People with university degrees are highly respected, and a doctorate is considered necessary for most political positions.

The German education system seems effective when compared with the other thirty-five first world countries in the Organization for Economic Co-operation and Development (OECD). In the 2012 Programme for International Student Assessment, or PISA, German fifteen-year-olds performed well above average in reading and math, ranking among the top fifteen OECD countries in 2012 in both categories—and higher than their American peers, who were below average, ranking seventeenth in reading and twenty-seventh in math. So if success is measured only in terms of math and literacy skills, the Germans have it, even with their slower approach to elementary school.

Like in the United States, German primary schools have undergone a great deal of reform, and in 2004, national standards were set for math, German, and foreign language. This move sounds similar to the U.S. Common Core standards (minus the foreign language), which focus on math and English skills, but the German schools have goals beyond just two subjects.

According to the government's online school guide, German primary grades should focus on "the development of self-learning strategies and skills, children are encouraged to learn by experience and interaction with their environment." This statement puts the child at the center of her own learning, with an emphasis on fostering independence in the process. In contrast, the U.S. Common Core talks only about what children need to learn, not about how they learn it, and as its critics have noted, the heavy testing involved leads to an emphasis on worksheets and direct instruction, not on children developing their own investigative process of learning.

Much of what is taught in German schools is overseen by each state or province, which in German is confusingly called a "*land*." I looked up the standards for the metropolitan area of Berlin, which is its own "land," and saw that Berlin has standards not only for math and German, but for history, geography, natural sciences, politics, art, music, languages

(English and French), social studies, sports, and traffic and mobility ed-ucation.

Given the few hours of the traditional half-day school, I had to won-der how all this fit into such a brief day of instruction. The short answer is that it didn't, not for first graders anyway. Many of the subjects are intro-duced slowly through the grades, and some subjects, such as politics, are only taught in the last year of elementary school. Still, you would be hard-pressed to find many U.S. states that push their public primary schools to teach such a wide range of subjects, even to fifth graders.

In Germany, the schools have some flexibility in how they arrive at teaching students these tasks. For instance, our school used projects to pro-mote learning, similar to the way Sophia's kita did. While the school, rather than the kids, picked the themes, the students did have the opportunity to explore a topic incorporating subject skills in the process. During Sophia's first year, the school projects had elemental themes: air, fire, and water. So, for example, during the air project, students learned the math and science around flight, they read stories about air travel, and they stud-ied birds. At the final stage, the kids were split into working groups that spanned all grades, and each group made a sculpture of a flying machine or animal—which could be real or imaginary. The results were hung in the hallways—giant hot air balloons, fanciful rocket ships, and strange unicorn-birds.

I helped out on the day the sculptures were created in what was essen-tially a school-wide papier-mâché project. Glue, colored paper, and sticky kids were everywhere. Still, the children were invested and engaged in the projects. Most of the kids had strong feelings about how things looked, or who got to make or paint which part. Each group had a fifth grader as a leader, and kids of all ages had to figure out how to work together.

These skills, leadership and teamwork, are a central part of the curric-ulum. The Berlin standards included not only a list of facts children should know about a given subject but also a number of "competencies" that sounded more like what a business guru might call "soft skills." For instance, the math standards stated that first graders should learn addi-tion, subtraction, etc., on up to such things as prime numbers in fifth grade—but the math standards also called for learning "social skills," such as communicating reasoning to others, and "personal skills," such as the ability "to take responsibility for their own learning, to critique their own results and process the criticism offered by others." Each subject had similar goals. By placing these skills at the center of every subject, the Berlin system seemed to recognize a critical truth about education and growing up: children need more from school than math and literacy skills; they need to learn how to become responsible, thoughtful people.

Homework, Food, and Protest

Despite the emphasis on responsibility, Sophia's school didn't assign much homework. In fact, in first grade, she had none. I knew homework would be coming because I heard the parents of third graders complain about the amount of *hausaufgaben* in yet another parent meeting. At our school, each class had its own type of PTA. We had elected officers and took votes. We also had multiple meetings with the teacher as an entire class, by grade, and one-on-one. All in all, the parents had a lot of opportunity to ask questions and give feedback to the teacher.

At this meeting, the issue was not about the amount of homework; many parents felt their kids shouldn't have any at all.

"It interferes with family time," one mother complained.

"If my son wants to play sports or take music lessons, then there is no time at all," a father said.

Frau Schneider deftly handled this problem by making sure there was enough time set aside in hort for the students to complete their homework before they got home. Her helper, Frau Müller, also worked as a hort instructor and was on hand at the meeting to assure the parents that the homework would get done.

It worked well. Sophia started getting some homework in second grade and more in third grade, at least three times a week, but I never saw a piece of this hausaufgaben actually done at our *haus*.

This is how it should be done according to Armin Himmelrath. A German journalist who often writes on education topics, Himmelrath called for an end to homework in his 2015 book: *Hausaufgaben? Nein Danke!* ("Homework? No Thanks!"). It set off a great debate among German educators and parents. Most German primary schools assign homework, and in greater amounts than our school in Berlin did. Homework is a long entrenched tradition, one which Himmelrath discovered goes all the way back to the 1400s.

Yet, according to the science, we shouldn't be assigning any homework in elementary school at all because it has no proven benefit. This is not the finding of one study alone, but of the vast majority of the research on the topic. Duke University psychologist Herbert Cooper led a review of 180 scientific papers published from 1987 to 2003 on the subject and found no strong correlation between doing homework and academic achievement in elementary school. There was some correlation in higher grades, but any benefit is lost after more than two hours of it.

The research Cooper reviewed was all conducted in the United States, and the German journalist Himmelrath found similar evidence in Europe. He pointed to the Swiss canton of Schwyz, where homework was abolished for four years in the 1990s. During that time, the performance of Schwyz students was compared with students in another region. The only difference researchers found? The children without homework were more motivated and less stressed. This should make sense to any parent who has had to push their reluctant children to do their homework. No one feels good about being forced to do anything. It does not exactly give them a warm, fuzzy feeling about school and learning.

Himmelrath also argues that homework exacerbates inequality. If a child hasn't understood a topic in school, she's unlikely to figure it out at home all by herself—which gives a distinct advantage to children from more privileged backgrounds who have educated parents with the time to help them over those who do not. Himmelrath said the best way to resolve this inequity was to have "homework" done in school, with an instructor nearby who can help—which, lucky for us, was exactly what was happening in our school.

The hort homework solution pleased the parents in our class, but some were much less pleased about other aspects of the school—namely, the food. No other issue was discussed more often and at greater length than the contents of the lunch menu: the food wasn't nutritious enough, there weren't enough choices, or it wasn't "bio" (organic). I watched these discussions with mild amusement. They didn't know how good they had it.

German food has a negative stereotype. People think it is all heavy sausage, potatoes, sauerkraut, and schnitzel. It's true Germans love these things, but I found greater variety and more healthy choices than I expected in restaurants and in schools. I was quite pleased by the school's lunch menu, which was light-years beyond the soggy hamburgers and tater tots from the school cafeterias I had known as a child. Yet I understood why the parents were concerned. None of the children brought lunch to our school. They had to eat what was served in the cafeteria.

Traditionally in Germany, lunch is the biggest meal of the day, as it is in many European countries. At Sophia's school this meant it was always a hot dish: casseroles and goulash, soups and pastas, and, yes, plenty of potatoes in all their varieties: fried, boiled, and mashed and pureed into a soup. Students always had a choice of vegetarian or meat entrée. Sometimes there were even special "sweet" lunches of German pancakes with applesauce or *milchreis,* a milky rice pudding usually served with cherries, but these were rare treats, not daily items. Notably, they never served chips, pizza, or chicken nuggets. Every once in a while, they did serve *wurst* (sausage). We were in Germany after all.

I liked the school cafeteria. For one, it meant I didn't have to pack Sophia a lunch, although I did pack her a small snack in her brotdose that she ate in class as a type of second breakfast around ten a.m. every day. Second, having to eat in the cafeteria forced Sophia to try new things. Of course, she loved the sweet stuff, but she also became used to eating vegetables she might otherwise have rejected. For instance, she informed me once that she really liked *krautsalat,* a cold cabbage salad, like coleslaw except without the mayo.

When she invited her best friend, Maya, over one afternoon, I asked the seven-year-old what her favorite meal was. I expected an answer like pizza or wurst, but without hesitation she answered, "*Spinat mit spie-*

geleiern und kartoffelbrei!" "Cooked spinach with fried eggs and pureed potatoes."

I about fell over. "*Wirklich*?" I asked. "Really?"

"Wirklich," she replied with a firm nod of her head. So when she came over, I presented the two girls with Maya's favorite meal, and they both cleaned their plates, cooked spinach and all.

Most parents weren't as pleased with the school menu as I was, and soon an email went around asking for concerned parents to come to an organizing meeting. I didn't go because I had no complaints about the food, but I saw the many emails that went around, and the number of meetings planned. And after some time, enough parents had gotten together to force an improvement, and the school changed its caterer.

I noticed that protest on all levels happened more often in Berlin than I'd seen anywhere I'd lived in the United States, and notably, it often had a real effect, especially when it came to children. For example, our kids came out on top when they went up against some developers, a normally powerful group in Berlin. The city's east side has seen a lot of renovation and new construction in recent years, and our neighborhood was no exception. At one point, five new buildings were going up at the same time on the street that led to Sophia's school, including one directly across from the school. The noise of hammering and sawing became so loud it became hard for the children to concentrate.

The principal wrote asking parents to call the city and the construction company. The fifth grade students hung a huge hand-painted banner from their window that read in German: "Quiet please! We are working here!" The pressure worked. The construction company gave in and agreed to stop the noisiest part of their work until two p.m. every day, when the instruction part of the school day was over for most students.

American parents and children can take a lesson from our German peers. Protest can work. For a long time, many Americans have been reluctant to protest—taking to the streets is often viewed as something only radicals do, and even objecting to the practices of a teacher or school is sometimes seen as overly critical or even rude. American culture places a high value on being friendly and polite. Germans don't have that baggage. For better or worse, they are known to be direct, even overly blunt in expressing their opinions.

The downside of Americans' politeness is that it has allowed the people in power at all levels to become complacent. A German parent living in the U.S. told me she found that teachers and administrators were less open to addressing parents' concerns than in her home country. To break this pattern, we have to get over our desire to be nice and start speaking up more often, not just to the people in the highest offices in our country but to the people in charge of our children's schools and classrooms. We don't have to be rude, but making change does require being direct and persistent.

If we gather enough parents together, we may be surprised by the results we can achieve. If we feel our children's classes are too test-focused and the subject matter too narrow, if there's too much homework or our kids need more time to play, even if we just want a better lunch menu, we can achieve change without waiting for political leaders to institute an entire school reform from the top down. Sometimes it just takes a few meetings, some phone calls, and letters—and involving the kids doesn't hurt. Children can have a lot of sway. After all, I've seen them stop work on an entire high-rise.

7

No Bad Weather

One winter afternoon in Berlin, I was having lunch with a Canadian friend when I saw a woman with a stroller and an older couple approach the restaurant. The woman rolled the stroller up next to the window, set the brake, and then walked into the restaurant—without her baby. The older couple, probably the child's grandparents, didn't give the baby carriage a second glance. The trio chose a seat by the window and picked up their menus.

"They're going to leave the baby outside?" I asked my friend.

"I know. They do that all the time here," she said in a low voice. "If the baby's sleeping, they don't want to wake her up. In Canada, you could never do that. It's too cold."

"I guess they aren't worried anyone would walk off with the baby!" I said. Even as I made that remark I realized how ridiculous that sounded. It was highly unlikely that a wacko would come up to the restaurant in broad daylight and make off with the infant, but I'd heard stories of baby stealing, and they loomed huge in my mind. Larger, of course, than the reality. In thirty-two years, from 1982 to 2015, 300 infants were abducted in the United States—that's less than ten a year—according to the National Center for Missing and Exploited Children. (Thankfully, the vast majority have also been recovered.) The odds of a baby getting hit by lightning are higher than her being abducted.

My reaction wasn't fact-based; it was cultural. The practice of leaving a sleeping baby unattended for even a short time is so antithetical to the American idea of safety that when a Danish mother left her small child outside a restaurant in New York City, she was arrested for it. But like many northern Europeans, Berliners place a high value on children getting fresh air, so leaving a baby outside is considered the healthy thing to do.

The importance of fresh air has deep roots in Europe. In one of the earlier versions of the *Three Bears* fairy tale recorded in the 1800s, Goldilocks is said to have jumped out the window, specifically left open because the bears "being good, tidy bears, always opened their bedroom window in the morning." Two centuries later, I found a clause in my German rental contract saying we should open the windows to air out the house on a daily basis. Every German I know did this, even in the dead of winter. They also made sure their children went outside every day for their required fresh air, no matter the season.

There's a German saying that translates roughly as "There's no bad weather, only unsuitable clothing." (*"Es gibt kein schlechtes Wetter, es gibt nur falsche Kleidung."*) When I left the restaurant that day, I saw that the sleeping baby in the stroller was under a puffy blanket and wearing a hat, mittens, and a snowsuit. She was definitely suitably dressed.

Germans love the outdoors. Berlin's restaurants and cafés keep their outside seating open as long as possible, leaving blankets out for customers who like to eat *draussen* even when it's chilly. Germans also celebrate Christmas outside at open-air fairs called *Weihnachtsmärkte*. (Germans call the holidays around Christ's birth *Weihnachten,* or "holy nights.") In public squares throughout Berlin, weihnachtsmärkte open up in late November and stay open through Christmas day. Many of the markets feature activities like ice skating and carnival rides, and all of them have rows of wooden huts selling crafts and food: bratwurst cooked on open fires and holiday treats such as *lebkuchen*, a spicy ginger cookie, and *stöl-len*, a sweet sugar-covered fruit bread too good to call fruitcake. To stay warm, adults drink steaming mugs of mulled spiced wine called *glühwein*, and kids have the choice of hot punch or cocoa.

We loved this tradition and went to as many of these markets as we could every Christmas. I have a picture of Ozzie at his first market, barely three months old, bundled in the stroller asleep. Then, another year, enjoying a cocoa with Sophia, and still later, jumping on a giant trampoline, soaring high into the fresh, cold winter air.

Granted, Berlin is warmer than you might expect. Like much of Europe, Germany benefits from the warm air brought by the Atlantic Ocean Gulf Stream. The snows only hit Berlin a few times a winter, and some winters have no snow at all. The only days that are truly bitter arrive when the winds shift and blow from the east—what happens, I've been told, when "Mother Russia lifts her skirts."

Even when it is cold, rarely does the temperature prevent German children from going outside. Year round, kita kids are playing in the garden for a good part of the day, and primary school children are sent out into the hof. They go outside even if it is raining or snowing.

At our kita, as soon as he could walk, Ozzie was bundled up along with the other toddlers and sent outside to muck around in the soggy play area. I was introduced to the necessity of having two pairs of raincoats, rain pants, and boots, so the children would never be without their full gear. In the winter, the children required snow pants or full body snowsuits as well as gloves, scarves, and *mütze* ("winter hats"), which covered the ears, or simply a knit stocking that covered the entire head with a hole cut out for the child's face. Around town, all those German grandmothers who were so prone to give my children candy were also quick to give me unsolicited criticism on how inappropriately I had dressed my children for current weather conditions.

The German value on the outdoors is reflected in the sheer number of outside places even within a big city like Berlin, which boasts 1,850 public playgrounds, not counting the play spaces found within the city's forests or next to its public pools. Compare this to the 1,700 recreation areas in

New York City, which has more than twice the population. While many U.S. cities have one giant park, Central Park in New York or the Golden Gate in San Francisco, Berlin has several huge green spaces in addition to the historic Tiergarten. Each neighborhood has at least one big park, such as Volkspark Friedrichshain in our neighborhood and Treptower Park to the south of us, which are both around 200 acres each. Berliners love their open space so much that they successfully fought off housing-development plans at the former Tempelhof airport in the southern part of the city, and in 2010, the city created a massive park out of the 984 acres of airfields.

As newcomers to Berlin, we visited a different park every weekend all over the city. We flew kites at Tempelhof, picnicked at Tiergarten, and climbed the waterfalls at Viktoria Park in Kreuzberg. One of our favorite discoveries was the *Arabian Nights*–themed playground at Volkspark Hasenheide in the southeastern district of Neukölln in Berlin. The playground features carved wooden figures of genies and sultans interspersed among the play structures, including a two-story wooden boat, a multi-sided climbing wall, and a "flying carpet" made of long stretches of bouncy rubber.

Sophia loved our weekend playground excursions and explored many play structures at the various parks. Just like at kita, she grew braver on the playground as she grew older. It took several visits to Mitte, the central district of Berlin, but she finally scaled the house-size rope-and-metal climbing pyramid we found there. By far her biggest challenge was still the dragon sitting in our own neighborhood park.

For nearly a year, she repeated her climb up and down that dragon without going into its mouth or trying the slides. Then one day while I was sitting with Ozzie in the sand, I heard her call out, "Mama! Mama!" I stood up and looked around. Where had she gone? I raced over to the tunnels thinking maybe she was stuck.

"Mama! Look up!" I did, and there she was waving at me from between the dragon's teeth. A few minutes later she came flying down the tall slide like it was no big thing. I couldn't help noticing the light in her eyes and the way she stood a little taller. She walked around like she was the queen of the park. She had conquered the dragon.

This courage was catching. It wasn't too long until I heard another "Mama! Mama!" over my head. This time Sophia was in the dragon's mouth with three-year-old Ozzie at her side.

America Inside

American kids don't have as many opportunities to conquer a dragon—at least outside of a video game—because our kids spend much more time indoors than their German peers do. About 77 percent of German kids ages three to ten play outside more than five times a week according to a 2013 Robert Koch Institute study. In contrast, out of a group of American mothers surveyed by physical education professor Rhonda Clements, only 31 percent reported that their kids played outside every day.

The American children who do get outside spend a short amount of time there. University of Michigan researchers surveyed 2,017 families with children and found that on average children ages six to seventeen spent less than an hour per week on "outdoor activities." (This excludes about three hours a week in sports, which may or may not be outside, and which are structured activities rather than free play.) What are children doing instead? They are spending increased time at school, studying, watching TV, and using the computer. These last two activities alone took up more than sixteen hours of children's time per week.

The problem with the loss of outside time is obvious in the size of our children's waistlines, but there are internal impacts as well. In a 2011 article for the *American Journal of Play,* psychologist Peter Gray noted that in the past fifty years, children's time for free play, particularly outdoors, has declined, while at the same time, "measures of psychopathology in children and adolescents—including indices of anxiety, depression, feelings of helplessness, and narcissism—have continually increased." In *Last Child in the Woods,* Richard Louv claims that our children are in danger of what he calls the "nature deficit disorder," an alienation from the natural world that has a host of ill effects, including diminished use of senses, increased crime rates, attention difficulties, and higher rates of physical and emotional problems.

The diagnosis rates of attention-deficit/hyperactivity disorder (ADHD) in the United States have increased 3 percent each year from 1997 to 2006. By 2011, approximately 11 percent, or 6.4 million, American kids (ages six to seventeen) had been diagnosed with the condition, according to the CDC. The disorder is defined as having trouble paying attention, controlling impulsive behavior, or being overly active. While many of these kids are treated with medication, a 2011 study published in *Applied Psychology* identified a simple, low-cost method to alleviating some of the symptoms: "exposure to green spaces."

It is interesting to note that while Germany has also experienced a surge of ADHD diagnoses, the rate is still lower than in the United States: 4.8 percent over a child's lifetime, according to research published in 2008 by German psychologist Michael Huss and colleagues. Could the difference be explained simply by the fact that German children have more free time to play outside?

In the United States, children can't get a break. When I went to elementary school, we had an outside recess at least twice a day, just as my children enjoyed in Germany, but that has changed. About 40 percent of U.S. school districts have cut down or eliminated recess, according to the Robert Wood Johnson Foundation. This has happened despite the studies that have found outside activity to be important to children's ability to learn. For instance, a 2009 study in the journal *Pediatrics* found that kids who had recess behaved better in the classroom and therefore were more ready to learn than kids who did not.

It used to be common-sense parenting in America to send kids outside to play every day. I remember many days when my mother would turn off the TV and tell me to go outside. I grew up in a town near Buffalo, New York, which is legendary for its record snowfalls, so in the winter it was a huge ordeal to get outside. I remember resisting efforts to get me out of the house, but once I was out, winter or summer, I played for hours. I suspect many kids growing up before the 1990s had this same experience. In fact in the survey by Professor Clements that I noted earlier, of the mothers who reported such low play rates in their own children, a vast majority, 70 percent, remembered playing outside themselves as children every day.

So what has changed in America that has driven children indoors? I've read an array of articles and books by child development experts and cultural observers who blame this change on a number of factors: the hyperemphasis on academics; the prioritization of organized sports over free outdoor play; increased time spent with electronic media, namely TV, but also smartphones, computers, and video games; and exaggerated fears that unsupervised children outdoors will be abducted. I say exaggerated because of these facts: an estimated 105 children were victims of the stereotypical stranger abduction in 2011, according to the U.S. Department of Justice. Each incident is horrifying to be sure, but as a statistical risk for the more than 70 million children in the United States, again it's in the "hit by lightning" territory. (It's more common that children will be abused or abducted by someone they already know, which is a problem that cannot be addressed by keeping children indoors.)

German culture has been hit with many of the same pressures and fears. As noted earlier, the country has had a number of academic "shocks," which has added to the already high stakes in German schools. Fussball (soccer) is a national obsession. Computers and smartphones are everywhere in the country, which is home to Europe's biggest telecommunications company, Deutsche Telecom. Germany has also had its share of child abduction cases. Although extremely rare, like it is in the United States, each incident is publicized in sensational German tabloids, stoking parents' fears. Yet, in Germany, parents and schools have not responded the same way that they have in the United States. There's been no mass movement by parents or educators to keep children inside for any of these reasons— most Germans seem to feel that the benefits of letting their children enjoy the fresh air outside far outweigh the risks.

Germans and Free Nature

Whenever I've posed the question directly to a German parent—"How can you let your children have so much freedom?"—I'd get a similar answer: it's difficult, they'd say, but necessary. It's what is best for their kids.

Cat Gerlach, a German mother of three children, two of whom have special needs, wrote to me after reading one of my articles to point out that giving kids freedom is probably the hardest thing a parent has to do. "Of course, I would have loved to shadow every single step my kids took (which would have been impossible since I've got three), but I forced myself not to," she said. "It's not good to stifle your child's interests."

Cat doesn't live in a big city like Berlin. She lives in a small village, the kind of place where everyone knows each other and doesn't bother to lock their doors. Cat told me she doesn't have to worry when her children play outside. Since two of her children have mental disabilities, they would occasionally get lost, but Cat felt confident that "if they end up in a place they shouldn't be, one of the neighbors will pick them up and bring them back."

This neighborhood trust may seem to apply only in a small village, but I've also seen it in action in Berlin. For instance, one time after leaving a playground with Sophia, we came across an anxious little girl no older than six, dancing with impatience on the curb. "Can you help me cross the street?" she asked me in German. I understood her words, but I was still confused.

"Where is your mother?" I asked. She pointed up, and there across the street was a woman leaning out of a third-floor window. She waved to me. This was obviously routine for them, even if it seemed odd to me, so I looked both directions to make sure the road was clear and sent the girl across.

"*Sag Danke!*" her mother shouted at her.

The girl turned back to me. "Danke!" she said.

The German culture at large seems to encourage children to feel free rather than afraid when they are outside in public, even when they are naked. In the summer, small children run around naked at almost every Berlin playground that has a bit of water. The first hot summer in Berlin, I supplied Sophia with a bathing suit to take to kita. The next day she asked me if she had to use it. "I'm the only one wearing one," she told me.

"Well, you don't have to wear one if you don't want to," I told her. And she didn't. On hot summer days, I would often come to pick up my kids at kita to find eighteen naked kids splashing in the outside water play area.

It was fun to see their joy. They were so comfortable in their own skins. There was no self-consciousness, no shame.

In Germany, nudity, in general, is much more accepted than it is in the United States. The German *freikörperkultur* ("free body culture") is more widespread and mainstream than the nudist movement is in the United States. Nudist sections are common at lake and seaside beaches in Germany, and they don't usually have any privacy screens to separate one area from the other. Even if it's not a nudist area, adults often change into their suits right on the beach.

Going to the beach, whether naked or not, is a favorite vacation for Germans. Every summer, they drive to the beaches on the north coast or fly south. So many Germans hit the Mediterranean beaches in Spain and Greece that in some places you can hear more German spoken than Spanish or Greek. Despite the hardworking stereotype, Germans take a lot of vacations. They have as many as six weeks off a year, and taking at least four weeks of vacation (twenty working days) is mandated by law. That's for everyone from doctors and lawyers to store clerks and garbage collectors— and generally, Germans take vacation for several weeks at a time. I remember once telling Kordula excitedly about the weeklong vacation we'd planned to the Spanish island of Mallorca. "Only one week!" she said. "You will have no time to relax before you have to go home again!"

The outdoors is a big focus for German vacations. While the beach is probably the most popular destination, many Germans go to the mountains or the countryside. Some Berliners even maintain small gardens with a one-room garden house that they rent or own. They go there on weekends to garden, barbecue, or just sit outside and enjoy the fresh air.

We owned no such special garden, and while we made it to the beach many times, I feared that my children were growing up as hopeless city kids. Sophia even once asked me what a lawnmower was, a natural question since we didn't have a lawn. However, it made me realize my children were experiencing a vastly different childhood than the one I had in the green suburbs of New York, or that of my husband whose memories are full of stories of camping in the wilds of California. *My kids,* I thought, *were growing up more like building-bound New York City kids.* Even with all the value on getting outside, I didn't think they would develop a deep love for nature in the middle of a huge urban place like Berlin.

Taking Away the Toys

Our normally democratic kita did push one project on the children that they would never choose, and it was a doozy: toy-free time. For three months, they took away all the toys. No more blocks, cars, and dolls. No puzzles or board games. No more dress-up clothes. Even the garden toys were put away—the scooters and tricycles, the shovels and buckets. All gone. It sounded like a punishment, but I was assured that it wasn't.

"It pushes them to use their imagination," Annika told me. "They have to use normal, everyday things around them to play with." The kids did make up games out of whatever they could find: lined-up chairs became a train. The nap-time blankets and tables became forts. They played house and pretended they were animals, all without the aid of any kind of toys. The children were also allowed to use what they found outside in the garden—chestnuts and small stones for coins to play store, sticks to build houses or use as pirate swords. Despite all this great creativity, they did become bored. Very bored.

"It's good for children to be bored sometimes," Annika told me.

When I first encountered the toy-free project idea, I thought it was an effort to battle consumerism. Already our kita seemed to discourage the "branded" and electronic toys that child development experts say can inhibit children's imaginative play. At our kita, there were no Star Wars figures or Disney characters—and no toys that beeped or sang at the push of a button. Instead the kita featured open-ended toys like blocks, generic cars, and small plastic animals. *Toy-free time,* I thought, *was taking this ethos a step further,* but I was wrong again. The toys themselves had little to do with the philosophy behind the project.

Toy-free time is a project aimed at preventing addiction. First developed in a Bavarian district in 1992, the toy-free kindergarten project is built on the premise that habit-forming behaviors start early. Children use toys sometimes to cover up "unsatisfied needs and frustrations." It is meant to be temporary. The teachers remove the toys for a short period of time and do not tell the children what to play instead. (Our kita already took a kid-directed approach to most things, so this part wasn't a new idea.) Taking away these external cues for play forces the children to rely on their own internal creativity and on each other.

The project received an expert evaluation in 1996 by a German social scientist, Anna Winner, who found that toy-free time helped the children get in better touch with their own needs, enhanced their creativity, built self-confidence, improved their communications with one another, and, perhaps most important, improved their ability to handle frustration. Following Winner's study, the youth nonprofit Aktion Jugendschutz published free instructional materials on its website, and hundreds of kitas and kindergartens throughout Germany, Switzerland, and Austria have implemented it.

At our international kita, toy-free time received mixed reviews. The first year Sophia was at this kita, the project was discussed at length with the parents, and everyone liked how it went. But the following year, the project landed at the end of a particularly long, gray winter, and some parents rebelled. They said their kids were so bored they didn't want to come to kita. Others reported that their children would come home and play madly with their toys in the evening. Sophia did this too, and I have to admit, it didn't seem healthy. The critics were so loud that the project was suspended the following year. Then it came back in a modified form just in time for Ozzie to experience it in the big kids' group.

After much discussion, the kita teachers and parents reached a very German compromise. Their solution: send the kids outside more. It fit with the traditional value of getting fresh air every day while still falling within the limits of the toy-free program—nature had no ready-made toys. The children had to use their imagination. As part of the compromise, the toy-free period was reduced from three months to six weeks and moved to the spring so that the extra outside time would be more pleasant. Even better, the kita teachers added field trips to the mix. Once a week, they would take the children into the *Wald* ("forest").

On the edges of Berlin, both inside the city borders and out are several large forests, all accessible by a short train ride. Toy-free time at our kita now seemed a bit like waldkitas, day-care centers that are literally located in forests and whose whole curriculum is focused on natural exploration. This type of kita also has few if any manufactured toys. (Waldkitas shouldn't be confused with the Waldorf schools, which were first developed in Germany by Rudolf Steiner and named after the Waldorf-Astoria cigarette company where Steiner opened his first school for children of company employees.)

At three, Ozzie had graduated from the toddler group and was now in the mixed-age group where Annika was the head teacher. He was excited to be with the big kids. As time went on, though, he started to have other worries. He told me he had no friends. When I asked his teachers about this, they reported to me the names of all the children he played with regularly, a group that included children younger and older, so what he said was not exactly true. What he seemed most concerned about was that he didn't have one single, close friend who played with him all the time, someone who paid attention to him like his sister, Sophia, did.

Ozzie had a bit of the second-child syndrome. At home, he played with his sister for hours. He was rarely alone, and Sophia, who is three years older, directed a lot of their play, so much so that if she wasn't around or wasn't interested in playing with him, he was at loose ends. I knew the minute this happened because he would be at my elbow. "Mom, what should I play? I don't know what I should do," he'd say.

I was still a parenting-book aficionado. I knew that I shouldn't always tell him what to play, that I should encourage him to come up with his own ideas. Sometimes I would turn the question back to him. "What do you want to play?" Or I'd try to point him in the right direction: "Why don't you go look in your room and see what you can find?" And it worked, for about ten minutes, and then he would be back again.

Of course, I'd occasionally pull out a puzzle or a game and play with him. It was nice together time, but I knew he needed to figure out how to play by himself. I didn't think he would learn that at kita with so many kids around, but that's how it happened with a little help from the modified toy-free time.

Ozzie did not like having no toys at kita. He joined the chorus of complaining kids for a while before the outdoors grabbed him. He spent most of his day in the kita's garden, gathering snail shells, chestnuts, acorns, and piles of rocks (each of these was "special," he told me). He and another boy counted red and black beetles that they called "fire bugs." They went on a hunt for the fox that supposedly visited the kita sometimes. I thought this was a made-up story, considering our urban kita was right next to the S-Bahn tracks, until I actually saw it one day.

By far, the forest trips were the high point of every week for Ozzie. He would remind me days ahead of time to help him pack his backpack. When he returned, he'd tell me it was "Great!" but like a typical kid, he'd provide few details:

Me: "What did you do on the trip?"
Ozzie: "We walked around."
Me: "Did you see anything interesting?"
Ozzie: "Bugs."
Me: "And?"
Ozzie: "There was lots of mud. I found some sticks. And rocks."
        Then he would show me his latest collection taken straight out of his pockets.

It didn't seem like these were life-changing experiences, at least at first. On our weekend family excursions, we'd visited a few of Berlin's forests, including Grunewald in the west and Plänterwald, a few train stops to the south. The kids enjoyed these trips—to a point. After some time, they'd start complaining that they were tired or hungry, and we would end up turning back without having hiked very far.

When Ozzie visited a forest we hadn't been to before with his kita, he insisted the whole family had to see "Bucher wald" because "it was a really good forest for exploring!" One weekend, we did just that. He was so proud to take us to his forest. I was impressed by how long a walk it was from the train station to the forest. There wasn't one complaint from him on the whole walk. In fact, he was quiet.

Once we got into Bucher wald, he couldn't remember exactly where he had been with his class. He wasn't sure where he wanted to go, so we walked around and looked at what we found on the forest floor. We found bugs, funny-looking mushrooms, lots of sticks, and plenty of mud. Bucher wald was large and far enough from the busy streets that once in the woods almost all outside sound faded away. It was easy to feel like we weren't near a city but deep in the wilds somewhere. I think that's what he liked.

Some weeks later, well after the toy-free project had ended, I showed up at kita on a drizzly day. All the kids were playing inside, except my son.

"Where's Ozzie?" I asked Annika. She pointed out the back windows. There he was in the garden with his raincoat on, all by himself.

"He does this quite often now," Annika said. "He'll go outside even when no one else wants to. He'll stay out there for maybe fifteen or twenty minutes, then come back in."

"What does he do?" I asked, joining Annika at the windows. Ozzie had a stick in his hand, and as I watched he squatted down and dug at something on the ground with his stick.

"He wanders around, looking at things," Annika said. "I think it's pretty cool."

"Me too," I said. I was amazed at how comfortable he was with being alone. It was clear that the extra time in nature had changed something for him. Somehow, in the forests near Berlin, Ozzie had found peace with himself.

8

The Freedom to Move

We bought Ozzie his first bicycle when he was four. It was small, but it was the real thing, a full-on pedal bike. Plenty of these tiny bikes can be found in Berlin, and many kids as young as three learn to ride. At four, Ozzie was among the last of his friends at kita to learn to ride, but it didn't take him long to learn—less than a minute in fact.

The day after we bought the bike, Ozzie couldn't wait to try it out. Zac and Sophia were going to a friend's birthday party, so I took Ozzie out by myself to practice. I figured Zac wouldn't miss much because Ozzie probably wouldn't get it right away. We went to "tire park," which in addition to tire swings had a large grassy area with a nice, paved circular trail perfect for a new bike rider. As I pushed him, Ozzie started pedaling and singing some nonsense song to himself, which sounded like "blah, la, do, do." I held on to the seat for about ten seconds before he pulled away and was pedaling on his own, blah-la-do-do-ing the whole time. He also rode all the way back home without falling once.

Ozzie found it easy because he had already been on two wheels for a couple of years. When he was two, his kita teachers expressed some concern about his coordination. He often ran into things and other children. I thought he simply didn't pay attention enough to where he was going, but our pediatrician suggested he try a *laufrad*—a walking bike (sometimes referred to as a balance bike in the United States). A laufrad has no pedals. Ozzie soon got the hang of it using his feet to make the bike move. His coordination improved so much that he left me far behind, and I ended up chasing that so-called walking bike many times through the sidewalks of Berlin.

Once Ozzie picked up both legs and flew down the hill near our house. I yelled, "Stop! Achtung! Ozzie!" None of it slowed his speed. I felt so helpless running behind him. I could do nothing to stop him from flying right out into the street. Only he did it himself, making this neat little turn at the corner and looking back up at me to see what all the shrieking was about. Eventually, I learned to do as many German parents do: give him rules about stopping at corners, then let him ride.

So when it came time to ride a real pedal bike, he was ready to take off. On a laufrad, a toddler learns not only how to balance a bike but also the rules of the road (or the sidewalk) before moving up to a faster pedal bike. It's a process of preparation, increased responsibility, and, for the parents, letting go.

I saw this same process underway all the time in Berlin. While walking to kita, we'd often run across tiny tots on two wheels seemingly by themselves. They were blocks ahead of their parents. One afternoon as I was walking to a birthday party with some other mothers, all of our kids started racing each other on foot far ahead toward a busy street corner. I was the only one nervous enough to chase after them and yell at them to slow down. "Oh, they know when to stop," my friend Susan assured me. Sure enough the kids finished their race well before the street corner and looked back. Susan smiled and waved them on.

This was just the start. I didn't realize that once Sophia entered first grade I was expected to teach her how to walk or bike there all by herself, even without me trailing a block behind. Before the first day, we received a pamphlet in the mail with a host of information about starting school. It also included a request that parents not drive their children to school. They should start learning the way on foot so that eventually they could go by themselves.

I decided that this did not apply to us. After all, we were Americans! I walked Sophia to school all through first grade—along with most German parents. In second grade, most of Sophia's friends started to walk on their own. By third grade, they were all on their own. Still, I held out.

The school was about 600 yards from our house, just up the street, but still, we were in a big city! She was only eight! She could get hit by a car or some crazy person could carry her off. I knew, intellectually, this last scenario was highly unlikely, but this fear loomed large in my mind. It didn't help that on one corner of the street, some seedy-looking characters gathered to drink in the afternoons.

"There's too much construction," I told Sophia. "The cars drive too fast. You're too dreamy when you're walking."

She didn't buy any of it. "All my friends walk to school by themselves," she said. "And they're fine."

It was true. Her friend Maya lived much farther away than we did, and at the age of eight, she rode her bike through crowded sidewalks and crossed busy intersections all by herself. She wasn't the only one. Every morning, hordes of children filled our neighborhood walking and biking to school without any attending adults. In the afternoons, they were there again walking home. They filled the playgrounds. They went in and out of the bakeries and stores with only other children for company.

German children learn how to navigate the streets from their parents and teachers. Along with math, reading, and all the other subjects, Berlin primary schools have a specific curriculum for "traffic and mobility education." Near the end of her first year, Sophia spent time learning traffic signs and rules of the road. Her teacher also took the entire class out for a walking tour of the neighborhood, showing them firsthand how the traffic moved, what the signs meant, and how to use crosswalks, or *zebrastreifen* ("zebra stripes"), as they're called in Germany. The parents back this up by walking and biking the route to school with their children for several months to an entire year before letting their kids try it on their own.

I had always thought I was a fairly relaxed parent, but I was starting to feel like maybe I was too overprotective. I knew it wasn't just me. It was my entire culture. While I was arguing with Sophia about letting her walk by herself, I was also reading about parents in the United States being arrested for doing that very thing. The most famous of these was the case of Danielle and Alexander Meitiv of Silver Spring, Maryland, who let their two children, ages ten and six at the time, walk home, about a mile, from a park alone. A concerned citizen called the police and the Meitivs wound up charged with "unsubstantiated child neglect"—a charge that was later dropped.

While this case gained the most media attention, there are plenty of other examples: a woman in Connecticut was arrested when she overslept and her stepson took it upon himself to walk the two miles to school. A mother in Florida was arrested for letting her seven-year-old walk to a park alone. In South Carolina, a mother trusted her nine-year-old nephew to walk her three-year-old son less than a quarter of a mile to McDonald's, and she was arrested. In any one of these cases, the parents' judgment could be disputed: perhaps two miles is too far for a child to walk or maybe nine isn't old enough to watch a toddler, but the reaction of the authorities in several different states made it clear that our culture had a strong stance against letting any grade-school child out in public without adult supervision. I also knew that most Germans wouldn't even think to call the *polizei* for any of these situations.

The Meitiv case probably earned the most scrutiny because they were deliberately letting their children out alone. They were "free-range" parents. That's the first time I'd heard the term, which had been coined by Lenore Skenazy, the so-called world's worst mom. In 2008, Skenazy, then a columnist for *The New York Sun*, let her nine-year-old son, Izzy, take the New York subway home by himself. He'd asked to try to see if he could find his way home on the subway, so she left him by the Bloomingdale's stop one sunny day, gave him a map and some money, and went the other direction. "Sure enough, he got home, and he felt very proud," Skenazy said. "I didn't write about it right away because it wasn't a publicity stunt, and to my mind it wasn't that big a deal. . . . If I'd thought it was dangerous, I would have said no."

When Skenazy did write about it, the world went crazy. Talk-show hosts and parenting experts condemned her for endangering her son. Skenazy launched her own counterattack starting a blog and later writing a hilarious book called *Free Range Kids: How to Raise Safe, Self-Reliant Children (Without Going Nuts With Worry)* lambasting America's paranoid parenting culture that sees a child predator lurking in every bush.

Skenazy makes a strong argument for giving children more freedom, based on common sense and statistics: for example, she often notes that the level of crime in America, of all kinds, is at the same level as 1963 when children regularly walked alone to school.

Eight years after her son's trip on the subway, Skenazy is still giving speeches about allowing children more independence and fielding calls from parents who have been investigated or arrested for letting their children walk places by themselves or even for leaving them in a car for a few minutes. Skenazy, who says she is simply an old-fashioned parent, is surprised that her ideas are still considered extreme.

"What continues to fascinate me is the idea that the second your child is unsupervised they are automatically in danger," Skenazy told me when I spoke with her in the spring of 2016. "And that's so obviously not true, because our parents let us walk to school and play outside back when the crime rate was higher than it is today."

Skenazy's free-range movement has gained proponents not only among parents but also with some policy makers. U.S. Senator Mike Lee (R-Utah) inserted a special clause in the 2015 Every Child Succeeds education bill that made it clear nothing in the law would "prohibit a child from traveling to and from school on foot or by car, bus, or bike when the parents of the child have given permission" or that their parents would face criminal charges for doing so. Unfortunately, these few lines in a federal law will not suddenly set thousands of American children free to walk to school. It doesn't preempt state or local laws, and it is extremely difficult to change a parenting trend that has been building for decades.

In 1969, 47.7 percent of kindergarteners through eighth graders in America walked or biked to school. In 2009, that number had dropped to 12.7 percent, according to a study on U.S. school travel headed up by University of North Carolina professor Noreen McDonald. While the study doesn't specify whether the children walked by themselves, anecdotally many people from earlier generations recall walking to school alone or with friends. Either way, it's clear that today our children are usually with their parents because they are in the car being chaperoned to school as well as to athletic activities, music lessons, and "play dates" with friends. German children also spend more time in the car than they used to, but according to the Policy Studies Institute (PSI), 61 percent of German primary school children were still walking to school in 2010, and if what I saw in Berlin is any indication, from about second grade on they are walking without their parents.

One of the most common arguments I've heard against letting children walk and play by themselves is that we are now living in "more dangerous times." Not only do U.S. crime statistics disprove that notion, but Germany provides a powerful counterexample. If another modern, first world country with its own share of crime and difficult problems can still let the majority of its children walk to school and around neighborhoods by themselves, then the dramatic drop in children's freedom to move isn't a fact of modern life but of culture.

People often assume that Germans and other Europeans let their children do more by themselves because there is less crime in Europe. I spoke with researcher Paolo Buonanno, who has analyzed crime rates in different countries, to find out if that's true. The vice chancellor for research at University of Bergamo in Italy, Buonanno helped author an in-depth paper comparing crime between major European countries and the United States. He told me that making such comparisons can be difficult because of disparate reporting rates among countries. For instance, crime seems to be awfully high in Nordic countries, according to official statistics, but that's primarily because people tend to report crimes more often in places like Sweden, Norway, and Denmark than in other countries.

Buonanno and his colleagues work to adjust for those differences. They found out that crime in both the United States and Europe has been dropping in recent years. Total crime in Europe, and in Germany, is actually still higher than it is in the United States—in all categories except murder. That's one scary category. Buonanno and his colleagues say one likely explanation is the prevalence of guns in American society and "the fact that many types of crime in the United States tend to be committed with the use of guns and that's very different from many European countries."

It's not like Germany has no guns. In fact, it has the fourth-highest rate of gun ownership in the world, but prospective gun owners have to pass many steps before they can purchase a weapon, including a criminal background check and a test of their knowledge of the weapon. If they are younger than twenty-five, they have to take a psychological exam. These measures seem to make a big difference. In the United States, there were 10.14 gun-related deaths per 100,000 people in 2014, according to GunPolicy.org. In Germany, the rate was 1.01. If we truly want to make our country safer for children, we don't need to lock kids indoors; we should enact gun-safety measures similar to those in Germany.

Regardless, most people living in American suburbs don't have to worry about their children being gunned down on the tree-lined streets of their neighborhoods, but I can imagine that in some neighborhoods that may be a real fear. Buonanno also pointed out that crime in the United States is very segregated to specific areas, with pockets of high-crime areas in a city that also has low-crime areas that are "as safe as many European cities." If you live in a low-crime area, you can be assured that it's probably as safe for your child to walk to school as it would be in Berlin.

I have to admit I didn't initially see Berlin as particularly safe, but the parents all around me thought the risk was manageable. While I was trying to convince myself to let my daughter walk the four blocks to her Berlin school by herself, my German friend Susan had started sending her two oldest children, now eight and eleven, to their Waldorf school, which was some distance from their apartment, on the bus, by themselves—and not the school bus, the public city bus. Judith's daughter started taking the bus to and from her school every day by herself in second grade. A colleague of Zac's let his nine-year-old son take the U-Bahn (the Berlin subway) to his school every day. They received no condemnation like Skenazy experienced, because this was a fairly common thing for children to do in Germany.

In a 2015 multicountry survey of children's independent mobility conducted by PSI, Germany ranked the highest out of sixteen countries in the practice of letting children take public buses by themselves. Overall in terms of the freedom to move independently, German children were second only to children in Finland, where children as young as seven walk and bike alone day or night. (The United States was not included in the survey, but notably three other English-speaking countries ranked poorly: England, Ireland, and Australia came in at 7, 12, and 13, respectively.)

Why German Children Walk Alone

German parents are not cavalier about sending their kids out into the big outside world by themselves. When I interviewed one German mother, Annekatherin, for a Mother's Day article in the German Sunday paper *Bild Am Sonntag*, she told me she hated it when her children, who were eight and ten, went by themselves to their grandmother's house, a trip that took them four stops on the U-Bahn in Berlin. So why did she do it? Her reasoning was quite simple: "I want them to be independent and proud of what they can do," she said. "If I'm always with them, they won't be."

PSI has been studying children's independent mobility since 1970 and can point to decades of research showing that children's ability to move freely outside of the home without adult supervision is important for their healthy physical, social, emotional, and mental development. You don't need to read the research papers to understand the reasons: when children can only go outside with an adult attendant, they go outside less, and they don't develop the physically healthy habit of walking places. They also have fewer opportunities to interact socially with friends. What might be less intuitive is that the presence of an adult can inhibit a child's learning process.

If an adult is constantly directing a child and watching over her every move, the child doesn't learn as well as when she is exploring on her own, including developing the important skills of finding her way and moving safely through traffic. Rainer Becker, CEO of Deutsche Kinderhilfe, a German nonprofit that advocates for children's rights and safety, frames this argument in terms of control versus responsibility: "How can a child learn self-reliance if at every moment he is under control and his parents always make decisions for him?" he said. "If we want to have adults who are self-reliant and responsible, they must learn how, but how can they learn if they have a childhood where they have learned control and nothing else?" It's a pattern that self-perpetuates, Becker argues, as controlled children grow up to become controlling adults because that's all they know.

The challenge is to teach children to be aware of dangers without terrifying them. My friend Susan told me that when she had her first child, she happened to watch a documentary about pedophiles that scared her so much she cried for five days straight. But as time went on, she overcame her fear for her children's sake. "I'm much calmer now but very much aware," she said. "The more you think about it, the more it freaks you out. That doesn't really help them, because your children get scared too and don't know what to do when something happens." Rather than chaperone her kids everywhere, Susan feels it's much better to prepare them to handle potential dangers on their own. "The smartest thing to do is to let go a little bit—and make sure they go to karate class," she said and laughed, but she was serious. Her two older daughters were both enrolled in karate classes.

Helping children learn to stand up for themselves, even against their own parents, is critical, according to Becker. If parents are truly concerned about someone abusing their children, Becker said that one of the best things parents can do is to respect children's right to say no, even to us.

"Your child has her own will. If you want to touch your child, sometimes she likes it, sometimes not, so if your child doesn't want to be touched by you, you have to respect that," Becker said, adding that parents should never force a child to hug or kiss any relative if they don't want to, even Grandma and Grandpa.

It's a matter of respect for children's right to control their own bodies.

It also helps protect them against people who would sexually abuse them, since most child abusers are not strangers, but people children already know, their neighbors and their relatives. (In the United States more than 92 percent of child sexual abusers are acquaintances or family members of their juvenile victims, according to the Bureau of Justice Statistics.) Becker argues that children who feel confident standing up to adults, no matter who they are, are more prepared to defend themselves against abuse.

"A lot of people who are child abusers will stop if the child says no, because the typical child abuser is not the man behind the tree who will knock a child down, he is the man who wants a relationship with the child," Becker said. Even in the more unlikely event of a stranger trying to convince a child to come with them, children who have been taught that they have a right to refuse adults are better prepared to resist than children who have been taught to always obey adults.

Deutsche Kinderhilfe puts out a cartoon-illustrated guide for kids about walking to school. The guide recommends children eat a good breakfast, and gives traffic safety tips and advice on how to deal with strangers. Some of this text sounds familiar—such as never get into a stranger's car no matter what the person promises, and if anyone tries to touch or grab you, shout "No! I don't want to!" loudly.

But here are a few pieces of advice Americans may not have heard: The guide suggests children have a password with their parents, so that if an adult, even one they know, ever says to come with them in an emergency, the children can ask that person for the password so that they know that their parents have agreed to trust this person. Also, if children ever feel that someone is following them or otherwise making them uncomfortable, they should seek help in a public place with a lot of people, such as a restaurant or a store. In other words, the guide advises asking strangers for help, instead of avoiding them.

We heard this same idea from other German parents: that the majority of people would help a child in trouble. For instance, Zac's colleague said he felt that sending his nine-year-old son traveling to and from school on the subway was relatively safe because there would be plenty of people on the train at that time of day, and if some crazy person tried to mess with his son, he expected the other travelers would interfere.

In the meantime, my daughter was nearing her ninth birthday and campaigning to be allowed to do more things on her own. After discussing it with Zac, I started to relent. On some mornings, I walked her halfway up the street and then let her go the rest of the way to school herself. We also sent Sophia to the bakery downstairs in our building to buy rolls for us on Saturday mornings. The first time she went, I hung out over the balcony watching her take the few steps to the bakery on the corner. She showed up with the rolls and an extra muffin the bakery clerks had given her. After that, she went nearly every Saturday and Sunday morning for us, often coming back with an extra special treat. She told me the bakery clerks called her *prinzesschen* ("little princess").

Then Maya's mother asked if her daughter could ring our bell some mornings, so the two girls could walk together the rest of the way to school. I agreed. They'd have each other, I reasoned, and in the mornings, there were all those other kids walking up the same street at the same time. Then came a day when Maya didn't ring, and I finally let Sophia go all by herself.

By the middle of third grade, Sophia was running most of her own mornings by herself: she would get up, get dressed, pack her bag and snack, and we'd say good-bye at our apartment door. She loved it, and as a parent, it was wonderful to see her so proud and taking responsibility for starting her day. Before I let her do this, it had been a battle of wills with me nagging and pushing her to get ready to go out the door together. I couldn't help noticing that aside from my own worries, it was much easier for me, especially since I didn't have to drag her little brother up the hill to school to drop her off, and then back down to the S-Bahn station for the ride to his kita.

Judith also told me that convenience was the primary reason she let her oldest daughter ride the bus to school by herself. It made mornings less complicated in a family with two full-time working parents and two younger kids who were still in kita. Like me, Judith worried about "creepy people who abduct children," but said that it was mostly the traffic that concerned her because that's the most likely reason a child gets hurt. Still, aside from the convenience, she thought it was a good experience for her daughter.

"If anything ever happened, of course, I'd feel so terribly guilty for not taking the time to go with her, but I think at some point they do have to learn it," Judith said. "If they want to meet with friends or go to sports, they have to be flexible and be able to do it on their own."

I wasn't quite as flexible. I still picked Sophia up after school at the end of the day. Hort, the after-school program, let children out at whatever time the parents indicated, so children were leaving school in ones and twos. There wasn't the strength in numbers that there was in the mornings with a great group of kids traveling up the street together. The idea of Sophia walking home by herself, past the group of seedy-looking drinkers, who were usually out by that time, was too much for me. On the other hand, her friends did it all the time. They left school and walked themselves to an after-school activity, or to the park, or home.

Freedom to Play

One spring day, I agreed to let Sophia go home with another friend, Katti, who lived nearby in an apartment across from Dragon Park. When I went to pick them up, I didn't find them at Katti's apartment. Instead, they were at the park, playing in the sand by themselves. Katti's parents were nowhere in sight. By then I knew this was normal. I had seen plenty of school-age children at playgrounds without their parents. Still, it was unsettling for someone who comes from a culture where parents are arrested for leaving their children alone. In a 2015 Pew Research survey, 66 percent of American parents said children shouldn't be allowed to be alone at a park until they were thirteen or older. Most (54 percent) also felt that a child shouldn't even play in their front yard unsupervised until they were at least ten.

Here again, the practices of German parents made me question my own parental instincts about safety. I started to consider the value of letting my child play outside without an adult present. I read articles by Peter Gray, a research psychologist at Boston College who has studied play in both animal and human development. As I mentioned earlier, Gray argues that there is a strong correlation between the decline of children's free play and the rise in mental disorders among young people in America. When I contacted him to ask him more about the importance of play, he told me that he doesn't really consider it "play" if an adult is present because the players, the children, have to be the ones in charge.

"Basically, the evolutionary purpose of play, from my analysis, is to allow children to practice controlling their own behavior, solving their own problems, planning and carrying out a plan—in a sense to practice being an adult because that's the situation where they're in control," he said. "When adults are around, they're not in charge of their own activities. There's an adult there either telling them what to do, solving their problems, or advising them."

In his book *Free to Learn*, Gray advocates for play-based schools that take this idea to its logical conclusion: schools without curriculum and children who are allowed to learn the way nature intended, through their own self-directed exploration—through play. While much of his book reminded me of our kita's democratic philosophy, I couldn't see the German public school system with its revered teachers and carefully tracked courses embracing the idea of primary and secondary schools totally based on free play. However, many German parents and educators do value and promote the ability of children to play without adult interference at almost every opportunity. We saw it every day in the freewheeling garden at kita and in the hands-off approach at hort—and simply in the frequent sight of children moving by themselves through our neighborhood.

Surrounded by this culture, Zac and I were forced to confront our relatively overprotective attitudes as American parents. We had many discussions about how much freedom we should give Sophia, and little by little, as situations presented themselves, we began to let her do more and more by herself.

One Saturday afternoon the whole family decided to go to Dragon Park. It was a sunny, spring day, and the playground was full. Sophia ran into a group of friends from school, including Katti, and none of their parents were with them. We let her go play with her friends on the other side of the playground and tried to give her some space while we stayed with Ozzie. After some time, we were ready to leave the park to get some coffee and ice cream, but Sophia didn't want to go. She asked to stay—playing with her friends was more important than ice cream! Zac and I looked at each other. We knew another time had arrived when maybe we should step back a little.

So we left Sophia behind at the park, while Zac, Ozzie, and I went around the corner to a café. The adults ordered frothy cappuccinos, and Ozzie had a giant cone with sprinkles. It should have been lovely, but something—someone—was obviously missing.

"I'm having a hard time enjoying this," I confessed.

"I know, me too," Zac said.

"Are we doing the right thing?"

"Of course we are," he said.

"What if she's climbing and falls and gets hurt?"

"She won't."

"But what if—" I said. It was really hard not to play that game.

"If she falls, someone will help her," Zac said. "They will send someone to get us."

She didn't fall or get hurt. Zac and I drank our coffees and waited the extra special long time it takes for Ozzie to eat an ice cream cone. By the time we returned to the playground, her friends had left, and Sophia was by herself swinging so high on the swing the chains went slack for a moment before they pulled her back. When she saw us, Sophia jumped off the swing, all smiles.

"Can I have some ice cream now?"

9

Dangerous Things

Every once in a while, a bomb is found in Berlin. With all the building going on in the city, construction crews inevitably uncover unexploded ordnance left over from World War II. Whenever this happens, everything stops until disposal teams determine if the bomb is still viable and, if so, neutralize it. The discovery of bombs shut down the S-Bahn trains many times while we lived in Berlin.

Once an old bomb was found near Zac's research institute, which is located in an East German town that was nearly leveled during the war. At lunch, the other scientists discussed the discovery, and realizing that Zac was among them, one of his colleagues tried to reassure him. "Don't worry, it's a Soviet one, not American," he said.

"Oh, I know," Zac quipped, "if it was American, it would have exploded." Only half the table laughed. Zac said he didn't think the scientists from East Germany appreciated his joke.

Unexploded bombs are dangerous reminders of the legacy of World War II in Germany. According to the magazine *Der Spiegel*, the Allies dropped an estimated 1.9 million tons of bombs on Germany during a five-year strategic offensive in the war, and seventy years later, Germans are still uncovering 2,000 tons of unexploded munitions every year.

With this history and the ongoing threat of buried bombs, you might think average Germans wouldn't enjoy the sound of anything exploding. But here I present the cultural paradox of the German New Year's Eve, the holiday they call "Sylvester." On New Year's Eve at midnight in Berlin, practically every man, woman, and child in the city goes out into the streets to shoot off their own personal fireworks. And I am not talking about sparklers or even Roman candles. They were the real thing. Rockets launched out of empty champagne bottles placed on the street that shoot high into the air and explode into huge flowers of colored sparks—ones that change color, sizzle, and dive in different directions. Then there are the ones that make a quick flash followed by an extremely loud bang that rattles the windows of buildings. People fire off so many that at five past midnight, smoke fills the streets in a dense fog. From above, it must look like the entire city is on fire.

We enjoyed our first New Year's in Berlin from the relative safety of our fifth-floor apartment, with the doors to our balcony securely closed. It was an amazing, beautiful, and terrifying experience all at the same time. (And later, annoying, because some people don't stop at midnight, so the early morning of January 1 is riddled with sudden random explosions.)

I do not have a good explanation why Germans like to start the New Year with a dangerous free-for-all display of fireworks. Another expat suggested that Germans love to do this because they are so reserved most of the time that they need one night a year to really cut loose. I've thought that maybe they like to celebrate with explosives as a way to defy their history with war and terror, a way to thumb their nose at fear. But that could be overthinking it. They may just really, really like fireworks.

New Year's is also one example of how Germans approach dangerous things in a much different way than Americans. I shouldn't have been surprised when Sophia came home from school with a piece of paper asking that she be allowed to play with matches. Following the air project that had them building flying machines, her school had moved on to the element of

fire. We were asked to let our children light candles and help them conduct experiments with fire at home to complement the other work they
were doing in the classroom.

Sophia was super excited and wanted to do it right away. We got some
candles out for dinner and handed her a box of matches. She'd already
learned how to light them at school and waved me off impatiently when I
tried to instruct her. She wanted to show us her new skill, so we stood back
and watched as Sophia lit the match. Delight danced in her eyes as she
carefully touched the match to the candlewick. Then she stepped back and
waved the match in the air until it went out. She looked at us across the
table and smiled. I shook my head. I couldn't believe we were letting our
eight-year-old daughter play with matches—something I was taught never,
ever to do.

The Art of Fire

This approach to fire education is partly the result of the work of Kain
Karawahn, a German fire performance artist turned fire-safety educator.
In 1984, Karawahn set a section of the Berlin Wall on fire. He told me his
intention wasn't to destroy the wall but to make art. He felt trapped in the
political island that was then West Berlin and the fire was his vision of
escape. "When you set a concrete wall on fire just for a few seconds, it's a
statement of freedom," he said.

Karawahn has worked in many mediums, but all of his art centers on
the theme of the human relationship to fire. He has put on fire performances
throughout Germany and held exhibitions in the United States, including
in New York and Seattle. Even with big budgets for his projects, Karawahn
felt unsatisfied with his ability to reach only relatively limited audiences
within the art world. Then in 2004, a German kindergarten asked him to
do a workshop on fire, and he found his best audience.

Karawahn's workshops go against the old wisdom that children should
never play with fire—instead he encourages them to engage with fire in
a safe way. In the language of children, he teaches five-year-olds to build
a "happy fire," one that doesn't destroy anything or burn anyone.

On the first day of Karawahn's five-day workshop, he has children light matches, a lot of them: about twenty children ignite 1,000 matches. "You have to go for saturation," Karawahn explained. "If you like ice cream and suddenly you get as much ice cream as you want, after ten ice creams you are sick, and you don't want to eat it anymore. It's the same with the fire."

By the end of the workshop, Karawahn has his young charges making their own mini campfires outside and attempting to cook sausages on them. This activity quickly teaches children that making a fire is a social activity, that they need to pair up so one can feed the fire to keep it going while the other one cooks food over it.

Karawahn's kindergarten workshops gained praise from teachers and parents and soon caught the attention of fire-safety organizations. Unfallkasse Berlin, an insurance company, and Das Sichere Haus, a non-profit comprised of governmental agencies, insurance companies, and associations focused on safety, partnered with Karawahn to produce a fire activity guide for children called "Fascination Fire!" which gives parents and educators the tools to help introduce children to fire in a safe way.

Although it might seem counterintuitive that insurance agencies would back such an approach, Karawahn says it directly addresses a pattern with fire accidents and young children. Our natural fascination with fire can be so strong that prohibiting children from using it just means they will do it in secret, for example, by lighting matches in their bedroom with the door closed while their parents are busy with something else. If they've never had any experience with matches, Karawahn said, the children don't know how to hold them or put them out, so they burn their fingers, drop the match, and perhaps catch a carpet or bedsheet on fire. In the most tragic cases, instead of calling out for help, young children who've been strictly told never to play with matches are so afraid of getting into trouble, they hide. By the time adults discover the fire, the children can die from lack of oxygen or smoke inhalation.

This is why Karawahn is so passionate about advocating for children to play with fire and learn how to manage it in a safe way. He has won awards for his fire education program and taught many teachers in kitas and primary schools how to bring these fire lessons into their classrooms.

Yet he has not won over everyone in Germany. While his approach has been accepted in Berlin and Brandenburg, the state surrounding Berlin, it has yet to spread to the other regions. Still, Karawahn's approach to fire reflects an ongoing shift in the German attitude toward children using dangerous things.

Tools

An old German nursery rhyme, which is also the title of a 1960s pop song, goes: "*Messer, gabel, schere, licht sind für kleine kinder nicht*," or "Knives, forks, scissors, and flames are not for little children." Siegbert Warwitz, a German psychologist and educator who has studied risk extensively, said this attitude was a thing of the past, from a time when children were told to avoid everything potentially dangerous. "The modern pedagogical method is for adults to teach children early on how to handle these objects safely," Warwitz said. "Otherwise children will explore them in secret, which is when they become truly dangerous."

This is the same idea behind Karawahn's fire project, and I've seen this approach to tools in action in Berlin. Both my children were given things in kita and at school that I'd never expect them to be allowed to use at such a young age.

At kita, children as young as three participated in cooking projects. Sophia's favorite was when they made a fruit salad. A group of students went to the store with the teacher to buy the food. They washed and prepared the salad, and cut the fruit themselves with knives. She was four at the time. She was so excited about the project, she told me all about it the moment I picked her up.

"You cut fruit? With a knife!" I exclaimed.

"It was a *kinder* knife," she assured me. "Not too sharp."

From then on she would often come into the kitchen when I was cooking and ask to help cut the fruits and vegetables. At first, I gave her a butter knife, but after a few rounds of frustration, I found something sharper and sat with her and showed her how to use it.

As my kids grew older, they participated in more projects that involved the use of tools that were either close to versions adults would use or were the actual, real thing. In primary school, Sophia had more cooking projects using real knives. On her school trip, the children in her class were invited to bring pocketknives so they could whittle wood.

At home, my attempts at introducing child-safe tools were rebuffed. I once bought Ozzie a pair of plastic scissors that were designed only to cut paper. I think he tried using these once before deciding they were lame (they were). He took to stealing his sister's scissors until I finally relented and got him a sharp pair of his own.

Adventure Play

The children also found a host of dangerous things at the *abenteuerspielplätze* ("adventure playgrounds") of Berlin. As I've mentioned, all German playgrounds tend to have more exciting and dangerous structures than American playgrounds, but adventure playgrounds are another thing entirely. These spaces are designed specifically to encourage children to experience the risk of wild, free play, even in the middle of a big city.

Adventure playgrounds come in many styles, but most feature opportunities for kids to build forts and tree houses, cook food on open fires, and try out a variety of tools. Some even let children take care of farm animals. Kids can also simply play in a space meant specifically for them. At each site, adult staff or volunteers are usually present, but they are there to help with projects or to teach classes, not to supervise the children's play.

Adventure playgrounds are not a German invention. They were first developed by the country's northern neighbor, Denmark, but Germans eagerly adopted the concept in the 1960s and '70s. Today, there are many such free-form play spaces throughout Germany. Berlin has one for nearly every neighborhood district. The adventure playground in our corner of the city was called "Forcki," nicknamed after the larger park, Forckenbeckplatz, that was its home.

Forcki is a *bauspielplatz*, a construction playground, where children are encouraged to build all kinds of things, including towering forts. Forcki was first opened in 1993 and seemed pretty well built out by the time we saw it—multiple handcrafted wooden towers crowded the grounds, creating a maze of plank boxes for children to explore. The playground advertises its attractions for kids in a long list: "Adventure, excitement, action, good moods, bad moods . . . making fire, building, destroying, axes, hammers, nails, screwdrivers, large and small saws, cold, heat, wind, sun, moon, chatting, laughing, being sad, running, jumping, playing . . ." It goes on that way for several more lines apparently offering the children a chance at playing in ways that are not always safe, not always happy, yet offer a lot of freedom and excitement.

Adventure parks like Forcki are aimed at children ages seven to thirteen. Sophia was at the start of that age range, and Ozzie was younger. Burdened by cautious American parents, both our children didn't visit these parks by themselves. Sophia did go to Forcki with groups from her school several times to play among the creaky towers and roast *stockbrot* ("stick bread") on an open fire.

We also visited several other adventure playgrounds as a family. Ozzie's favorite type were *kinderbauernhof* ("child farms"), which had all kinds of farm animals on site: rabbits, ducks, geese, sheep, goats, pigs. Some even had horses. One of the best was Pinke Panke, located north of Berlin. We visited this child farm on a cold misty day in March, when it seemed the whole place was nothing but a huge mud puddle. Little kids like Ozzie seemed particularly drawn to these places, and there were plenty of parents at Pinke Panke, ferrying their young ones around to see the animals like at a visit to the zoo. But several primary school children were also there on their own, helping feed the livestock and mucking out stalls with pitchforks and rakes.

When we went into the main building for cocoa and coffee, we shared a long table with a large group of teenagers who were half playing board games but mostly talking and joking around. Clearly they thought of this old barn as their space. I thought it was incredible that any type of "playground" could hold the attention of such a wide range of young people from wide-eyed toddlers to wisecracking adolescents.

Even for older kids, adventure playgrounds offer an enticing mix of freedom and risk. They are allowed to do almost anything they want and are openly invited to try out tools normally reserved for adults. At Kolle 37, an adventure playground tucked between trendy restaurants in the bustling Prenzlauer Berg neighborhood, someone had set out a marble block on a stump, along with a chisel and a heavy metal hammer. Just lying there. No instructors hovering nearby. When we visited, Sophia picked up the tools gingerly, feeling their weight before putting them down again. A few moments later, two children about nine or ten years old came running by. They skidded to stop at the block, and a girl picked up the hammer and gave the block a few resounding blows before tearing off again. This struck me as an accident waiting to happen.

Accidents do happen at adventure playgrounds, even bad ones. The German courts haven't often sided with people seeking to sue for damages or to change the playgrounds to make them safer. In a 1978 case, which the play-advocacy group ABA Association calls "the adventure playground judgment," a German federal court ruled against an injured person in part because the purpose of adventure playgrounds is to educate children about the "existence of risk" and teach them through daring how to manage "the dangers of daily life." In other words, the dangers in these play spaces are real, on purpose, and no one is responsible for managing the risk but the child.

Necessary Dangers

The German risk researcher Warwitz told me that such playgrounds "are a good way of self-testing for children," providing places where they can try out skills and take risks, enhancing their knowledge of what they can do safely. Although Warwitz studies the benefits of risky play for children, he has a low opinion of amusement parks which feed children "pseudo-adventures" passively to induce the thrill of danger with things like roller coasters without any of the responsibility of taking a true risk.

"Real adventures do not have to be spectacular," he said. "They have to involve independent initiative, responsibility for oneself, the potential for failure, and the willingness to accept any possible consequences." Everyone needs to learn to manage risk, Warwitz contends, and children should start learning as early as possible how to identify and handle dangers.

Jörg, one of the fathers I met through my children's kita, grew up in Wolfsburg, a city famous for its huge Volkswagen plant, and he told me he rode his bicycle to kita at age four. By elementary school, he often played outside all day, unsupervised, with a group of kids at a playground across the street from his house. "And we only enjoyed it if there was risky stuff to do," he said. He described doing things like jumping off the top of the swing set, and "this terrific game" in which all the kids would help each other climb on top of a six-foot-high block and then try and push each other off. None of this Jörg considered too dangerous, and while he'd broken a couple of bones in his life, it was from doing other things—such as gymnastics—not during this wild play with his peers. "I find it really dangerous when kids are protected from risk taking, because that's how you learn how much you can trust yourself," he said.

The importance of children engaging in risky play is an idea backed by research—and not just from Germany. In 2015, the University of British Columbia and the Child & Family Research Institute at BC Children's Hospital in Canada published a systemic review of twenty-one papers on the subject. The review determined that risky outdoor play was not only healthy for children but encouraged the development of creativity, social skills, and resilience. In particular, playgrounds that offered natural elements, changes in height, and freedom for children to choose their own activities helped bring about these positive results. "These spaces give children a chance to learn about risk and learn about their own limits," said Mariana Brussoni, the lead author of the study and an assistant professor at UBC.

Brussoni's study looked at three types of risky play: heights, rough-and-tumble play in which children have the potential to hurt each other, and play in which there's a perceived risk of the child disappearing or getting lost—in other words, play or movement without adult supervision. These three categories of risky play are among six that were first defined by the Norwegian early childhood education professor Ellen Sandseter in 2007. She created the categories after interviewing preschool teachers and the preschoolers themselves about what they saw as risky play. Sand-seter's categories, which have since been much cited in the field, also include play involving great speed, dangerous tools, and dangerous elements, such as something a child could fall from or into.

In her 2011 paper titled "Children's Risky Play From an Evolutionary Perspective: The Anti-Phobic Effects of Thrilling Experiences," Sandseter theorizes that there are evolutionary functions for these types of play that help children manage their own fear later in life. She points to studies that indicate that children who engage in climbing have less fear of heights as adults, young children who engage in rough and tumble play are less aggressive when they are older, and children who experience multiple, positive separations from their parents before the age of nine have less separation anxiety symptoms at age eighteen. She cautions that reducing or eliminating risky play could result in increased mental problems. "Overprotection through governmental control of playgrounds and exaggerated fear of playground accidents might thus result in an increase of anxiety in society," she writes. "We might need to provide more stimulating environments for children, rather than hamper their development."

Overprotection has definitely sucked the life out of most American playgrounds. In recent decades, the equipment has become extremely tame in the name of safety—and a fear of lawsuits, which journalist Hanna Rosin detailed well in a 2014 article for *The Atlantic* called "The Over-protected Kid." Rosin describes the lawsuit mania that started in the late 1970s with a prime example: In 1978, a toddler named Frank Nelson fell through a gap between a tornado slide and the railing, and landed on his head on the hard asphalt below—because that was what covered the ground of most playgrounds in those days. Tragically, the fall caused permanent brain damage. His parents sued the Chicago Park District and two companies involved in manufacturing and installing the slide—and won. This and similar suits caused a sweeping change in playgrounds across the country.

Gone were the tall metal climbing structures and towering slides, replaced by plastic play structures of modest heights. Gone also was the asphalt, replaced by soft surfaces that almost bounce underfoot. Arguably, some of these hazardous things needed to disappear, but it's hard not to notice that the kids have also disappeared from playgrounds. Most of the small, safe plastic playgrounds I've visited in the United States have few if any school-age children on them.

Even with all these safety measures, the number of playground accidents in the United States is still high. In 1980, the rate of emergency room visits related to playground equipment, both public ones and home equipment, was one visit per 1,452 Americans, according to what Rosin calculates using statistics from the National Electronic Injury Surveillance System. In 2012, even after all that plastic and soft padding, the injury rate stood at one per 1,156 Americans.

It is interesting to note that the rate of injury in the European Union is a bit lower, even though many countries tend to have riskier playground equipment and parents don't monitor their children as closely. An estimated 119,000 children per year in the entire EU required emergency medical treatment due to injuries related to playground equipment, according to a study by EuroSafe. That's about one for every 4,235 EU residents (based on the EU population in 2012, the last year of the Euro-Safe study).

It's difficult to compare the playground injury rates with those in Germany, because the country's national statistics office does not keep that statistic separate from other injuries, which is perhaps indicative of the lower concern about making playgrounds perfectly safe. However, Mario Ladu, CEO of the playground inspection firm Spielplatzmobil, told the German press agency DPA in 2013 that about 16,000 playground injuries are reported every year. If that's an accurate number, that would mean the injury rate is even lower in Germany at one per 5,039 residents.

There can be many reasons for a higher injury rate in the United States—children following their natural inclinations will often be more careful on playgrounds that feel more dangerous and likewise if a playground is too safe or boring, they will make something risky to make it more fun. They will go up a slide backward or throw themselves down the slide headfirst. They will climb on the outside of a structure not meant for climbing on or stand up on a swing. This behavior fits with the risk compensation theory, which argues that people adjust their behavior according to the level of risk—taking more risk if they perceive that something is safer. So since all the safety equipment has been put in place, children may be more likely to misjudge the danger involved. For instance, they might think it's safer to climb higher if the surface below them is designed to soften their fall.

Risk researchers argue that normal children have a natural instinct for self-preservation and will usually only dare as much as they think they can manage. Warwitz says that children's "fear acts as a natural brake." The really dangerous situations happen when something interferes with that normal instinct; for instance, when other people, such as older kids or adults, pressure children to try something they aren't ready for.

Sports writer Mark Hyman found that this damaging outside pressure often comes from the parents themselves when it comes to organized team sports. Hyman wrote about the phenomenon in his book *Until It Hurts*, showing that the pressure to win from coaches and parents cheering on the sidelines can cause children and teens to play past the point of pain to injury. His own son, a high school pitcher, wound up with a rare injury requiring a surgery normally used on professional baseball players. Sometimes it seems that parents watching can be more harmful than when we let children play on their own.

So what can parents do in America with our ultrasafe playgrounds and culture of controlling children to encourage kids to take reasonable risks? It's pretty simple. Do as the Germans do. Send your kids outside to play, and don't watch everything they do. Take them to the playground and leave them on their own for a while. Let them climb trees and ride bikes. Seek out playgrounds with creative and riskier structures. They are few and far between in the United States, but they can be found. There are even some adventure playgrounds, including ones in New York City and Berkeley, California. We also can urge our parks and recreation districts to create more exciting play spaces for our kids.

Most of all, we parents can help by turning off the "Achtung" in our heads. If we can break the habit of constantly telling our school-age kids to "Stop!" and "Be careful!" then they'll have a better chance to test their own limits and rely on their natural "fear brakes" to judge what they can and cannot do. "Kids are supposed to do things that make their parents nervous," my husband told me once. I remind myself of that almost every day.

Another thing we can do is to let our children engage fully in the parts of our culture that do encourage risk-taking and facing fears—in my opinion, the best thing for this is American Halloween.

A Celebration of Fear

When I was a young kid, Halloween was the biggest, most scary-fun night of the year. This was a night to dress up like frightening creatures, to overcome shyness to ring a stranger's doorbell, and threaten them with tricks unless they gave you treats. Despite all the razor-blades-in-candy scares, Americans have still preserved much of that Halloween spirit, and at least for one evening a year school-age children are still allowed to roam the streets with only light adult supervision.

I thought Germans would be all over this holiday, since it seems to embrace so much of what they teach their children. After I experienced a German Halloween, it was clear they didn't understand the concept. Halloween, I didn't realize, is really an American holiday. While Halloween has roots in Europe, starting out as a Celtic tradition that was later modified and picked up by Christianity as the day before All Saint's Day, Germans have not formally celebrated it until recently. It is seen as an imported holiday, not from Ireland, but from the United States.

In my opinion, Germans don't know how to do Halloween right. Part of the problem is that October 31 falls close to a traditional German holiday called Saint Martin's Day. Usually celebrated on or near November 11, Saint Martin's Day is built around the story of a Good Samaritan, Saint Martin, who gave half his cloak to a freezing beggar. To mark this act of mercy, German children make paper lanterns, often lit with candles, and then parade through the streets and sing songs. While this is a lovely idea—children spreading the light of mercy and kindness through their neighborhoods—in practice, it's not exactly a thrilling children's holiday, at least compared to Halloween.

We celebrated Saint Martin's Day several times at our kita and at Sophia's school. November can be a cold time of year in Berlin, and the party usually started out with a bonfire in the kita's garden or schoolyard, with some food and drink. The school served the parents warm spiced wine, which was a major plus. Still, for the parents, the holiday was simply a lot of time spent standing and walking around in the cold. The kids would march around the block with their lanterns, singing—and that was it. No scary costumes. No candy.

Since Germans already had one holiday that meant walking around at night in the cold, I could see why they weren't eager to adopt another. Halloween got short shrift in Berlin. First no one seemed to know that Halloween had to be celebrated on the actual day of October 31. Parties at the school or in the neighborhood would happen on a day near Halloween that was most convenient, so that meant nobody celebrated it at the same time. While some stores gave out candy, none of our neighbors expected children in costumes to come knocking on their doors demanding treats.

One year, we went to a Halloween party held at Forcki, our neighborhood adventure playground. It was packed. There was pumpkin soup, cooked apples, hot cocoa for the kids, and warm spiced wine for the adults. Children in scary costumes were running everywhere. In the middle, some adults and teenagers had built a crude dragon statue out of wood planks, fabric, and paper. It was quite large, about six feet tall and ten feet long. At first, I didn't understand what it was for—an art project perhaps for the teenagers.

Sophia, dressed as a witch, ran around the whole place, trying out the haunted house that other kids had made out of the wooden huts. Eight years old and above it all, she declared it to be "not scary." When I asked her what was inside, she said, "Just some kids in costumes who jump out at you."

Ozzie, who had recently turned four, wouldn't go near the haunted house. He was dressed up as a Spiderman–alien (he couldn't decide on one costume) and stuck to my side. He kept asking to go back to look at the dragon. There was a circle around it marked with a single rope strung between stakes, so the little kids wouldn't get too close. Ozzie gripped that rope and stood wide-eyed as a teenager set up a dry ice machine, which made the dragon look even scarier.

After some time, a couple of guys with drums and, for some reason, bagpipes, started playing music—a signal for all the kids to line up. Then we all paraded in one big mass down the city streets. People in apartments opened their windows and threw candy down on the kids, who scrambled to pick it up. It was completely crazy and, I thought, missed the entire point of Halloween! Where is the daring if the kids didn't have to go to the doors by themselves and ring the bell? Essentially, as one big roiling group of kids and parents walking down the street, it was a lot like Saint Martin's Day, except with scary costumes instead of lanterns. My kids barely got any sweets, but only Zac and I knew what they were missing out on. They'd never experienced the excesses of an American Halloween.

After walking around a while in the cold, we went back to Forcki. They lit the dragon on fire. All the kids who had been running around and yelling were suddenly still and quiet. Ozzie watched as the sculpture that had fascinated and terrified him turned into a raging bonfire and started falling apart. The head with its open jaw full of teeth flamed for a moment and then broke and fell to the ground. The children laughed and cheered. The adults and teens that were managing the fire picked up bits of fallen dragon and threw them back onto the growing bonfire.

Sure, my German neighbors had got all the details of the holiday wrong, but they got this part of the Halloween spirit right. They created something monstrous and scary—then they burned it down.

10

Tough Subjects

When you live in a country where your language skills are less than perfect, you miss a few memos. One of the first important memos I missed was about sex education. I'm sure it was discussed at a parents' meeting, probably right after a long conversation in rapid-fire German about the lunch menu. So my daughter was introduced to the birds and the bees in school at age seven via a picture book called *Mummy Laid an Egg*, by British author Babette Cole. Sophia, of course, heard it translated into German. It's a silly book—perfect for giggling children.

I only learned what she knew when I saw her pull the same book out at the library and start showing it to Ozzie. I glanced over at the pages and saw childish cartoon drawings of all the ways Mommy and Daddy "fit together." I turned as red in the face as the embarrassed parents in the book. I took the book and flipped through the pages. It was about a wise child counteracting her parents' white lies about how babies are made: like a stork brings babies or that they are grown in a cabbage patch. Then the child explains how it really happens with cartoon drawings.

"Um . . . I'd rather you not look at this right now," I told Sophia. "We can talk about it later."

"*Mo-om*," Sophia said with a hand on her hip. "Frau Schneider already read it to us in class."

"She did? When was this?"

"A couple weeks ago. It's really funny."

I showed the book to Zac and explained what happened. He raised his eyebrows. "Well, now she knows," he said.

I found myself battling conflicting reactions: someone else had that dreaded conversation with her first, and on the other hand, someone *else* had that dreaded conversation with her first! I had always thought I'd be the one to talk to my daughter about sex, but quite honestly, I wasn't sure when and how I was going to handle the topic. Now that the subject had already been introduced, I found it much easier to talk with Sophia about it, to find out what she knew, what questions she had. While she was still quite giggly, she seemed at ease with the idea. She was less embarrassed than I was. She saw sex as a normal if silly thing to do, and I couldn't help affirming that truth. "It's OK to laugh," I told her. "It is kind of funny."

Another huge benefit of having the teacher read this book to her students meant that all Sophia's friends knew the same basic information that she did. There were no secrets or weird stories floating around. When I was Sophia's age, I was one of the only kids in my neighborhood who knew the facts of life. My mother had told me straight out fairly early. I didn't go around telling all my friends, but I did feel obligated to inject some truth when other kids told crazy stories of how babies are conceived. For instance, I remember having a heated argument with a neighbor girl who insisted that women got pregnant when a man peed on them and then the baby came out of their belly button. She told me this with a mixture of seriousness and horror and refused to believe what I told her. She was already convinced by her own odd version of sex, which she probably got through a combination of TV, overheard conversations, and kid logic.

Sex is an open secret in American culture. Kids see signs of it everywhere—in advertisements, on billboards, in magazines, on TV, in movies, in the lyrics of pop songs, and in a million jokes. Today's children also have the Internet, which makes it even more likely they will see or read false, misleading, or disturbing information about sex. Yet it's still difficult for American kids to get an honest, unbiased discussion of sex in school—and ignorance can have disastrous consequences.

Sex education in the United States has been divided between two approaches: comprehensive sexual education, which strives to provide information on anatomy, puberty, contraception, sexual orientation, and sexual health, in addition to the basic facts of how a baby is conceived; and abstinence-only education, which has a primary focus on discouraging sex before marriage and leaves out almost all of the other topics. Until recently, the federal government continued to fund abstinence-only education, to the tune of $1.5 billion over twenty-five years, despite the fact that no evidence exists that such programs have any impact on teen sexual activity.

This has meant that fewer than half of U.S. high schools cover all of the topics that the CDC has identified as critical to ensuring sexual health, and only 20 percent of middle schools address them. In 2016, fewer than half the U.S. states required public schools to teach sexual education, and thirty-five states allowed parents to opt their children out of the courses, according to the National Conference of State Legislatures.

In contrast, comprehensive sex education is considered a right in Germany. The way sex ed is taught still varies from state to state, and parents must be informed by the school about what is being taught, but no parent can opt their children out of sex education, not even for religious reasons. Many Americans might object to that loss of parental power, but it's hard to argue with the results the German approach achieves. In comparison, the German teenage birth rate is three and a half times lower than it is in the United States; the abortion rate is about four and a half times lower; and the HIV prevalence rate is three and a half times lower, according to figures compiled by Planned Parenthood.

Germans also do not wait until high school or even middle school to introduce the topic. "Sex education cannot begin early enough," said Dr. Heike Kramer in an article on the city of Berlin's official website. Kramer said that children need a cushion of information well before puberty, with its attendant hormones and mood swings, overwhelms them. Many

American programs start in fifth grade or later. That's much too late by Kramer's standards, especially considering that doctors now place the average start of puberty around age ten or eleven, and many fifth graders are already in the midst of it.

In Berlin, sex education usually begins in first and second grades with basic biology, body differences, and sex abuse prevention. My children had some education even earlier than that in kita, including setting boundaries around touching, which was meant to help protect them from abuse, and learning the differences between male and female bodies—although in kita to learn about body differences, all they had to do was look around them. Kita bathrooms have no stalls, just rows of toilets in an open room with no door. I was taken aback by this at first, but it soon made a lot of sense. The children are safer when there's no door that can be locked and where something secretive could happen. And children that age don't really care who sees them on the toilet.

We adults sometimes forget that body shame is learned, not something we're born with. The rows of toilets in the kita also meant there was rarely a wait in case they had to pee, and they all saw each other's naked bodies regularly. In America, long before we went to Germany, I once changed my infant daughter's diaper in front of a young cousin who had grown up with only brothers. He gasped and asked me worriedly, "Where's her penis?" This was funny at the time, but in retrospect, it reveals how American modesty is somewhat problematic. Our children can grow to be five, six, or even older before ever understanding the basic biological differences between the sexes.

Once German children start school, more formal sex education begins. The Berlin Department of Education, Youth, and Science provides only a general framework of what students should be taught about sex, but its goals are ambitious: schools should convey a "comprehensive, holistic, and personal concept of human sexuality." Kids should be taught about sexuality as "a force that affects human beings physically, mentally, emotionally, and socially throughout every stage of life."

In practical terms, this means German kids learn much more about sex than conception. They talk about things like body image and gender

stereotypes. They learn about preventing pregnancy and sexually trans-
mitted diseases and about the pleasure of sex, including masturbation and
orgasms. They are also taught about homosexuality. The Berlin guidelines
emphasize that teachers should respect cultural and religious differences
and take a neutral stance toward sexual issues, not impose their own opinions or morals on the students. I have to wonder if this is truly possible
given the difficulty of the topic.

Sex education is not without controversy in Germany, but as with a
lot of things, the debate is in a whole other place than it is in America.
German parents are more concerned with how sex ed is taught rather
than keeping information out entirely. For instance, in 2011 materials that
were much more explicit than *Mummy Laid an Egg* were pulled from
the Berlin primary schools after parents' objections. Yet few people in
Germany would call for a morality-laden "abstinence-only" approach the
way it has been taught in the United States.

Regardless of your beliefs around sex, I think there's a strong case for
American parents to start pressuring our legislators for German-style
comprehensive sexual education in schools. Why? Because by age seventeen, the vast majority of American teens will have had sex. Religious
prohibition does not necessarily prevent young people from engaging in
sex. According to a 2009 study by the National Campaign to Prevent Teen
and Unplanned Pregnancy, 80 percent of evangelical young adults have
had premarital sex. The fact is the majority of young people are sexually
active, and they need good information to protect their health and prevent
unwanted pregnancies.

If our school districts won't provide this education, we owe it to our
children to help them find good sources of information, in addition to
ourselves, because quite frankly children and young people don't want
to discuss some of these topics with their parents. Did you? Outside of
school, we can guide our children to ask questions of trusted health-care
providers and nonprofits. We can also give them good books, movies, and
appropriate sources on the Internet that let them learn by themselves without us even having to be there.

I know culturally America is a bit prudish compared to Germany. It's part of our Puritan heritage, but the urge to keep our children "innocent" is not just impossible, it's dangerous. Our children will eventually grow into adults and they have a right to know about their own bodies. When I told Sophia that many parents in America would be angry that a school had taught their first grade children about sex, her response was to the point: "Well, somebody has to tell us some time!"

Death

Sophia was always one for asking the hard questions, and at age four, she hit me with this one:

"Do I have to die?" she asked.

How did this come up? I thought, as I struggled to formulate an answer. Somehow Sophia had suddenly realized that death is permanent. (Young children usually have trouble recognizing that death and sleep are different.) This bomb of a question was possibly one of the toughest moments Zac and I had ever faced as parents. Long ago, we had decided that we would be as honest as possible with our children when they asked difficult questions. What we didn't realize is how much trouble honesty can get you into.

"Everybody dies," I said. "But most likely you won't die until you are very, very old. Older than your grandmother." This was the wrong thing to say. Her eyes grew wide.

"Grandma is going to die?"

"Not right now," I said. "But, yes, eventually she will die. Everyone dies, Sophia."

"Will you die?" she asked.

"Yes, but hopefully not for a long time."

"What happens after someone dies?"

I took a deep breath. "Nobody knows for sure," I said. "Some people believe that there's a heaven, a place where your spirit goes. It's a happy place where you can be with all the other people who died."

Despite this rosy picture of the afterlife, she obviously didn't think it was good enough. "I don't want to die," she repeated, her eyes filling up with tears.

"Nobody does, honey. Nobody does," I said and hugged her, still feeling that somehow I had let her down.

She repeated a version of this conversation with Zac and me for a couple weeks, and no matter what religious explanations we proffered about what might happen after people die, she was not comforted. Oddly enough, she finally calmed down after Zac gave the biological explanation of what happens to a dead body. Ever the scientist, Zac carefully explained the process in which the body is broken down by decomposers like worms, insects, and bacteria, and then becomes part of the earth, and eventually all the atoms and molecules that once made up your body become part of the world, the dirt, the water, the plants, and the air. Sophia asked him to repeat this story several times. At four, she seemed to like this idea a lot, even though it said nothing about what happened to her spirit. I think in her mind she imagined that to be happening not just to her body but also to her "self," which is a rather poetic way of thinking about death.

Then as things often do with kids, she dropped the subject. In second grade, it popped up again. Sophia came home with a video link she was excited to show me. She had me look it up on the website for RBB (which is like the German version of a local PBS station): it was a cartoon showing two children on a roller coaster. As we watched, a child's voice explained that bad times come in life, people get sick or have accidents, but in the end, we all die. The cartoon kids grew older, until their heads hung to the side. Crosses replaced their eyes, and their tongues hung out in classic cartoon death. Then two springs ejected them from the roller coaster ride. I looked at my daughter in horror. Sophia just smiled.

"Watch! This is the really funny part!" Sophia said. The roller coaster cart was now filled with an array of animals and plants, who as they traveled all soon had crosses for eyes too and then were ejected by springs. It was a simple, clear message, and one of the hardest truths I had told her at age four: everything that lives must die. Only this time Sophia seemed to take it in stride.

The public broadcasting station first ran this cartoon called *Leben mit dem Tod* ("Living With Death") as a "subject week" in 2012, encouraging schools to view the videos and participate in related activities. Not all schools adopted it like ours did. It was an optional activity, though German psychologist Christoph Student thinks it shouldn't be. While the subject of death is often taught in religion classes, Student thinks that's too little, too late and argues that death should be taught with the openness of sexual education in German schools. "Adults want to protect children from fear. But that's nonsense—keeping children away from death is like keeping them away from life," Student said in an interview with RBB.

This doesn't mean that parents should sit down with their toddler and have a "death talk"; Student advises that parents should respond to children's questions about death with "What do you think?" and let the child's own beliefs stand. They should only correct them if they have destructive ideas. And there will be plenty of opportunities to talk about death, Student points out, as children see pets and other animals die and, of course, sometimes their own relatives.

As part of the death project, the children in Sophia's class were asked to draw pictures of someone they knew who had died. A lot of her classmates drew pictures of their grandfathers. One showed an uncle going to the hospital. Sophia drew a picture of her fish. At that age, she'd been fortunate enough that her only direct experience with death had been through the aquarium in her room.

Sophia seemed almost nonchalant about the topic of death, even as she examined it closely with her class. She'd accepted that death was part of life, and the death project reaffirmed that for her. When the class visited a museum that had everything to do with death, she was almost bored by it, even the section on the Day of the Dead, which I thought looked cool and scary at the same time. The project also touched on some religious ideas about the afterlife.

At one point, Sophia told me she had "decided to believe in heaven," and then another day, she said she wanted to come back as a bird or a dolphin in her next life. They had discussed reincarnation in class. It was obviously a child's understanding of it, but it should have been clear to us then that she would choose a course called "*lebenskunde*" (which translates to lifestyles or life skills) over religion, both of which were offered in her public elementary school.

Religion

Germans teach religion in public school. The country's law stipulates only that "there is no state church," which is currently interpreted to mean that the government does not advocate for any one belief system. So religion is taught as a stand-alone class in public schools.

Until the 1970s, most German children went to either Protestant or Catholic religion class, but as times changed, more and more parents opted their children out of the course. This happened for a variety of reasons: either the parents weren't religious or perhaps they didn't like the way it was being taught. German children who have an immigrant background often come from another religion entirely—Islam. So the German school systems in the various states have started offering other choices. Currently, religion class comes in several flavors, depending on the region and the preferences of the parents at the school. In many German states, religion is a mandatory class; the only alternative they offer for parents who want to opt their children out is an "ethics" class, a philosophical course that takes a neutral stance toward religion. (Ethics itself becomes a mandatory course starting around seventh grade.)

In Berlin, which was once dubbed the "atheist capital of the world," more than 60 percent of the population identifies as *konfessionfrei* (literally "confession-free" or nonreligious). This is nearly the mirror opposite of the statistics for the entire country: more than 60 percent of the German population claims a religious affiliation. In the United States, the percent of the faithful is closer to 77 percent. We are one of the most religious nations in the developed world, but keep in mind that believing in God is no casual affair in Germany. Upon entering the country, we were presented with an unusual tax form asking us whether we belonged to any religious faith. If we checked one of those boxes, our earnings would be taxed at 9 percent, which would go directly to the religious organization we named. Most churches in America ask their members to tithe around that amount, but in Germany, the government makes the religious put their money where their belief is.

In Berlin and Brandenburg, the large population of nonreligious people have had an impact on the schools, and one of the most popular alternatives to taking a religion course in primary school is *lebenskunde*, a class that is sponsored by the German Humanist Association, which is an atheist and agnostic group.

I didn't know this when I first saw Sophia's primary school schedule. All I saw was an hour blocked off for "Religion/Lebenskunde." I thought that it was all one class: a generalized course on different "lifestyles" that included education about the world's religions. But it wasn't. Religion at our school was full-on Christian instruction, like Sunday school, except rather than on the weekend at church, it was during the week at public school. At our particular school, the class was neither Protestant nor Catholic, but a generalized course on the basic tenets of Christianity.

This made me nervous. Being an American, I was used to coming across a wide variety of faiths, and I knew that some could be more extreme than others. I wasn't eager to have my daughter indoctrinated into some brand of religion I knew nothing about. Zac came up with an equitable solution; he told Sophia that she could try out each class and decide for herself. I thought she might choose religion because of how nice heaven sounded to her, but instead, Sophia told us she preferred lebenskunde, mainly because she liked the teacher better. (Here's a hint to the religions of the world seeking new members: hire fun teachers.)

Although it was an atheist-sponsored course, lebenskunde taught Sophia about religions—all of them. Around the holidays, she came home with colored crèche scenes and a menorah. She also learned about Hindu gods, Buddha, and Mohammed, as well as Jesus Christ. The course didn't focus on religion but covered a wide range of subjects, from children's feelings to the change of seasons. It involved a lot of artwork, which Sophia loved, and games. Never did she come home saying that the teacher had told her not to believe in God.

That's not the primary focus of the class, according to Jaap Schilt, the head of lebenskunde training and education at the German Humanist Association. The class is more focused on teaching the children to ask questions and find their own answers. "One of the main goals in leben-skunde is to teach children to believe in their own capacities and to believe in themselves," he said.

Schilt said there were four themes to the lebenskunde course: learning about human rights, especially the rights of children; skeptical thinking; responsibility toward society and the environment; and the history of humanism, world religions, and other "life stances."

While these are the broad themes, what is actually taught in each primary school class is mostly guided by the children and their questions. Since they are so young, big discussions about religion or atheism are not such pressing issues for them. Instead, the children want to learn about things like how to handle friendships, take care of a pet, and deal with other matters that are important to them at the moment. Because of this, and because in Berlin, the teachers "are all a little bit like free thinkers," Schilt said there probably is not a big difference between lebenskunde and a religion class.

For my part, I was quite happy with Sophia's lebenskunde class, but not all Germans are happy with the way religion classes are offered in their schools. The teachers of each religion or lebenskunde class are certified by their respective organizations, but they also must meet the standards of the education system, including having the right degree and certification. Some people think this amounts to too much government interference in religion, or they don't like the way the subject is taught in their school. The mere existence of the class also has a peer-pressure effect on students. More than one parent told me that their children's desire to take religion class was based not so much on what they believed but on whether their friends were in the class.

My friend Judith is raising her kids in the Christian faith, and while her daughter takes religion class, Judith is indifferent to it. "Going to worship and Sunday school is much more important," she said, adding that sometimes the information her daughter gets from the class doesn't fit with her church's teachings. "It may be better to just teach all the kids together, and teach different religions or the different ways of living that there are," she said. "I don't know if it makes a lot of sense to separate kids. The parents who are Christian and bring their kids up in a Christian way, they will do it anyway. They don't need to depend on the class."

The German example is instructional for Americans who wish to insert religion into public schools. It's not as easy as it may seem. For one, the religion that is taught in school may not fit the beliefs of every family, and then there's the problem of providing an appropriate class for the many religious sects in the United States. Most religious Germans are either Roman Catholic or Protestant—and most of those Protestants belong to one of the churches united under the banner of the Evangelical Church in Germany or EKD. Even though there are fewer differences among them, many German Christians still are not happy with the religious courses offered. The introduction of an Islamic religion class in Germany has also proved controversial. (Roughly 5 percent of the German population is Muslim compared with less than 1 percent in the United States.)

On the other hand, teaching religion in such a public place as a school brings it out into the open, allowing students to ask questions and learn from one another. It may seem odd, but the atheist organization in Berlin actually prefers that religion is taught in schools. "We think it's better when we can discuss religion on a public platform, and it's not hidden in some private organizations," Schilt said. "It's better when there's an open debate about these themes for both parties. . . . Maybe they can learn something from each other."

Through all these tough subjects, I was struck by the incredible amount of intellectual freedom Germans gave their children and the trust they had in their children's ability to handle what we might consider sensitive or difficult facts of life. As my children grew, I became less and less afraid of their tough questions, not because I had the perfect answers to all of them, but because I soon found I could often best address their questions by turning it back to them and asking, "What do you think?"

I started to trust my children more to be able to absorb information and come up with their own ideas, as they developed their own sense of right and wrong. I know now that if I truly value their independence, I should allow them freedom of thought. I also have to come to terms with the fact that they are not always going to think or believe what I do. Ultimately, when children separate from their parents, they not only physically move away from us but also intellectually and, often times, spiritually. A significant portion of American adults, 44 percent, do not practice the faith of their childhood, according to a 2011 Pew Research study.

This spiritual separation doesn't always lead to less religiosity. Judith is a case in point. She grew up in East Germany, the daughter of atheist parents, but she is a Christian, and her parents remain close to her. They live nearby and are actively involved with their grandchildren.

Being open about ideas and beliefs with my children has also been a source of joy. My children are constantly bringing back the many interesting concepts they've discovered, and in Germany, there was always a lot available for them to discover. Information about a number of topics that would be more controlled in the United States is easily accessible to children. The *Mommy Laid an Egg* book just sitting on the shelf in the children's section of the library is a prime example. I have yet to find that book on any U.S. library shelves.

At the age of four, Ozzie became a big fan of audio books. I usually let him pick whatever CDs he wanted from the children's section at the library. He would listen to them while he played in his room. They were meant for children and were in German, so I often tuned them out when he had them on. For a while, he had a favorite one that was all about life in the Arctic and the Inuit people. He played it over and over.

One day he asked me out of the blue, "Mom, do you think you are a lucky person?"

"Absolutely," I said, and thinking this was a teachable moment, I began to launch into a list of things I was grateful for. "I'm happy and healthy. I have two fantastic kids and—"

"Great!" Ozzie interrupted. "If you're lucky, that means when you die you get to come back as an orca."

Who knew?

11

Facing the Past

Sophia was climbing on a tall rock at a playground near our house when she called me over. "Mom, what is this?" she asked. I walked around to where she was pointing, and there set in the stone was a plaque with two names, dates ending in the 1940s, and a Star of David. Oh.

"It's a memorial," I said.

"What's that?"

"For people who died," I said. "So they would be remembered."

Sophia seemed to accept that at face value, and I thought I'd dodged a difficult question, but it was only for the moment.

Some weeks later while walking through the streets of Berlin, Sophia stopped in front of two golden stones. They were small squares, the same size as other paving stones on the street, but they were golden and stood out. "Mom, what are these?" A pair of names were engraved on the stones, side by side, a husband and wife. Then the dates: birth, deportation, and death at two different concentration camps. It was hard not to imagine the scene of the couple being torn from their home, which we were standing in front of right now, how they were taken away to separate camps to die not ever knowing what had happened to the other.

"These people used to live here, and they died," I said to Sophia. "People put these stones here so they'd be remembered, like the plaque we saw in the playground."

"Why are they in the sidewalk?"

"They wanted to make sure no one forgets," I said, realizing that was the point of these stones—that even children would ask. I knew I shouldn't skimp on the truth. We were in Germany after all. I took a breath: "So there was this big war back when my grandparents were young. . . ." I began to explain to my daughter the basics of what happened with the Nazis, how they sent the Jews and other people they didn't like to camps, and how many died there, like the people named on these two stones.

We talked about World War II with our children many times when we were in Berlin, not because Zac or I brought it up on purpose, but because it was everywhere. It was in those golden "stumble stones" set right into the sidewalk, at memorials in the middle of parks, and in all the museums, not just the ones focused on the war and the Holocaust. For instance, we once visited the Deutsches Technikmuseum, a great place for kids because it features all kinds of transportation, including full-scale planes, ships, trains, and automobiles. On the floor dedicated to trains, there among all the shiny engines from different periods of history sat a humble wooden railcar. It looked like the kind used for cattle, only this one had been used for humans. So we talked about that cruelty, right then and there.

"In Germany, it's such a big topic you can't really avoid it when you have kids, especially when you have kids who are interested in things," Annekatherin told me. As a teacher, Annekatherin said she'd never encountered kids who were new to the topic. They'd already heard about it early on from their families, at museums, in books, or on TV. When I asked my German friends about World War II, they also told me they could not remember a time when they didn't know what their country had done.

The toughest subject of all for German parents might be their own history, but no one I met in Germany tried to hide the topic from their children. Remembering World War II and its atrocities is seen as a culture-wide activity, and as with many things in the German language, there is a long, special word for this: *Vergangenheitsbewältigung*, which means "coming to terms with the past."

In addition to the museums, monuments, TV programs, and films, German children are formally taught about the Nazi years in depth at school, and not just in history class. It's often taught in courses such as German literature, ethics, and even English-language class. "I felt like in all subjects, there was always some point when we were talking about it," Jörg said. High school students also often visit memorials and the sites of former concentration camps.

Oddly enough, I heard from several Germans that part of their education involved a book and film based on a true American story, called *The Wave*. In 1967, Palo Alto teacher Ron Jones decided to conduct an experiment in authoritarianism in his high school history class. He instituted some simple discipline routines, and they quickly caught on. Within days students were saluting each other in the hall and wearing shirts to show they were part of the group. He ended the experiment by telling the students they were part of a national movement, and then revealing their leader at a packed assembly. He played them an old movie of Adolf Hitler speaking to his Nazi youth. The effect was devastating.

A fictionalized version of the events was made into an ABC After-school Special in 1981, and author Todd Strasser turned it into a novel that same year. In 2008, German filmmakers made a modern adaptation called *Die Welle*, turning the tale into a thriller that challenges the notion that the rise of Nazi-like authoritarianism could never happen in today's Germany.

It's a compelling story that makes the dangers of authoritarianism real for teens, and it's an appealing tool for teachers to use—perhaps too appealing. As a student, Annekatherin encountered the story in three different classes. "Now, there's a movie, but I can't see it," she said. Although *Die Welle* is a new interpretation, Annekatherin couldn't stand to see any version of *The Wave* story told one more time.

As a teacher, Annekatherin felt the most powerful experience she could arrange for her students was to have a concentration camp survivor speak with them directly. "This is always very moving," she said. "The boys, who are maybe fourteen or fifteen years old, are at an awkward age, and they usually laugh things off, but here they are really solemn. And they ask good questions."

As time passes, German students have fewer opportunities to talk with survivors face-to-face. In fact, the whole way that Germany treats its past is evolving as the years put more distance between the present and 1945.

The History of Memory

Immediately after World War II, there was a lot of denial in Germany around what had happened. Harold Marcuse, a German history professor at University of California, Santa Barbara, said that three myths surfaced at the end of the war: victimization, ignorance, and resistance. Many Germans said they were victims of the Nazis too, that they were not active supporters but were forced to do things by the people in power. Many also said they had no idea what was going on at the camps, and it was popular to claim that they or their family resisted Nazi power in some way and offered help to Jews or other victims of the camps.

The Germans who were born immediately after the war are known for challenging their parents and these myths. What is often called the '68 generation rejected almost everything associated with their parents' generation. This was also the era when some of the biggest Nazi war crime trials occurred, and as more light was shone on their horrific acts, the younger generation felt an incredible amount of shame and guilt over what their culture had done.

Even at this point, Marcuse said the myths of victimization, ignorance, and denial still existed, but they morphed. For example, some Germans now saw themselves as victims of the Allied powers. These entrenched myths didn't really come crumbling down until much later. Marcuse points to the airing of the American-produced TV series *The Holocaust* in Germany in 1978 as a key moment, when much that was hidden had to be faced. "It really inoculated a whole new era of dealing with the Nazi past, in the schools," he said. "It had a huge impact. It just bowled people over."

Interest grew in uncovering the past, no matter how difficult. A "dig where you stand" movement began, which purported that anyone could discover history. In 1976, sixteen-year-old Anna Rosmus dug a little too far. Her Bavarian town of Passau had a reputation for being part of the resistance to Nazism, and this is what Rosmus had expected to find when she started digging into the town's past. Instead, she uncovered evidence of anti-Semitic fervor and that current prominent people in Passau, including priests, had been active Nazis. She won an award for her first essay, "Passau and the Third Reich," and followed that later with a book. For her efforts, people called her *das schreckliche mädchen*, or "the nasty girl," and in 1990 a fictionalized account of her discoveries was made into a popular movie of that name.

Rosmus's story is emblematic of the intergenerational strife in Germany, when the younger generation was openly questioning a still-powerful older generation. In the face of all the historical facts that were being uncovered, no one could claim ignorance. Not everyone had been part of the resistance, and many Germans had to come to terms with the fact that their relatives, friends, and neighbors hadn't all been victims but perpetrators. They were culpable.

Around this time arose an interesting controversy about the nature of that culpability. On the one side is the argument put forth in books like Christopher Browning's *Ordinary Men*, published in 1992. Browning showed that average men willingly committed mass murder in Poland, even though they had a chance to opt out of the duty with no repercussions His book put forth the idea that when regular people are placed in a certain setting, they will generally follow the orders of the designated authority. (The *Wave* experiment in Palo Alto backs up this theory as well.)

Daniel Goldhagen took issue with this argument and launched a huge controversy with his book *Hitler's Willing Executioners: Ordinary Germans and the Holocaust*, in which he essentially contends that it was not that they were ordinary people, but that they were German and part of a long history and toxic culture that hated Jews.

The Germans ate it up. Or a certain segment of the population did. Goldhagen made appearances on many German talk shows, and he was even given the Democracy Prize in 1997 by a prestigious German political journal because he had "stirred the consciousness of the German public." Yet others called out Goldhagen for cherry-picking his evidence to make his case—and for making an essentially racial argument that there is something distinctly German about people committing these atrocities, rather than seeing a capacity for evil and hate as a danger among all people in every society.

The idea of the specific cultural menace of the Germans was even reflected by such revered German figures like the novelist Günter Grass. Grass won a Nobel Peace Prize for his novels that explored the Nazi years. Once seen as Germany's conscience, Grass famously fought against the reunification of the country after the fall of the Wall for fear that the nation would again become a belligerent force in the world. He ultimately lost credibility with many people when late in life he admitted that as a youth he had been briefly part of the Waffen-SS at the end of the war, a particularly aggressive and violent military unit.

Grass was a prominent example of a divide in how Germans see themselves. He was part of a generation that sought to come to terms with the past through a type of cultural penance (even while perhaps still hiding its own personal crimes). The younger generations, on the other hand, have a different struggle: what do they do with this cultural identity, this horrible past that they had taken no part in, but yet belonged to them? Many Germans born in the 1960s and later see a need to play an active role in the political world, both personally and as a nation—not to remain a country forever divided or humbled into silence, but to face the past, accept responsibility, and, with that knowledge, move forward. When Grass died in 2015, journalist Jochen Bittner wrote an opinion piece in *The New York Times* about this generational conflict, saying that Grass came from a different Germany than he did.

Yet the argument that Grass represented can still be seen in Germany today. In Berlin, I was always puzzled by a banner that hung off a balcony of a building in Friedrichshain that read: "I still don't believe Germany has a right to exist." This struck me as hypocritical in so many ways, and even more so because the banner was in English. I wanted to argue with the banner's creator—because Germany did exist, they were in it and obviously benefitting from it.

Banners like this are fine to fly in Berlin, yet many Germans are reticent to fly their own country's flag. "You will only see flags during the World Cup," Kordula told me. And it was true. During the much-revered global soccer competition (which occurred twice while we lived in Germany), everything was black, red, and gold: flags, shirts, Hawaiian-style leis of flowers; even the Berlin punks dyed their hair in the colors of the German flag. Then, a few days after the games ended, even when Germany won the championship in 2014, all the flags and colors disappeared again. While the far-right has started flag-waving again, most Germans today are uncomfortable with any sustained outward displays of patriotic pride, perhaps because of their history with disastrous nationalism, and how the outside world might view such displays.

Yet the world at large has started to view Germany differently. In 2014, Germany knocked the United States out of its longtime position in the top spot as the most admired nation in the world, according to the Anholt-GfK Nation Brands Index. This was partly due to the World Cup win, but it also stemmed from the country's rising position of power in the world. In 2016, *U.S. News & World Report* ranked countries on a variety of criteria, including openness to business, cultural influence, and quality of life. Again, Germany came out on top. Nevertheless, I found Germans to be more mildly amused by this than proud. Outright national pride was not an emotion I saw often in Germany, outside of the World Cup. In his satiric song "Be German," comedian Jan Böhmermann aptly summed up the feeling that Germans today "are proud of not being proud."

Modern Germans have been brought up with the humbling weight of their country's past. Even though most people today were not even born during the rise of Hitler, they still feel a sense of responsibility for what their culture did—and an obligation to the future. On his visits to classrooms of German students studying the Nazi years, Marcuse said one of the most striking things he witnessed was the reaction of the few students with an immigrant background in the class. "It was interesting to see how they felt it was part of their history," Marcuse said. "They hadn't grown up in Germany, and they were in their mid-teens, and still they felt, 'This is part of my history and I'm reaping the legacy and the benefits of the Nazi period in a way. So I'm responsible too.'" This is the same sentiment Michael Moore captured on his film *Where to Invade Next?* when a brown-skinned teenager sitting in a German class claims his country's past "because I'm German too."

The Germans I spoke with also expressed a similar sense of responsibility, even though all of them were born well after the end of World War II. Axel, a German actor whose youngest son went to kita with mine, felt that it was important not to dismiss the crimes of World War II as something belonging to the past: "Only when you say, 'I'm German. It's partly my fault. It's part of me,' then we can start to actually deal with it," he said. At the same time, he acknowledged that it's something that's "very hard to get across when you talk to kids."

Ulrike Jureit, a German historian with the Hamburg Institute for Social Research, told me that many consider Germany's treatment of the past as exemplary. "Hardly any other country in the world has confronted its criminal past with such thoroughness and commitment—not only from political and criminal-justice standpoints but also in terms of collective cultural memory." At the same time, she noted that critics see problematic aspects with the education around Nazism, including "a certain level of oversaturation" of the topic.

I heard this sentiment, too, from Germans who felt the country's Nazi past was almost overtaught, as a topic that was in every classroom and all around them. Still, I found no one who advocated for less instruction. "It's better to talk too much than too little about what happened," Annekatherin said, even though she was the one who had had to read *The Wave* three times.

Jureit suggested that perhaps it's time to place more focus on the Holocaust's significance today. "We have spent decades investigating what happened during the Second World War, but now the question of what the Holocaust means for us and our current political, social, and economic challenges is becoming ever more prominent. What can we really learn from this time in history to help us shape our future?"

It's clear from the response to the Syrian refugee crisis that many Germans have already asked themselves such questions—and not just prominent leaders like Chancellor Angela Merkel, but ordinary Germans. In 2015, when nearly a million refugees arrived in Germany, thousands of citizens came out to greet arriving trainloads of asylum seekers. When the surge of asylum seekers started, a survey by the broadcasting association ARD found that 88% of Germans were willing to donate to help the refugees, and 67% were willing to volunteer their time to help.

This is not to say all Germans are welcoming and accepting of refugees—and in the wake of terror attacks and sexual assaults blamed on immigrants that support has eroded. The relatively new right-wing group AfD (Alternative for Germany) has ridden a wave of anti-immigrant feeling with its calls to tighten borders and a return to German nationalism. While the rise of the AfD is alarming, it is still not close to becoming a major political party. A large majority of Germans still reject any politics that appeal to prejudice. A January 2017 ARD poll found only 12 percent of voters supported the AfD. Instead most Germans were either still backing Merkel's center-right Christian Democratic Union party or the left SPD (Social Democratic Party) that has taken similar stances to the CDU on the refugee crisis.

Even though right-wing, anti-immigrant populism seems to be triumphing in the United States, the United Kingdom, and many countries in Europe, Germany so far remains a steadfast, if somewhat lonely, champion of liberal democracy. The fact that the country has largely rejected politics based on prejudice has a lot to do with the keen awareness many average Germans have of their country's historical crimes and their responsibility for them. As Peter Schriever, a German janitor, told *The Washington Post* in 2015: "We caused so much suffering many years ago during the war, when we invaded other nations and did many horrible things," he said. "Now it is our time to heal those who suffer."

Historic Crimes and Responsibility

We have our own myths in America. If I compare Germany's approach to its past with my own education in U.S. history, it is easy to see a clear effort to portray America as always the hero with only cursory treatment of our country's historical crimes. For example, I learned of the mass killing of Native Americans only within a narrative of "conquering the West." I also remember a long lecture about the economics of slavery, the "triangle trade," but no in-depth discussion about its inhumanity.

History teaching has changed in the United States since I was in school, but it is still subject to a variety of political pressures. The way it's taught also varies from state to state and even from one school board to another. Still, history education in general has moved away from the old style of teaching "names, dates, facts, and heroes," according to James Grossman, the executive director of the American Historical Association. "We've moved toward understanding that the history of ideas is not just the ideas written down by a small group of people, but that history is written across a wide range of people within a society," he said.

That broader understanding opens up the study of U.S. history to more than the single narrative line, which troubles those who want to keep the idea of American exceptionalism as the main point of the story: the idea that the United States was (and remains) a model for the rest of the world. In 2014, Oklahoma state legislator Dan Fisher introduced a bill to ban U.S. advanced placement (AP) history courses, saying they focused too heavily on "what's bad about America." While that bill was eventually withdrawn, legislators in Colorado, Georgia, North Carolina, South Carolina, and Texas all made similar moves to modify or dump the course. Then a group that called itself the "National Association of Scholars" issued an open letter opposing the AP history framework developed by the College Board because it "downplays American citizenship and American world leadership in favor of a more global and transnational perspective."

Part of the uproar was the misconception that the document in question was a full curriculum. Instead, it was a framework, a set of guidelines to help teachers prepare students for the AP test. School districts and teachers were left the task to populate it with actual content, so they were fairly free to include or exclude what they liked.

Some of the language in the AP framework was eventually changed to satisfy the critics. Grossman said that while the changes were needed, they were relatively minor. The basic narrative remained, and the way history is taught will continue to evolve.

"The challenge is to move from thinking of ourselves as teaching history to a view of ourselves as teaching students how to learn history," Grossman said. Today, in many history classes, students are learning how to use the "tools of history," which involves understanding historical context and examining evidence and how that evidence is used to make a historical narrative.

My friend Carrie, a high school history teacher in a large Michigan district, has been part of that change in education style. "The big transformation in history is now there's more emphasis on doing history and uncovering history in different ways," she told me. Carrie now teaches in a very different way than she herself was taught. "There's more primary source use, instead of the way it was before, which was 'Here's the textbook, read these pages, and you'll have a quiz on those pages,' and not a lot of discussion," she said.

Carrie felt it was important to provide the students with a number of different sources that bring a subject alive, then have the students debate and discuss it. She described the process of how she once taught her American students about the Holocaust, a topic that was framed around the issue of remembering historical atrocities. The students did a study of monuments around the world, visited a local Holocaust memorial, and heard a survivor speak. They looked into how the Holocaust was taught and remembered in Germany. They compared two famous books on the period: *Night*, by Elie Wiesel, and *Maus*, by Art Spiegelman. After the students had worked with all this information about the Holocaust, one of history's worst atrocities, Carrie presented her students with a hypothetical situation about another real historical atrocity, slavery, asking them to debate if and how they would build a memorial to the victims of the slave trade in a fictional place in West Africa.

Carrie's teaching plan used numerous sources, gave many chances for discussion, and allowed the students to apply the concepts they had learned to a new situation. It sounded fabulous. Only she can't do it anymore.

Michigan has since revised its standards, which now limit her flexibility in terms of what she can teach and for how long.

"I have less time to do things like that," she said. "I couldn't do it now because I wouldn't have a week and a half or two weeks to focus just on the Holocaust. Those days are gone."

The Holocaust is still taught in Michigan, and the state recently mandated that every student learn about the Holocaust in World War II and the Armenian genocide that took place between 1915 and 1920. The law recommends six hours of instruction, not exactly the two weeks Carrie originally had, and nothing close to the coverage Germans give the topic, but it's something. Carrie and her colleagues don't shy away from American historical crimes, such as slavery or the Jim Crow laws. Those subjects are also mandated in the Michigan standards.

Yet Michigan is a state with a fairly open approach to history. Not all states have come that far. Take, for example, Texas, whose State Board of Education passed regulations in 2010 on how the Civil War was to be taught, emphasizing "states' rights" as the primary cause and designating slavery as a side issue. This decision and other controversial ones, like omitting any mention of the Jim Crow laws, have a large effect, because Texas, with its huge purchasing power, influences the content of many of the nation's history textbooks. So any remaining "teach from the book" instructors out there will be giving their students a decidedly limited view of U.S. history—one that not only fails to come to terms with the crimes of the past but neglects to even mention them.

This limited perspective on history education has consequences in the present day. As German historian Hans Heer once told the *Telegraph*, it's essential to tell young Germans that "while you have no guilt, you must have a view. You must know what happened, and you have a responsibility to make sure this doesn't happen again."

Jureit was hesitant to say that the United States should learn from the German example of teaching about their past. "Each society has to find its own path, to develop and maintain its own discussion formats, debate cultures, and constellations of conflict," she told me. However, she did feel that it was crucial for democratic societies to always allow the widest possible range of opinions, even if they seem radical, ideological, or absurd. "There is no long-term benefit to suppressing those types of opinions; and in these types of debates, it's more important to ensure that everyone is treated fairly, no matter how controversial or hard the discussion becomes."

Regardless, I can't help wondering what our history education would look like if we followed the German example. What if our students were taught not only about slavery and Jim Crow but also about their responsibility for it? What if such historical crimes weren't taught in just one class, but in several subjects, and we were reminded of slavery not just at one museum but in many and in our media and with memorials set in our sidewalks? It might change our current discussions around race relations today.

What if we chose to erect monuments to the innocent victims of our wars? Not the soldiers, but the noncombatants—the women and children hit by napalm in Vietnam, or the ordinary citizens killed by atomic bombs in Japan. Wouldn't it change our view of current and future wars?

This is perhaps why some people are afraid to tell the negative sides of American history. Their children might reject them, as the Germans did their parents and grandparents. They might even refuse to go to war. If we did as Germans do, and refused to allow ourselves to escape the responsibility for our country's past, we might change what it means to be American.

As the descendent of German immigrants, I had never felt particularly proud of my heritage. This background wasn't talked about all that much in our family. In 1985, U.S. President Ronald Reagan made an ill-advised visit to a German military cemetery in Bitburg, a visit he later defended by saying the soldiers buried there were "victims of Nazism just as surely as the victims of the concentration camps." His statement buys right into the myth of German victimhood, seeking to somehow absolve even those who had willingly taken up arms for the Nazi cause.

I remember reading an article about Reagan's visit, and there listed among the names of the SS members buried was one Georg Zaske. Not a close relative for sure, but given my uncommon last name, probably somehow related. I was horrified. Never mind that he was only seventeen when he died. He'd signed up for one of the worst, murderous jobs a Nazi could do. This was not a relative I wanted to be associated with, and through most of my youth, I downplayed my German heritage, even denied it, saying at times that my family was Polish.

And as an American, I could also rationalize away any personal responsibility for U.S. misdeeds. My ancestors arrived well after slavery had ended. The West had already been conquered and the land taken from the Native American tribes. For the most part, my relatives had lived in the North, not the South, so they took no part in Jim Crow.

Now, after learning from today's Germans, I will own my cultural heritage, all of it. As a German American, I have some connection to what my German relations did in the past. With that, I can also now take some pride—without being too proud, of course—to have heritage from a country that has owned its mistakes and is continually working to make sure they never happen again.

Closer to home, I see now that if I claim to be American, I need also to claim all the things the United States has done wrong, even before my time. I need to say, "I'm American. It's partly my fault. It's part of me." My ancestors and I have benefited from stolen land, forced labor, and a number of historic crimes. As many Germans know, only when we accept this responsibility can we start to move forward to make changes for the better.

Even more difficult, I have to talk to my children about these things, and about their responsibility as Americans. I didn't have to wait until the United States established an entire culture of remembrance to do this. Berlin did it for me. One sunny spring day, Sophia, ever the one with the hard questions, hit me with this one:

"Mom, I learned in lebenskunde that people haven't been very nice to black people—they put them in chains and forced them onto ships?" She said that last part with a question in her voice, as if it was too outrageous to believe.

This was the beginning of the conversation, one I found more difficult than any other talk. I took a deep breath. "So in America . . ."

12

Big Kids, Big Worries
(Grosse Kinder, Grosse Sorgen)

I arrived at Tine and Axel's apartment in Prenzlauer Berg carrying bribes—homemade poppy seed cake and sweet bread from a nearby bakery. Tine met me at the door and invited me into the kitchen where Axel made us all cups of strong coffee. We sat together at a thick wooden table and got ready to discuss one of the most difficult subjects around: teenagers. They had two of them, and I had none, yet, so I asked them to share their insights. At one point, Axel mentioned that their eldest daughter, who was almost sixteen at the time, was usually gone the entire weekend.

"She's now pretty much allowed to do whatever she wants to do as long as she keeps us informed, and during the week, we want her to sleep at home," he said.

I gaped at them. "She doesn't sleep here on the weekends?"

"She tells us where she's going to be. And I trust her," he said. "It used to worry me a little more than Tine probably. Then Tine said we have to relax a little."

Axel and Tine may not be typical middle-class German parents (if there is such a thing). They're both artists—an actor and a fashion designer, respectively. Axel was raised in a small industrial town in West Germany. Tine grew up in East Berlin during the GDR days. But they have similar views on raising teenagers, espousing values that I've found fairly common among German parents: that teenagers should be able to manage a lot of their own lives, including their schoolwork and social lives.

As you might expect, in a country where eight-year-old children are free to roam their neighborhoods, German teens roam the city. Some even take vacations with only their peers as company. When I spoke to Axel and Tine, their daughter was in the midst of planning a camping trip with her friends—with no parents in attendance.

Like American parents, Germans know full well that unsupervised teenagers are likely to engage in risky behaviors. And they worry too. That's at the root of the German saying *kleine kinder, kleine sorgen; grosse kinder, grosse sorgen*—essentially the bigger the child, the bigger the worries. Teenagers face many dangers as they try to become adults, and the consequences of making bad choices during this time—unwanted pregnancy, STDs, alcohol or drug addiction, academic failure—can have lasting impacts on the rest of their lives.

In the United States, parents typically respond to these threats by clamping down on adolescents, imposing strict rules and even laws in an attempt to dictate their behavior, but in Germany, they take almost the complete opposite approach. There are fewer prohibitions, legally and culturally, on what adolescents can do, and many German parents seem to feel that teenagers will behave more responsibly if they are given more freedom and a greater ability to control their own lives.

The Space to Be Young

Every day on the way to my son's kita, we would walk through an odd little park. It was made out of a space between two buildings. The park didn't have many structures: a few benches, some low cement blocks, a wooden platform off to one side that looked like a stage, and a couple of ping-pong tables. I thought it was a lame kids' park until I realized it wasn't intended for young children at all; it was for teenagers. Just down the street was a *gymnasium* (pronounced with a hard *g*), a public high school for university-bound students.

When gymnasium got out, I would often find a few teenagers at the park—trying out skateboard tricks on the cement blocks, playing ping-pong, or just hanging out on the wooden platform drinking a few beers.

This was in the Prenzlauer Berg neighborhood, which has many desirable apartments, popular shops, and restaurants. I couldn't imagine a space like this made on purpose for adolescents in a similar area in the United States. The neighbors would have shut it down; developers would have long ago filled that space with a tower of luxury condos.

One of the things I remember well about my own adolescence in the United States was how there never seemed to be any place for us to just be, outside of school or home. So we went to the mall even though we had nothing to buy. We hung out in parking lots and watched our friends illegally grind their skateboards onto curbs. We drove around in cars chasing rumors of house parties at homes where the parents were away. We snuck beers onto golf courses and hopped into pools after dark. It was alternately boring and risky, and when alcohol was involved, downright dangerous.

In Germany, teenagers have space to be themselves. In addition to park areas designed for them, adolescents can go into almost all places in Berlin, including dance clubs and bars. There are some rules, including a curfew: teens under sixteen must be out of the clubs and restaurants by ten p.m., those under eighteen must leave by midnight. Parents are supposed to help oversee that these rules are observed, but businesses that violate Germany's youth protection laws can be hit with fines or even jail time.

At sixteen, teenagers can buy their own beer or wine, and traditionally in Germany, parents give older children their first glass of champagne or beer even earlier, around the age of fourteen. (When I was this age, my German American grandfather surprised me by pouring a small glass of beer for me at Thanksgiving dinner. I had no idea this was a German thing until now.)

Isabell, one of Zac's graduate students, said that her mother always told her, "When you learn to drink at home you know your boundaries." She had her first glass of champagne at Christmas when she was fourteen and claims that she has only "overdone it" four or five times in her life. "I always stopped before it got too bad," she said. "I think if you forbid it until twenty-one it feels like something scary. So you do it because you're a teenager, and you do things that are not allowed. If it's allowed, it loses a lot of its—maybe *magic* is the wrong word—but then you do it for fun and with your friends. It's not like you are just drinking until you fall over."

Of course, some Germans do drink in excess. After all, this is the country that prides itself on its beer and has entire festivals dedicated to drinking the stuff in large quantities. Yet, while teenage binge drinking is a rising concern, the problem is at a lower level than it is in America. In a 2015 survey by the German health education agency (abbreviated BZgA in German), 12.9 percent of German youth ages twelve to seventeen reported getting drunk at least once a month. In comparison, 18 percent of American high school students reported they'd binge drank within the last month, according to a 2015 CDC survey. Even further, two studies published in the 2012 Lancet Series on Adolescent Health found that American teenagers have the worst problems among their peers in the Western world, not just with alcohol but also with drugs and violence. With such results, it doesn't appear that our strict controls on teenage behavior result in the best outcomes.

Perhaps we should look at the benefits of the German model, where the culture and the law give children more freedom and rights at the age of fourteen. This age is a huge milestone for Germans: it's the point when kids are no longer considered children but teenagers, not quite full adults but on their way. Typically there's a public and private celebration marking this turning point. In religious families, fourteen is usually when young people have a religious confirmation. In the East, many people still hold a secular *jugendfeier*, or "youth party," for their fourteen-year-olds, a tradition that started during the GDR days as a substitute for confirmation. It fell out of favor when the Wall fell, but it has been making a comeback, and I saw plenty of jugendfeier invitations alongside religious confirmation cards in the shops in Berlin.

Turning fourteen also means more responsibility too. Under German law, fourteen-year-olds can be held criminally responsible for their actions (whereas children under that age can never be tried as adults, as they sometimes are in the United States). Fourteen is the age of "spiritual maturity," and young people can decide for themselves whether to take religion classes or not. It's also the age of consent, meaning at fourteen they can legally have sex—as long as their partners are also fourteen years or older, and there's no coercion involved.

This may be shocking to Americans, since the age of consent in most states is sixteen or higher, but Germany is famously liberal about sex and sees little wrong with young people having sex as long as they are safe about it. Some German parents will even let their teenager's boyfriend or girlfriend spend the night. In a parenting article on T-Online, Germany's most popular online portal, Simone Blass advises parents on how to respond to having "a stranger in the bathroom" when their son or daughter has an overnight guest. Allowing such sleepovers, Blass contends, is ultimately safer for young people since it removes the need for secrecy and for rebellion. She points out that parental restrictions can have the opposite effect: "Parents often forbid their children to do certain things—rules that will most likely be ignored anyway. In the worst case scenario, they will drive young people to do things out of spite that they otherwise would have held off on."

Many parents fear that this kind of openness will encourage teens to engage in sexual activity earlier, but there is little evidence to support that. A 2015 study by the BZgA showed that only 6 percent of German fourteen-year-olds had engaged in sexual activity. On the other hand, more than half of young Germans had their first sexual experience by age seventeen, which is about the same percentage of sexually active seventeen-year-olds in the United States. More than half of German young people also said they speak openly with their parents about sexuality and contraception.

I've always told my children they can talk to me about anything, and I plan to be honest and nonjudgmental when it comes to questions of sex and relationships—but I can't say I'm comfortable with the idea of having a boyfriend or girlfriend sleep over. I think few parents are—even the liberal Germans, but they are still more reluctant to be strict and squelch their children's freedom.

"Often parents don't agree about the boyfriend staying overnight in the home, but the children usually win," said psychologist Heidi Keller, who pointed out that since teenage children are free to do many things on their own, they expect their independence in this area as well. "One of my friends was very embarrassed that a strange young man was having breakfast with them, but eventually he became a full member of the family."

To allow our teens this freedom in American society, which is so heavily laden with moral judgments about sex, seems nearly impossible. On the other hand, I can see that the American taboo on teen sex hasn't been working out very well: as I noted earlier, American teens have much higher rates of unwanted pregnancies, abortion, and HIV than Germans do. I want my kids to be safe and make good decisions for themselves—not to rush into having sex as an act of rebellion against their parents. Their safety is more important to me than pushing my version of sexual morality on them.

As parents, we might have to admit to ourselves, despite laws and all the parental threats in the world, most American teens are drinking and having sex well before they leave our homes. They are also going to places where no adults are on hand to supervise them. We can try and stop them, but most likely our efforts will just drive teenagers to do these things in secret. Even if we succeed in controlling their movement, we aren't preparing them well for making decisions on their own. After all, there's not a huge difference between a seventeen-year-old at home and an eighteen-year-old on their own.

My friend Aimee lives in a college town in the United States and sees firsthand what happens when those young people are released into full freedom after years of being restrained by their parents. "It feels like the students are just starting to test out independence—but at eighteen! And then in big ways, with big consequences, in a society of equally irrational age-mates where no one is asking for trust in response," she said. "I honestly think the German system feels safer for kids to learn how to test boundaries."

Aimee isn't comfortable with everything she sees children doing in Germany—the free-for-all of the playgrounds, the dangerous things like sharp knives and fireworks that kids are allowed to use—but ultimately she felt the Germans better prepared young people to be on their own. "If they're more used to responsibility at a younger age, and getting larger pieces of it as they go, then when they finally have a solid grasp of it as college students, they might make better choices," she said.

An Extra-Long Adolescence

To learn more about Germany's youth, I met with the noted social scientist Klaus Hurrelmann at the Hertie School of Governance in Berlin. Hurrelmann has studied and written extensively on adolescence and has helped put together several Shell Youth Studies, a huge survey of Germany's young people that comes out every three to four years.

Hurrelmann told me that German history with its "tides of authoritarianism and anti-authoritarianism" in the past century affected how children were raised, and up until about ten years ago, the remainders of these two extremes could still be felt. "Only recently are things moving to a more normal and relaxed style of children's education," he said. "I think all of this has not happened in the United States."

I had to agree, as the pattern of parenting in America has seemed to be a slow and steady march toward more supervision and control. While not exactly authoritarian, there certainly isn't anything very "relaxed" about how Americans parent today.

Raising teenagers has become even more complicated since adolescence has become a lot longer than it used to be—no matter which side of the Atlantic you are on. According to Hurrelmann, in the 1800s, puberty typically started around seventeen, now it begins at twelve (and according to some estimates even earlier than that). That's at least an additional five years on the front end, and more years have been added to the other side. Hurrelmann claimed the average adolescence is now fifteen years, extending well into the twenties.

How we mark the end of adolescence has also become less clear. In the past, adulthood meant moving out of your parents' house, becoming financially independent, getting married, and having kids. Many adults today don't do some of these things at any point in their lives.

"This is the difficult job of educating, of parenting, teenage children living in your house on their way to becoming adults in a situation where nobody knows what adulthood really is any longer," Hurrelmann said.

So young people in Germany have a lot in common with their peers in America. They are all growing up at a time when it is less clear what being a grown-up means. More German and American young people are staying at home with their parents long after the age of eighteen. In the United States, the rate climbed to 32.1 percent for adults ages eighteen to thirty-four in 2014, according to the Pew Research Center. In Germany, however, it's even higher, with 43.1 percent of young adults in the same age group living at home with their parents in 2015, according to an EU survey.

Yet adult children living at home is not a new trend in Germany, since it's more culturally accepted for young people to live with their parents. That doesn't mean they are completely dependent. As *Slate* columnist Rebecca Schuman pointed out, it's not the fact that a grown child is living at home that matters, it is *how* they are living at home. Schuman notes that German young adults usually act more like roommates with their parents: they do their own shopping and laundry, come and go as they please, and help pay the rent.

In fact, German young people, living at home or not, are much more likely to be employed than their American peers. Germany has one of the lowest youth unemployment rates in the world. Only 9.3 percent of Germans ages twenty to twenty-four were not in employment, education, or training in 2015, according to the OECD. In the United States, it was 15.8 percent for the same age group.

Hurrelmann argues that achieving independence means learning to run your own life and having the "capacity to be your own self-manager and to organize your life by yourself." This is the difficulty we have as parents: to teach our children how to manage their time, their activities, and schooling for themselves, to help them figure out what they want and how to get it, but without telling them directly how to do it or, worse, doing it for them. "All this has to be done by the children themselves," Hurrelmann said.

The Academic Question

Zac and I weren't even close to having to deal with these teenage problems, but both Ozzie and Sophia were still coming up on a few critical turning points. Ozzie was now five and in his last year of kita, eagerly awaiting his own einschulung celebration to mark the start of school. That winter we filled out the forms for him to enter first grade at the same school Sophia attended. Sophia herself would be moving on to fourth grade, out of the comfort of the mixed-grade class of younger kids into a more academically challenging year, and looming ever closer to the time when it would be decided whether she was university material.

Despite the relaxed approach in the early grades, the academic stakes get very high by the end of German primary school. Traditionally, students are set onto academic tracks by fifth grade. This means that at the tender age of ten, many German students are placed on one of three paths: children who are clearly university-bound go to gymnasium; students who don't perform quite as well are placed on a middle track and go to *realschule*, which can still lead to university or a shorter technical college program; and a third track, the *hauptschule*, emphasizes vocational education. All three tracks are meant to lead to viable careers, and this strategy has worked well for Germany's economy in the past.

Today, some see this system as antiquated, and naturally, not every parent is a big fan. "It's kind of a traumatic approach to what life has to offer and say, 'Look you are ten years old, and we have to decide if you are going to be an academic,'" Axel said. "I don't like that at all. Coming from a family of teachers, we've always discussed this separation. We all know where it's coming from and what it's based on, but I don't think it's appropriate anymore as a society."

Yet the system is so entrenched in German culture, it's a hard thing to fight. Axel and Tine's daughter is in gymnasium, and most upper- and middle-class parents want to be sure their children are on that top track so that they will have the best opportunities available to them. And going to gymnasium by itself is no guarantee. To be accepted at a university, graduating high school students have to pass a series of tough exit exams called the *arbitur*. Many students take three or four of these exams, in different subjects, and each one can be four to five hours long—sort of like taking the SAT, but longer, and repeated three times, in more subjects than just math and writing, such as the sciences, history, and languages.

Even though the stakes are high, many German parents fight the impulse to monitor their children's study habits. Annette Turowski, an educator and parent who lives outside of Düsseldorf, said she used to hover over her son's schooling like a *helikopter-eltern* ("helicopter parent") until she went on a trip to Sweden and visited some schools there. "Sweden had a completely different approach to the education of children: any child who wants to learn needs to have interior motivation," she said. When she came back, Annette told her oldest son, who was twelve at the time, that she would no longer interfere: he was in charge of his own schooling. "He turned out fine," she said. "Maybe his marks could have been better, but the other possibility was that he could have left home at sixteen and ended up in some gutter."

Annette's approach is also indicative of the national change in education in Germany in another way: She is an educational director at a comprehensive school, called a *gesamtschule*, one that includes teenagers of all abilities, sort of like an American high school, but without any tracking. This is a new thing in Germany, one of the changes that came about in response to the "PISA shock" of 2000, when Germany's fifteen-year-olds tested below international averages in math, science, and reading on the Programme for International Student Assessment, commonly known as the PISA test.

After the poor performance, German policy makers and educators took a look at how top-performing countries like Finland ran their schools and instituted major reforms, including mandating at least two years of kindergarten for all children, longer days for primary school students (which are still short by comparison with American standards), more centralized testing and assessment; and they introduced alternatives to the heavy-handed tracking system, such as comprehensive schools like the one where Annette works.

The PISA results revealed that students from countries where children of all abilities were taught together through more grade levels did best. As Amanda Ripley details in her book *The Smartest Kids in the World*, children feed off each other when they learn and where the value of hard work is emphasized over innate talent. While many Americans may not realize it, U.S. schools track children even earlier than Germany does through our "gifted and talented" programs, and it starts at the earliest grade levels in elementary schools. This tracking goes on through high school. Some students can take advantage of magnet schools or ones with special honors or AP classes. Other children, too often from low-income and minority communities, are left with lower quality schools with less experienced staff that don't offer the advanced classes. Even if all the students are in the same building, they are divided into remedial, standard, and advanced tracks. Ripley argues that the American approach is especially problematic since it emphasizes that doing well at school is a gift or a talent rather than something that can be attained through hard work.

While America has tried to implement its own school reform with programs like No Child Left Behind and Common Core, these efforts have resulted in a lot of high-stakes testing for teachers and schools—but not for the students themselves, which is an interesting transfer of responsibility for learning. We've done little to flatten our tracking system or improve access to quality preschools.

While America's PISA scores have remained stubbornly mediocre, Germany's reforms have yielded results within a little more than a decade, proving it can be done. By 2012, German fifteen-year-olds had moved up in the PISA rankings, rising to about seventh in math and twelfth in reading and science among the thirty-four countries that participate in the OECD. German students outperformed the test average and left the Americans well behind. (On the 2012 test, U.S. students ranked around seventeen in reading, twenty in science, and an abysmal twenty-seven in mathematics.) Most of the improvement in Germany's test scores was attributed to a better performance among low-achieving and disadvantaged students. In other words, Germany had made its education system more equitable.

Still, the social scientist Hurrelmann felt the chances for mobility are not very high in Germany, meaning children from lower income families have a tough time rising out of their socioeconomic class. He felt that the system of separating children so early often locked their status into place. Yet international comparative research shows mobility in Germany is still better than it is in the United States, even though, as Hurrelmann put it, we are "the entrepreneurial country where a dishwasher can become a millionaire. That's a typical idea in your culture, but that isn't the regular case."

Kai, another graduate student who studied with Zac, illustrates how the German system can work well for a student with fewer advantages. Kai grew up in a small town of fewer than 500 people. He had the advantage of a quality preschool/kindergarten. He was the first in his family to go to gymnasium, a university-tracked high school, and he did well, even though no one at home could really help him with his homework.

His gymnasium served a rural population, but it was still a good school—good enough to give him the education he needed to pass three difficult arbitur tests in math, chemistry, and history. While his parents were supportive of his studies, they couldn't afford to pay his living expenses when he went to university, so he received a stipend from the state. (He paid no tuition because German universities are free for qualified students.) He is now on his way to a PhD. A similar student in the United States would have faced many more obstacles to this achievement, starting with limited access to an affordable preschool, continuing with low-quality primary and secondary schools, and ending with the huge cost of attending college.

Achieving Adulthood

Turning eighteen isn't the bright dividing line in Germany, at least for young people who go to university or other education after high school.

They've already enjoyed many freedoms that American teens are denied, including the ability to manage their own time and movement. But most German university students are still financially tied to their parents. University tuition is free in Germany, but parents who have some means are expected, and required by law, to pay the living expenses for their children who are still in school up to age twenty-seven. If they cannot afford it, as in Kai's case, the government provides a student stipend.

This parental obligation galls some American expats I know, because they can't refuse to pay, even if their children perform poorly at university or decide to major in something like basket weaving (not that German universities have such a major, but you see my point). Regardless, I imagine that many middle-class parents in the United States would be relieved to pay only the living expenses for their college-age children and not tens of thousands of dollars in tuition as well. The German approach leaves young adults financially dependent on their parents, but those parents cannot control their grown children with threats to withhold funding. They are free to make their own life and educational decisions.

Which brings back that question of what makes an adult in our modern world? After so much independence as children and teens, are the young adults in Germany more responsible than their American counterparts? Young Germans do participate in society more than Americans by volunteering and voting in much greater numbers. About 35 percent of Germans ages fourteen to twenty-four are involved with nonprofits, according to a German ministry survey. Less than 22 percent of America's sixteen- to twenty-four-year-olds volunteered in 2015, according to the U.S. Bureau of Labor Statistics. As for voting, young eligible German voters, age eighteen to thirty, had participation rates of 60.3 percent to 64.2 percent in the 2013 German parliamentary election, according to the BPB. In contrast, only about 50 percent of eligible American youth ages 18 to 29 voted in the 2016 presidential election, according to the Center for Information and Research on Civic Learning and Engagement.

Perhaps even more important is how young people feel about themselves and their future. The Shell Youth Study of 2015 indicated that the vast majority of German young people, from ages twelve to twenty-five, were feeling good about their future, with only 3 percent having a bleak outlook. The study described young Germans as being a "pragmatic generation" who at the same time were eager to make the world a better place: ". . . this is a young generation who is more adventuresome: their attitude extends beyond a sober orientation towards success. Rather, they pursue idealistic visions. They want to get on with the job, be movers and shakers and explore new horizons. And they are willing to run risks in doing so." This description sounds like a confident group of young people well prepared to take on the challenges of the future.

American young people are also optimistic, but then optimism is a core part of our cultural character, whether it is realistic or not. A 2013 Gallup survey of American teens found that almost all of them felt they were very likely or somewhat likely to have a better standard of living than their parents. (Yet the adults were decidedly less optimistic on the topic. They were almost evenly divided on whether the younger generation would do better or worse.)

However, many young Americans have trouble maintaining this sunny outlook when they hit college campuses. In a 2013 survey by the American College Health Association of more than 100,000 college students, over half reported that they felt "very sad," "very lonely," or "overwhelming anxiety" within the past twelve months. In 2015, the *Chronicle of Higher Education* ran a series of articles addressing a reported mental health crisis among college students. Campus counseling centers have been inundated by students in need: 89 percent of the centers reported a rise in anxiety disorders and 58 percent saw an increase in clinical depression.

Anecdotally, college educators are reporting that students lack "resilience." They are easily devastated by small setbacks and need more handholding to make it through a course. It's not hard to see how this range of problems from lack of resilience on up to serious mental health problems might be the result of our overprotective parenting culture. Many parents supervise and control their children's behavior while at the same time pushing hard for achievement—as defined by the parents, not by the children for themselves. Then, once these grown children are released into the adult world, they don't have the skills or the internal strength to handle the challenges of being on their own.

Former Stanford dean Julie Lythcott-Haims blames the many intelligent but fragile college students she saw on campus on overparenting in her book *How to Raise an Adult*. She feels that parents who escorted their kids from "milestone to milestone" did more harm than good. "It can leave young adults without the strengths of skill, will, and character that are needed to know themselves and to craft a life."

In contrast, mental health among the generation of the "pragmatic" German youth appears to be stronger. The percentage of German young people with diagnoses of depression is half that in the United States (7 percent of Germans compared to 14 percent of Americans ages eighteen to twenty-nine according to Gallup's 2011 Health and Well Being Index). Anxiety also appears lower among all German adults. Studies place the lifetime prevalence of anxiety disorders in the United States as among the highest in the world at between 23 percent and 28.7 percent; in Germany, it's 13.4 percent, according to a review of anxiety studies published in the journal *Brain and Behavior*. In addition, fewer Germans of all ages commit suicide (9.2 per 100,000 Germans versus 12.1 per 100,000 Americans according to the WHO). There are many factors that may influence these numbers, but it does point to a healthier mental state and a stronger resilience among adults in Germany than in the United States.

Taken together with the fact that German youth are more likely to be employed or in school; more likely to avoid problems like unwanted pregnancies, binge drinking, drug abuse, and violence—and that they are more likely to participate in society than their American peers—a strong case can be made that the German approach to raising children results in more positive outcomes.

It's also simply logical that young people will be more self-reliant and responsible if they've been raised to be that way from a young age: if as children, they walked to school by themselves, played freely, dealt with risk, managed their own relationships, discussed difficult subjects, and pursued their own ideas and career goals. Children who are encouraged to test out independence and freedom all along grow up to become young adults who are better equipped to handle their own lives.

We American parents have the best intentions: We want to protect our children from danger, to shape them to be good people, to give them the tools to succeed in life. We're just going about it the wrong way. Many of these things require less interference from parents, not more. Ultimately, the children have to do it for themselves. Otherwise, we risk having whole generations of young adults who are overly dependent—who do not have, as Hurrelmann puts it, the ability to become their own "self-managers," the ability to run their own lives.

I was beginning to embrace this German approach, to feel strongly that selbständigkeit ("self-reliance") and independence were vital for our kids, when Zac got a call from California. He was offered a position located at a research lab in the Bay Area, not far from where his family lived, and not far from where Zac and I had first met in a bookstore all those many years ago.

We were going home.

13

Coming Back to America

The California dream is the American dream of opportunity writ large. California is gold in the hills; it's the farming paradise in *East of Eden*; it's the promise of fame in giant bold-faced type placed on a hill with lights on it. It's an app that will make you a Silicon Valley billionaire.

I had swallowed the California dream whole when I was twenty-three. Now as I returned older, wiser, and with my family in tow, I was not so sun-struck. When our airplane banked over San Francisco, I still felt some of that old excitement, but after so long away, I knew the opportunities in California were not as golden as they seemed, that most of the beauty in the Bay Area was on the surface. In reality, Berlin, even with its long, dark winter nights and grimy streets, was a much friendlier place for families than that shining city by the bay.

In comparison to Germany, the United States can be a hard place to live. Just making ends meet is difficult for many Americans, and it's particularly difficult in the Bay Area with its soaring rents and high cost of living. The safety net in America is very thin, and nowhere is that more obvious than in San Francisco, where the ugly side of the American dream is out in the open, homeless, and sleeping on the streets.

The kids didn't know about any of that yet. All they saw was sunshine and blue water and more opportunities for fun. We stayed first with my mother-in-law, who showered the kids with attention and treats. Aunts, uncles, and cousins came to visit, and everywhere there were flags, which the kids kept pointing out. "American flag! American flag!" It was a game they used to play in Berlin, yelling out whenever they spotted a different country's flag, but in the United States there was only one kind of flag, and with the Fourth of July approaching, the game got really old really fast.

Yet this is something we'd wanted for our kids. We wanted them to feel American. We wanted them to spend time with their grandparents and get to know their extended family. In Berlin, we had talked a lot about whether we wanted to stay there forever. It was such a great place for families, but in spite of all the things we loved about living in Germany, we still felt very much American, and we wanted our children to be American as well. Only now, I also wanted them to be a little German too.

I wanted Sophia to be able to walk to school every day by herself and go to the park with just her friends. I wanted Ozzie to have an einschulung that launched him into his school career. I wanted his first-grade experience to be full of play as well as learning. I wanted them both to grow up with selbständigkeit, to be able to make decisions for themselves, to believe what they wanted to believe, and to find their own path in life. I only hoped we could make that happen for them in the United States because things were quite different here when it came to raising children.

We eventually found a house to rent near Zac's new job in a suburban neighborhood in the far eastern reaches of the Bay Area. The house had a nice-sized backyard and an elementary school that was less than a mile away. There was even a park with a playground down the block. It looked like the ideal place for kids. Only after moving in, we couldn't find any other children.

When we first arrived, our neighbor Melissa went out of her way to introduce herself and her two children, which was nice, but after that, we didn't see much of them. They were keeping their distance—out of politeness or a desire to keep their own privacy, I wasn't sure. After a few days at our new home, I packed up a lunch and took the kids to the park down the street, intending to stay there for a while so Sophia and Ozzie would have a chance to meet some of the neighborhood kids.

The playground at the park was empty. It had a plastic, multipurpose structure with two short wide slides. Ozzie dutifully climbed the short six-rung ladder and slid down one of them, slowly. The monkey bars were so low Sophia had to fold up her legs to avoid touching the ground. Within ten minutes, they were done playing there. I offered them sandwiches, and we ate our picnic under a tree looking out at the basketball court and the vast green playing field, both also empty. It was the middle of summer. Where were all the kids?

We did see other children around town—at the community pool and on the sports fields playing Little League and soccer games. Occasionally, we heard them playing in fenced-in backyards on our street. It almost felt like they were sequestered from us. Apparently, access to the other kids required a special invitation, a playdate, which of course is arranged by parents. Because we were new and school hadn't started yet, I hadn't met any other parents. So my kids were friendless.

Sophia and Ozzie found ways to amuse themselves, which was a good thing because I still needed to do some freelance work. I tried to find child care and camps in the United States, but I soon discovered that one week of camp in California cost more than three months of kita or hort in Berlin. I knew private child care would be pricey too, but I checked any-way through a local child-care network. The only spots available were in "home child-care" settings, where one caregiver watched fewer than eight kids at their personal residence. This wasn't much better for my kids than staying home while I worked, and certainly not worth the cost.

So all summer long, Sophia and Ozzie played in our big backyard, which was a novelty after apartment life in Germany. They built huts using the empty moving boxes and played on a makeshift zip line and swing Zac set up for them. We held "morning circle" like they'd done at their schools in Germany. They voluntarily chose projects to do (Sophia picked hum-mingbirds; Ozzie rattlesnakes). We went to the library and took breaks at the pool. I got up before they were awake to interview people on the phone for articles. Occasionally, I broke down and turned on a movie or handed out tablets so that I could make a deadline. It was less than ideal, but we made it work. It would be easier, and harder, once school began.

Starting American School

Even though we had left Germany, we gave Ozzie an einschulung. He'd been taught to look forward to the start-of-school party ever since he could remember, so we promised to hold him one in the United States. While Ozzie didn't have the big celebration at his school, he did have something that Sophia had missed—a party with his extended family. His older cousins even put on a show for him, just as the kids had done for first graders in Germany.

Ozzie was eager to start school. He already knew how to read. Like Sophia before him, we'd taught him early, but we had another problem. Ozzie was only five. In Germany, that wouldn't have mattered because all the kids born in a particular calendar year started school at the same time. In California, first graders were expected to be six by the time school started, and Ozzie's birthday was in the fall. Anticipating some trouble, I came armed with a letter from Ozzie's kita teachers saying he was ready, but no one questioned his registration—well, no one official. The other parents did.

We walked to school that first day. A few other parents and kids were walking and biking as well, but as we approached the school it was clear by the car-lined streets that most parents drove their kids to a nearby street, parked, and got out to walk their children onto the school grounds. The California school was almost the structural opposite of Sophia's urban four-story stone building in Berlin, with an open, outside layout comprised of portable buildings loosely arranged around a central office and gym that doubled as a cafeteria. The school also had a large grassy yard and a black-top area with two plastic play structures on it.

On the first day of school, children streamed onto the blacktop with their parents following at a leisurely pace behind them, most of them wearing flip-flops, shorts, or yoga pants—casual clothing rarely seen on the streets of Berlin. They grouped on the blacktop and chatted with other parents as their kids formed loose lines near their designated classrooms. I almost relaxed looking at them. This was California after all! It's supposed to be alternative, innovative, and laid-back. It was hard to imagine that the school that served this community would be a traditional, highly structured institution, focused on driving the kids to achieve well on state standardized tests.

We had two nervous children, but Sophia boldly waited with a group of kids she had never met, while Zac and I walked Ozzie over to his line for first grade. At first I didn't think we had the right line. Ozzie was tall for his age, and he had been one of the biggest kids in his kita. Yet here most of the boys were bigger than him, much bigger. Some did not look like first graders at all.

Another mother introduced herself to us and started up a conversation. She soon got around to asking Ozzie's age. "I don't think that's allowed," she said in a confidential voice and then informed us of the state cutoff date. Her son was on the cusp of that date, but she had still held him back. He was seven, a head taller than Ozzie and a full year older. I explained that Ozzie had been well prepared in Germany to start first grade this year. The mother smiled politely, but I could see the doubt in her eyes. She was wondering if our son would be able to hack it.

Later, another mother told me that many parents "redshirted" their children, boys in particular, holding them back for an extra year of kindergarten or simply starting them later, so they would be more ready for the demands of first grade—and for a possible advantage in sports later on. She sounded like she thought that this practice was ridiculous, but I also noted that her seven-year-old first grader was already heavily involved in several organized sports.

Academic redshirting, which borrows its name from the college sports term for postponing competitive play to lengthen a player's eligibility, used to be rare in the United States. In 1968, only 4 percent of children starting kindergarten were six or older, but according to census data, that figure rose to 20 percent by 2013. I'd heard redshirting was becoming even more popular as academic pressure was being ramped up at all grade levels, but it was strange to see the trend illustrated so dramatically in real life.

As Ozzie clung to my hand that first day, I tried not to be anxious too. I should have realized that since kindergarten was the new first grade in America, first grade would now be second. I was confident that Ozzie was ready for first grade, but second? Then the teacher came out, a young woman with a brilliant white California smile. "Good morning, everyone!" She introduced herself and had all the kids respond loudly, "Good morning, Mrs. Tyler!" which was incredibly cute. Then she told the children to hang their backpacks, find their desks, and start their morning work. Clearly, she wasn't going to waste any time. She motioned the line of kids into the classroom. Ozzie finally let go of my hand and, with only one nervous glance back, went inside.

It would be all right. Ozzie did well in his American school, even though the work was quite demanding. For instance, the first-grade math ranged from basic addition to word problems and simple algebraic concepts by the end of the year. He didn't have much time to play, though— only one short recess and another tied to his lunch period. His desire to play was so strong he often didn't eat much of his lunch. He also had homework.

Fortunately, Mrs. Tyler wisely assigned worksheets that involved games, coloring, and cutting and pasting. I also had to sign his sheet to ensure that he completed it. I had to do this for Sophia too. This didn't feel right to me as it moved the responsibility from the children to the parents as enforcers. However, it was relatively painless to get Ozzie to do the homework, so I didn't raise a fuss. Yet I couldn't help wondering about all the other kids in his class. What happened to the six- and seven-year-olds who struggled with the academics or resisted doing homework? Surely that would affect their attitude toward school.

Luckily, Mrs. Tyler also encouraged a lot of individual and group work in her class. While not the same as the self-directed learning the kids had in Germany, it kept Ozzie engaged, and he loved school. Sophia was not so lucky.

Fourth-Grade Blues

Sophia's teacher, Mrs. Alexander, was old-school. She made the children in her fourth-grade class sit with "bubble-gum hands," fingers laced on top of the desk, while she lectured. There was a spelling and math test every Friday. Students who misbehaved wrote a sentence over and over again about why what they did was wrong. I understood why Mrs. Alexander felt she had to run a strict, traditional classroom. She had thirty active kids—none of whom got enough playtime during the school day—and no assistant to help. But that didn't make it any easier to watch Sophia struggle in her class.

The worst part was the homework. It took Sophia two hours to complete every evening. We knew our daughter had a steep learning curve. Her self-directed Montessori-style education in Berlin had meant that she had self-directed away from math, and her skills weren't up to the U.S. fourth-grade standards. Her spelling would have been wonderful, if the English language followed German rules. She spelled lots of words with *ei* and could not grasp the need for a silent *e*. Sophia was also expected to know how to type. Her school had no formal art, music, or theater instruction, but it did have a computer class. This was the exact opposite of her German school, which emphasized the arts in almost every subject and had only one computer for the teacher to use.

All this seemed a lot for Sophia to take. I watched as my daughter, who used to love school, began to wilt. "It's boring," she complained. "There's just so much talking and talking."

"The other kids are talking in class?"

"No, Mrs. Alexander talks. We listen, *all* day."

I felt for her. She was used to more creativity and active learning in her school. She had also had a lot more opportunity to play. Here, she had two short recesses and no hort—so that meant no free playtime after school. I'd tried to get both my children into the after-school program on the campus, not just so I could work more but so that they would have more opportunity to play with other kids. I was told there was no space and that the wait list was so long that some parents even registered their kids as soon as they were born to ensure they had a spot by the time they entered first grade.

Not that Sophia had much time after school anyway. She would come home from school, have a snack, do her homework, have dinner, finish her homework, and then it would be almost time for bed. I feared that the year was going to be completely miserable for her until suddenly the homework got a lot lighter. I found out later that one of the other girls' parents had complained. It wasn't just Sophia, the new kid, who had been suffering. Other parents wanted things done differently, and the teacher had listened. This meant there was a chance for change!

This was also my clue that I had to learn from all those parent meetings at Sophia's school in Berlin. The parents there did more than complain: they got together, organized, and actually changed things. We didn't have class-level parents' organization at our California school, but there was the school-wide parent-teacher association, the PTA.

I went to a meeting ready to participate in good old American local democracy. Besides the elected officers, I was one of three parents in attendance. The rest of the small crowd was made up of teachers and administrators. The parents were too busy or not interested enough to attend. As I listened to the meeting, I soon learned that all the PTA decisions had been made at the executive meeting the month before, then voted on at this session. The topics they discussed mostly had to do with raising money for PTA-sponsored events and training opportunities for teachers. Good things, sure, but this clearly wasn't the place to have input into how our children were educated. I left discouraged.

I wasn't ready to give up, so I did what I do best. I wrote. I wrote a note to Mrs. Tyler about Ozzie not eating lunch and a letter to the principal requesting she try to add more recess time for the kids, including an adequate lunchtime that didn't interfere with recess. I wrote to the school district and the park service board that ran the after-school program asking that they open more spaces in their program and look for funding to subsidize it. I even wrote to the PTA and suggested that they sponsor a walk-to-school day.

In the meantime, Zac and I met with Mrs. Alexander to talk about Sophia. She expressed confidence that Sophia was improving, which was encouraging. I asked her if she could scale back the Friday tests because they were making Sophia anxious, especially when a third subject like social studies was tested on the same day. Mrs. Alexander did agree to not put three tests on one day, but that was the only concession she made on that point. "We have to get them ready for the state standards testing," she emphasized.

My letters yielded some results. Mrs. Tyler arranged for Ozzie to stay longer in the cafeteria to finish his lunch. Although this didn't solve the problem of his not having enough time to play, at least I knew he wouldn't be going hungry. After I sent my letter to the parks board, the after-school program suddenly found two spaces for my children in the summer—but without any subsidy. The school and the PTA agreed to hold a walk-to-school event in the fall, if I volunteered to lead it.

Sophia survived her first year in an American school and even managed good grades. Her success was a testament to her own hard work, but it also called into question the value of pushing academics so early in elementary school. She did not have four hard-driving years of academics behind her, as most of her peers did, yet she caught up relatively easily.

Some of Sophia's classmates didn't do as well, and not because they weren't intelligent. Rather, I think they struggled because they couldn't handle the boredom of the classroom. Sophia would tell me stories of other kids misbehaving in class, reading in their laps while the teacher lectured, or passing notes and whispering. There was a group of boys who would always get in trouble for joking around and doing silly things like "using the force" to levitate their desks. They also once had a glue bottle battle using their feet to squirt each other when the teacher's head was turned.

It's hard to blame them. They had no say in what they were learning, and they hadn't much chance to play not just during this year but also in the previous three years (four if you count the new academic-focused kindergarten)—and that means they had fewer opportunities to develop their skills in self-control and concentration.

Even though my kids are doing well in American school so far, I'm preparing to do battle with the teachers and administration, even the district if I have to, next year. Sophia has had one year of disliking school. I don't want that dislike to harden into a dislike of learning in general. She deserves the opportunity to have a child-centered classroom, where she can engage her own curiosity and learn independently and from other kids, not just listen to lectures and take never-ending tests. I think many modern American teachers know that group and independent learning is important. I just have to make sure my children are put into their classrooms.

Freedom for Kids in the Land of the Free

Once I took the kids to a bagel shop, and we chose a place to sit outside. After the meal, I started to excuse myself to go to the restroom, leaving them at the table by themselves, when Sophia stopped me. "Is that allowed in America?" she asked.

"I don't know," I admitted. Still, the thought of hauling my two responsible children into the restroom with me was too ridiculous, so I risked it. Luckily, there was no concerned citizen (or worse a police officer) waiting to scold me when I returned.

When I renewed my driver's license in California, I learned that it is illegal to leave a child under six unattended in a car and that only another child who is older than twelve can supervise a younger child. In other words, I couldn't leave my nine-year-old and five-year-old alone in the car for even a few minutes. I remembered reading stories about American parents being arrested for leaving children in cars, so I dragged my kids on every errand no matter how small until Ozzie turned six. Now whenever I leave my children in the car for a few minutes, I'm more worried about some well-intentioned citizen making trouble for our family than about an evil-minded stranger snatching them. I know which one is more likely. I've already seen it in action.

I once let Ozzie sit on a bench at the park down the street from us while I biked back home two blocks to get the lunch he'd forgotten. In the five minutes that it took me to do this, an elderly woman out walking in the park stopped to question him. I returned while she was still talking to him. "Hi," I said. She gave me a disapproving glare and returned to her walk.

On most days, I bike with Ozzie to and from school. Sophia bikes on her own, usually leaving a few minutes before we do. (Ozzie is a little slower to get his stuff together.) One afternoon, Ozzie wanted to stay later after school so he could play with a friend on the playground. I waited for him at a picnic table area where some other mothers and children had gathered to meet up for an after-school club.

"Where's Sophia?" one mother asked me.

"She's at home," I said without elaborating.

"Oh, she biked there by herself?"

Other parents' heads turned.

"Yes, she's used to doing it by herself," I said. "She did it all the time in Germany."

I thought that would end it. They could dismiss me as the exotic parent who'd lived in Germany, but the mother kept pushing the point. "So is your husband home?"

"No," I said. "She's there by herself."

Before anyone could question my judgment, the mother's own daughter, a nine-year-old girl, interrupted, "No fair! You won't let me stay at home by myself until I'm twelve!"

Her mother's mouth opened and closed.

"Everybody's different," I said. The mother looked relieved.

At the time I thought I'd said the right thing, that I shouldn't contradict another parent's rules in front of her child, but on the other hand, I felt like I let that girl down. I knew her. She was in Sophia's class and very responsible. She lived even closer than we did to school and yet her mother drove her almost every day.

I don't mean to imply this mother is horrible. She is quite the opposite. She is a caring, educated, and attentive mother who would do anything for her children, but in our parenting culture, that means doing almost everything. And she wasn't alone. As my children brought friends for playdates, I could see the results of the parents who were trying so hard to do the right things for their children that they were interfering in their ability to do things for themselves. One child informed me of his attention diagnoses in one fast breath. He loved coming to our house to play, but we rarely saw him because his parents had him scheduled into an activity nearly every day after school. Then there was the little girl who couldn't think of her own ideas of what to play and kept asking me, instead of the other kids, what to do, or the other little boy who couldn't concentrate on playing—on playing!—at any one thing but kept hopping from one activity to another. Yet he was already on an organized sports team at age six. (I can only imagine how organized those games really were.)

None of my children's German friends had these problems. They usually fell right into playing from the moment they came over to the moment they left. American kids obviously didn't play the same way. Some didn't understand my children's games, which were primarily based on pretending to be things and acting out stories. "Do you want to play pretend animals?" Sophia shyly asked one girl. She looked at Sophia like she was nuts.

"Can we watch music videos?" she countered. Almost all the children who came over to play would do that at some point: ask for media, for video games, TV, music videos, or movies. I wished I could take them all and give them enough outside unstructured playtime until they figured out how to play again.

It wasn't all like this. Sophia and Ozzie both found friends who enjoyed playing like they did, at least some of the time, and there were plenty of kids who were interested in building forts in the backyard and trying out our zip line. I also heard other parents say they would like to give their children more freedom. One father commented on the fact that Ozzie and I rode our bikes every day. "When I was young, my parents would just point to our bikes and say, 'Better get going!' " he laughed. "And off we went!"

"You know you could probably let your kids do that now," I said. "It's a safe neighborhood, not a lot of traffic."

"Not in today's world," he said, and I thought he was going to warn me how there were so many dangerous child predators nowadays. Instead, he told me how his young boys like to go to the corner of the street in the morning to wave good-bye to their mom when she left for work, but people in passing cars would slow down to make sure the boys were being supervised.

My neighbor Melissa also told me that she sometimes sends her boys to the park down the street by themselves, but that other parents asked her, "How can you do that?"

Still, I was encouraged by a recent neighborhood gathering, where I met several parents who expressed a desire to get more kids out together at the park more often—usually with some parents present, but it's a start.

Like Melissa, we try to let our kids play in the park by themselves whenever there's a good opportunity. If a few more parents did the same, it would become normal, and the park would be more fun and safe for all of the kids. It just takes a tip in the right direction.

Lenore Skenazy, the founder of the free-range kids movement, says that all a parent has to do is to try it once. "You have to steel yourself to let your kid do one thing on their own, particularly if it's something you loved doing as a kid, like ride your bike to the library or walk to school," she said. That experience can be transformative—for the parent as well as the child. It's wonderful to see your child learn to do something independently for the first time. "The joy that you feel is hardwired," Skenazy said. "Just like the fear, the joy of seeing your kid grow up, succeed, blossom, mature, will surprise you. Those things are extremely powerful, and they break the grip of fear."

I already knew this joy. Before we left Germany, we had already let Sophia do a number of things by herself, from walking to school and playing in the park to buying bread at the bakery for the family.

Here in America, I let her do things by herself as much as possible. I am still beset by irrational fears of someone kidnapping her off the street, and the slightly more realistic fears that she will get lost or be hit by a car. But I've come to realize my fears have more to do with me, and the parenting culture around me, than what is best for her. She needs to learn how to navigate her world. So when she asks to do something by herself, I try to assess the real risk and her ability to handle it—and more often than not, I let her do it.

I've also seen that the simple act of letting my child have this freedom

has encouraged others. Sophia's friends have a sudden new interest in riding their bikes more, and when school started up again this last fall, there
was a whole new pack of kids in our neighborhood riding bikes by themselves to school. I can't say Sophia was the inspiration, but I'm sure it didn't
hurt to see her flying by their houses every morning and afternoon. I like
to think that as more people see this group of kids do it, it will expand and
expand until it's the norm and not the exception. While protest, activism,
and writing articles and books can have an influence, cultural change often
happens just by the actions of a few people emboldening others.

Of course, the freedom also caught on within our household. I had just
gotten used to Sophia riding through the streets of our neighborhood by
herself when Ozzie asked to walk home from school alone. *He's six—too
young!* I thought instantly. Yet here he was asking me, telling me he was
ready to try it.

We were standing on a side street near the school where many parents
parked their cars. I had to push aside the nagging worry of what the other
parents would think. It's all relative, I reminded myself. If we were in
Berlin, the other parents wouldn't bat an eyelash at the sight of even a
six-year-old walking alone. Since it was near the end of first grade, most of
the German parents would be preparing their kids to get to school by
themselves for the next year.

It was late spring and we'd gone this route at least a hundred times
together on foot and by bike. I had only driven that day because I'd had a
work appointment. It was a hot day, and Ozzie didn't want to get into the
hot car, and Sophia didn't want to walk with him.

"OK, if you think you're ready. . . ." I said.

"I'll run!" Ozzie said excitedly. "I bet I'll be home before you are." This
was a distinct possibility because we lived so close, and he could cut
through the open park on his way, while we had to go around with the car.

"But don't run when you cross a street, right? You'll be extra careful
crossing the streets?"

"Yes, I'll be super careful."

"OK, but listen," I said and leaned down near him for one last warning. "Most Americans aren't used to seeing little kids walking by them-

selves so they might say something to you. Don't let them bother you. Tell them you are walking home from school, and your mother knows where you are."

Ozzie nodded, the picture of seriousness.

And off he went. He got to the first corner, and I could already see one of the other cars slowing down by him to make sure he was all right. I got in our car with Sophia and drove slowly down the street, watching him in my rearview mirror.

"He's fine, Mom, go!" said Sophia impatiently.

I went. We arrived home before him, but he showed up a few minutes later very sweaty. He had indeed run most of the way home.

"You OK?"

"Yeah, I'm fine. Michael's mom asked me if I wanted a ride, but I said no," he told me with pride. I've told my children many times never to get in anyone's car without checking with me first, so at least this was reassuring that he knew enough to refuse—and that he stuck to his plan.

Later, that mother asked me if Ozzie was all right. She'd seen him running on the street and said he looked scared. I told her he was fine, but now I was worried again. Maybe it was too early to try? Was he terrified?

He didn't say anything about walking home again for a while. Then a couple weeks later, he asked to walk home again. I let him. When he arrived this time, he announced, "I wasn't even scared this time!"

"You were scared before?" I asked.

"Yeah, I was a little scared at first when I was all by myself, but then I saw that nothing bad was going to happen. This time it was easy."

Boom. There was the joy. My six-year-old had just reminded me what learning *selbständigkeit*, real independence, was all about. It wasn't about my child never being afraid when trying a new thing. It was about feeling that fear and doing it anyway. Ozzie hadn't just walked home by himself. He'd faced a personal challenge and conquered it. He'd taken a major step toward growing up.

EPILOGUE

German Lessons

From the moment my first child was born, I wondered who she would become, what kind of person she would be. I also felt this awesome responsibility. I couldn't believe someone had let us out of the hospital with this tiny creature who only knew how to eat, sleep, poop, and scream if any of those things didn't happen in the right way—and somehow we were supposed to teach her how to become a real human being. I was so afraid I would screw her up royally.

I overestimated my influence. If there is any relief to be found in these pages, it should be that we, as parents, are not in control of our children's lives. Sure, there are things we can do that will hurt them, but if we've got the basics down—love, food, shelter, and some general guidance—that's all that's required. Our children will do the rest of the growing up all by themselves.

The biggest lesson I learned in Germany is that my children are not really mine. They belong first and foremost to themselves. I already knew this intellectually, but when I saw parents in Germany put this value into practice, I saw how differently I was acting. I often treated my children, even as they grew older and more capable, as beings who needed to be constantly supervised—and, in effect, controlled. I lectured and pushed them until they would behave the way I wanted them to, so that they would do what I wanted them to. I yelled "Achtung!" way too often.

Once I started to treat my children as individuals, growing and coming into their own, it changed the way I viewed my role as a mother. I'm still a source of love and support, but rather than being an "authority"—an enforcer of all rules and teacher of all things—now I try to act as more of a guide and a helper. I also try to make space for the many other people they can learn from: other family members, child-care givers, school teachers, friends, and neighbors.

I've been actively trying to step back more and more as they get older, even though this requires pushing back against my culture that still assumes that I, as their mother, should be the "primary caregiver." This is a particularly hard thing to do as a woman. Motherhood has been both a source of power and a prison for us: in the past, the home was where women ruled, and slaved, and where we were given the great responsibility of bringing up children. Feminist activism has expanded women's rights and our role in the workforce, but it hasn't changed our roles as mothers all that much.

While many mothers wish for more equity in parenting, it's tough to let go of the power that role also gives us. Many men will acquiesce nearly all parenting decisions and care to their wives. Indeed, some American fathers are working such long hours, they are barely present in their families' lives, except on weekends. I know a lot of men who strive to have a greater role in their children's lives, and things are changing slowly.

If we want to make things better for our children, we need to start making things better for ourselves, for parents. We need to push for better policies: universal preschool, subsidized child care, school policies that allow more play in school and don't allow school work to creep into family time. Even more than that, we need to push our politicians and employers for benefits that Germans, and frankly the rest of the developed world, take as rights: paid parental leave, work hours that don't extend into evenings and weekends, and a guaranteed amount of sick and vacation days. We simply need more time to be families.

This is not just for parents now, but for our children, so that we can create a better world for them when they grow up. I think a good piece of our anxiety around academic achievement is that having a middle-class income isn't enough to make it in the United States anymore. We fear that if our children aren't extremely successful, they won't enjoy a good quality of life and will have to struggle their entire lives. Americans now work more hours than any of our peers in the Western world. Our Puritan work ethic and capitalist value of competition has gotten so out of hand that work has subsumed almost everything else.

I remember sitting in a café meeting with a potential client, a young woman from South Africa who worked at a large international start-up based in Berlin. She told me she had lived in the States but didn't like it at all. I was taken aback. Not like America? I'd just assumed that the United States would be the number-one destination for any immigrant around the world, especially young people. "Why not?" I asked her.

"I couldn't stand that whole 'work is life' thing. You are defined by what you do for a job," she said. "You work evenings, weekends. There's so little vacation."

At home in the United States, benefits like a guaranteed four weeks of vacation sound virtually impossible to achieve, but when you go abroad and talk to people from other countries, you realize it is possible. In fact they see such breaks from work as normal, even necessary to enjoying life. Sure, it will take a sustained political and social effort to make it happen, but the first step is a simple shift in values: to place something other than a job at the center of our assessment of what makes a good life.

If we can remove the heavy weight of the "work is life" value, it will remove a lot of the pressure in our parenting. We can let our children grow and learn what they are interested in—a surer path to a fulfilling life than one focused on just learning what will fit the career path we've picked for them.

But an even bigger step would be to reduce our parental power in general—to give over the main control of raising children to the people it belongs to the most: our children themselves.

The Rights of Children

Researchers in child development tend to lump parents in Western societies together as valuing "independence" in raising their children, as opposed to other cultures, often in the developing world, which place a higher value on interrelatedness—meaning children's obedience to their elders and connectedness to their community are more important than their autonomy. Parents in many of those cultures don't rely on parenting books. As the German cultural psychologist Bettina Lamm pointed out to me, adults in these places often learn parenting skills from their own parents and grandparents. This doesn't happen as much in Western cultures anymore. We tend to break from previous generations. (Take a moment, and think what happens when your mother or your mother in law tells you how to raise your kids.) Instead, parents try to learn from books and peers.

And I think we can learn something from our peers in Germany. As I've said earlier, German culture is not monolithic. The psychologist Heidi Keller would probably argue with many of the assumptions I've made about German parenting culture (politely, of course—she is a lovely person to talk to). She co-wrote a chapter with Hiltrud Otto titled "Is There Such a Thing as German Parenting?" in which they point out, among other things, that so many influences are affecting German parents that it's hard to pick out one approach to raising children that is distinctly German.

The United States is no doubt one of these influences. Our culture sits heavily on cultures all over the world, and its presence is obvious in Germany. Our movies, music, and even our consumer culture are everywhere. I once asked my language partner, Kordula, why so many Berlin stores had English names: "Because it's the language of America, and America is the land of shopping!" she said.

Our overparenting trend has also made inroads into German culture as well, and helicopter-eltern can be found there too. They are not prevalent in Berlin, and Rainer Becker of Kinderhilfe insists such parents are in the minority in Germany. My friend Taska recently sent me an article from *Der Spiegel* decrying the rise of helicopter parenting. The article tells parents to give responsibility back to their children, to let them play on their own, to get them outside and away from computers, and to stop overscheduling them with team activities and organized playdates. It reads like a free-range parenting article you might find on an American blog, only with one significant difference: the author is not a parenting activist but a teacher. He's part of the official, mainstream world that governs the education of children, and that official world is strongly in favor of raising children with self-reliance and independence. There is no surrounding culture of control in Germany.

As I researched this book, I realized that a lot of the differences I'd noticed in Germany around raising children had to do with the fact that Germans believe children have rights—or more precisely, Germans believe children have more rights than Americans are willing to give their children. The rights of children are encoded into German law and in the everyday actions of ordinary people.

I've met many German parents who expressed the same anxieties Americans have over how best to raise their kids and keep them safe. Whenever I told them about how brave I thought German parents were to let their children go around unsupervised, I was met with surprise.

"Really?" said one mother I'd met at kita. "I thought we watched our children too carefully!"

Annekatherin, the mother who let her two children take the subway to their grandmother's house, used strong language to describe how she felt about them doing so: "I hate it," she said. Yet she let her kids do it anyway because she felt her children had the right to learn how to move about in their world.

In America, we've let our worries over kids' safety and future eclipse our children's most fundamental rights. The United States is the only country in the world that has not ratified the United Nations' Convention on the Rights of the Child (CRC). The opposition to the CRC has come primarily from "parents' rights" groups. Never mind that ratifying the CRC will do nothing to change U.S. law—it's an aspirational document, and countries with much more restrictive cultures, such as Saudi Arabia and China, have ratified it—look at the central objection these parent groups have against the CRC: they feel that giving children rights would deprive them of their own power as parents over their children.

These groups name specific rights they find alarming such as a child's right to express their own religious beliefs and the right for children to have leisure (which I guess means they want to make sure their children are working all the time, whether in school or out). The parents' rights groups also worry that the CRC's statements about "the right of the child to protection from corporal punishment and other cruel or degrading forms of punishment" means they cannot spank their children.

I'm willing to bet many of these same American parents have flags in their yards and believe strongly in the idea of freedom and in raising responsible, respectful children. Yet there's an essential conflict between these ideals and a parenting style that doesn't respect the rights of children. We cannot raise free and responsible children by trying to restrict what they think and believe, and beating them for misbehavior. We raise free and responsible children by giving them freedom and responsibility. Likewise, teaching children real respect for others, as opposed to the facsimile of respect meant to avoid punishment, requires first treating our children with respect.

You can find a lot of practical ways to give children more physical freedom in this book, such as by leaving your baby alone when she is happy, sending children outside every day, and giving them time to play without parents hovering. You can send your school-age child to the store by himself, or let her walk or bike to school with friends—all of these things are great. However, none of these activities will create confident, self-reliant children if we don't first see our children as growing people with rights, not as beings we should control. If you want to parent like a German (or, if that hurts your patriotism, like a true freedom-loving American), you should start with a foundation that values children's rights.

Freedom of Ideas

Perhaps the hardest thing to do is to give our growing children intellectual and spiritual freedom. We all want to raise children to become adults who hold the same values as we do, but no matter what we do, there is no guarantee that they will. Imposing our own belief systems on our children is likely to backfire, causing them to rebel, or may permanently damage our relationships with them as adults.

Do you think exactly like your parents do? On every topic? There's a good reason it's a cultural cliché to never discuss politics or religion at Thanksgiving dinner. Some of the most diverse and conflicting ideas are found among members of immediate families. So why then do we hang on to the practice of trying to mold our children into smaller versions of ourselves?

As parents, we can exercise an enormous amount of power over our children if we want to. We have physical, legal, and financial control over their lives for quite some time. If we misuse that power to try to force them to think the way we do, or do exactly what we want, our children may not forgive us when they get older.

"I'm looking at the long-term picture," the German father Axel told me. "I'm looking at me at eighty. How do I want my kids to be with me? I'm not talking about them taking care of me when I'm fragile . . . but the emotional connection to them."

With two teenage children just a few years from adulthood, Axel realizes that they will soon have their own lives, and other people and activities will become more important to them than their parents. Still, he would want them to know that he is always there for them, without judgment. "I would love for them to have that connection that if they have problems or find themselves in a really bad situation, they know they can come back and not have me say, 'Oh, I told you so,'" he said.

I like Axel's vision of the parent-child relationship, which builds respect and trust to last a lifetime. I hope I can do this with my children as well. I no longer expect to raise children who will agree with me. I know many adults who spend most of their lives working in a profession chosen by their parents or trying to overcome guilt for not living up to a parent's expectations. I do not want to do that to my children. I want to support them to grow into the people they want to be.

It has been a decade now since my first child was born. I still don't know what kind of adults either of my children will become, but I have seen some trends. Both children are adventurous and curious, two qualities Zac and I are happy to encourage.

Sophia is still "a sunshine girl," a peace maker who gets along with most people. She is also a creator and loves to make things. She is constantly drawing, painting, sewing, and using whatever materials she can get her hands on to make all kinds of things. She's told me she wants to be an artist and live near the beach in Santa Cruz. I smile at this and let her dream—I don't see a need to discourage her with the realities of artists' paychecks and the price of California beachfront property. Besides, who knows? Things could change by the time she's twenty-three.

For Ozzie, I see a certain tenacity in him —a stick-to-it quality that I've tried to stop calling stubbornness. Ultimately I think it will serve him well in life. He's the kind of kid who can concentrate on one topic for a long time but can't remember to put his clothes on right side out and front side forward. Right now, one of his main obsessions is Vietnam, an interest he chose for himself when he discovered a love of Vietnamese food in Berlin. (He was won over by a dish of crispy duck and a glass of sweet mango lassi.) For some reason, he wants to learn everything about the country he can, including the language. So far, he's taught himself how to say hello and a few numbers. In keeping with our effort to be honest about the past, we've told him the basics of the Vietnam War, but that hasn't dampened his enthusiasm.

I wonder sometimes if his Vietnam fascination will be a passing phase, like the way some kids are fascinated by dinosaurs for months, then find something else, but it has been over a year since this obsession started. Perhaps he'll be on to the next thing soon, or maybe I'm raising a future ambassador to Vietnam. I don't know. He also still likes rattlesnakes.

For now, I'm letting both my children roll with whatever interests them. Zac and I certainly won't tell them they need to be doctors or lawyers, or even writers and scientists like their mom and dad. Instead, we'll try to support them in their choices as much as possible. After all, it will be their lives to live.

Bibliography

ABA Fachverband. "Das Abenteuerspielplatz-Urteil." 2008. http://www.aba-fachverband.org/fileadmin/user_upload_2008/recht/TD_01_Auflage7_ASP-Urteil_IN.pdf.

Ahnert, Lieslotte, Michael E. Lamb, and Katrin Seltenheim. "Infant–Care Provider Attachments in Contrasting German Child Care Settings." *Infant Behavior and Development* 23, no. 2 (2000): 197–209.

Aktion Jugendschutz. "Toy Free Kindergarten." Accessed October 13, 2016. http://www.spielzeugfreierkindergarten.de/fr_engl.html.

Albert, Mathias, Klaus Hurrelmann, and Gudrun Quenzel, in cooperation with TNS Infratest Social Research. *The 17th Shell Youth Study.* Hamburg: Deutsche Shell Holding GmbH, October 2015.

Albes, Jens. "Damit Spielen nur Spaß macht: Firma prüft Schaukeln und Gerüste auf Spielplätzen." Deutsche Press-Agentur (DPA) on T-Online, January 14, 2013.

Allen, Taylor Ann. "Children Between Private and Public Worlds: The Kindergarten and Public Policy in Germany 1840–present," in *Kindergartens and*

Cultures: The Global Diffusion of an Idea, edited by Roberta Wollons, 16–41. New Haven: Yale University Press, 2000.

Allensbach Institut. "Einstellungen und Lebensbedingungen von Familien 2009." Bundesministerium für Familie, Senioren, Frauen, und Jugend, 2009. http://www.ifd-allensbach.de/uploads/tx_studies/7407_Monitor_Familienleben_2009.pdf.

Alpers, Philip and Marcus Wilson. *Germany—Gun Facts, Figures and the Law*. Sydney School of Public Health, The University of Sydney. GunPolicy.org, October 13, 2016. http://www.gunpolicy.org/firearms/region/germany.

—*United States—Gun Facts, Figures and the Law*. Sydney School of Public Health, The University of Sydney. GunPolicy.org, June 20, 2016. http://www.gunpolicy.org/firearms/region/united-states.

American College Health Association. *American College Health Association–National College Health Assessment II: Reference Group Undergraduates Executive Summary*. Spring 2013. Hannover, MD: American College Health Association, 2013. http://www.acha-ncha.org/docs/ACHA-NCHA-II_UNDERGRAD_Reference Group_ExecutiveSummary_Spring2013.pdf.

ARD-DeutschlandTrend. "Ostdeutsche haben mehr Angst vor Flüchtlingen." September 3, 2014. https://www.tagesschau.de/inland/deutschlandtrend-395.html.

ASP Forcki. "Informationen zum Abenteuerspielplatz ASP." Accessed October 17, 2016. http://www.forcki.de.

Barros, R. M., E. J. Silver, and R. E. Stein. "123, no. 2 (2009): 431–6.

Bassok, D., S. Latham, and A. Rorem. "Is Kindergarten the New First Grade?" *AERA Open*, 1(4), 2016: 1–31. doi: 0.1177/2332858415616358.

Berwick, Carly. "The Great German School Turnaround," *The Atlantic*, November 3, 2015.

Bittner, Jochem. "Günter Grass's Germany, and Mine." *The New York Times*, April 14, 2015. http://www.nytimes.com/2015/04/15/opinion/gunter-grasss-germany-and-mine.html.

Blass, Simone. "Wenn plötzlich ein Fremder im Badezimmer steht," *T-online*, June 24, 2016. http://www.t-online.de/eltern/erziehung/id_18919842/erster-freund-wenn-ploetzlich-ein-fremder-im-badezimmer-steht.html.

Browning, Christopher. *Ordinary Men. Reserve Police Battalion 101 and the Final Solution in Poland.* New York: Harper Collins, 1992.

Brussoni, M., R. Gibbons, C. Gray, T. Ishikawa, E. Sandseter, A. Bienenstock, G. Chabot, P. Fuselli, S. Herrington, I. Janssen, W. Pickett, M. Power, N. Stanger, M. Sampson, and M.S. Tremblay. "What Is the Relationship Between Risky Outdoor Play and Health in Children? A Systematic Review." *International Journal of Environmental Research and Public Health* 12, no. 6 (2015): 6423–54. doi: 10.3390/ijerph120606423.

Bundeszentrale fuer Politische Bildung (BPB). "Foundation and Development 1952–1961." November 5, 2012. http://www.bpb.de/die-bpb/148017/foundation-and-development-1952-1961.

Buonanno, Paulo, and Francesco Drago. "How Much Should We Trust Crime Statistics? A Comparison Between UE and US." LIEPP Working Paper 19 Paris: Sciences Po./LIEPP, February 2014. https://spire.sciencespo.fr/hdl:/2441/f6h8764e-nu2lskk9p48i5a4sj/resources/wp-19.pdf.

Bureau of Justice Statistics. "Sexual Assault of Young Children as Reported to Law Enforcement: Victim, Incident, and Offender Characteristics." U.S. Department of Justice, 2000.

Bureau of Labor Statistics. "Labor Force Statistics from the Current Population Survey." Household Data, Annual Averages. Last modified: February 10, 2016. http://www.bls.gov/cps/cpsaat11.htm.

—*Occupational Outlook Handbook: 2016–17 Edition, Childcare Workers.* U.S. Department of Labor. http://www.bls.gov/ooh/personal-care-and-service/childcare-workers.htm.

—"Volunteering in the United States, 2015." February 25, 2016. http://www.bls.gov/news.release/volun.nr0.htm.

BzgA. "Aktuelle BZgA-Studie zeigt Trendwende beim Rauschtrinken junger Männer—Alkoholkonsum bei jungen Menschen aber weiterhin zu hoch." June 30, 2015. http://www.bzga.de/presse/pressemitteilungen/?nummer=996.

—"Jugendsexualität 2015: Erste Ergebnisse." November 12, 2015. Accessed October 16, 2016. http://www.forschung.sexualaufklaerung.de/4923.html.

Carlsson-Paige, Nancy, Geralyn Bywater McLaughlin, and Joan Wolfsheimer Almon. "Reading Instruction in Kindergarten: Little to Gain and Much to Lose."

Defending the Early Years/Alliance for Childhood. 2015. https://deyproject.files. wordpress.com/2015/01/readinginkindergarten_online-1.pdf.

Carlsson-Paige, Nancy. *Taking Back Childhood.* New York: Penguin, 2009.

CBS News. "Nasty Girl Still at Work." April 3, 2000. http://www.cbsnews.com /news/nasty-girl-still-at-work.

Centers for Disease Control and Prevention. "Attention Deficit/Hyperactivity Disorder: Data and Statistics." http://www.cdc.gov/ncbddd/adhd/data.html.

—"Fact Sheets Underage Drinking." October 20, 2016. http://www.cdc.gov/alcohol/fact-sheets/underage-drinking.htm.

—"Infant Mortality." Updated September 28, 2016. http://www.cdc.gov/repro ductivehealth/maternalinfanthealth/infantmortality.htm.

—"New Findings From CDC Survey Suggest Too Few Schools Teach Prevention of HIV, STDs, Pregnancy," news release, December 9, 2015. http://www.cdc. gov/nchhstp/newsroom/2015/nhpc-press-release-schools-teaching-prevention. html.

—"Pregnancy Mortality Surveillance System." Updated January 21, 2016. http://www.cdc.gov/reproductivehealth/maternalinfanthealth/pmss.html.

Chen, Alice, Emily Oster, and Heidi Williams. "Why Is Infant Mortality Higher in the U.S. than in Europe?" National Bureau of Economic Research (NBER) Working Paper 20525, September 2014. http://www.nber.org/papers/w20525. pdf.

The Chronicle of Higher Education. "Today's Anguished Students—and How to Help Them." Fall 2015.

Clements, Rhonda. "An Investigation of the Status of Outdoor Play." *Contemporary Issues in Early Childhood* 5, no.1 (2004): 68–80.

Cohen, Roger. "The World; The Germans Want Their History Back." *New York Times,* September 12, 1999. http://www.nytimes.com/1999/09/12/weekinreview /the-world-the-germans-want-their-history-back.html.

Cohn, D'vera, and Andrea Caumont. "Seven Key Findings About Stay-at-Home Moms." Pew Research Center, April 8, 2014. http://www.pewresearch.org/fact-tank/2014/04/08/7-key-findings-about-stay-at-home-moms.

Conlon, Kevin. "Oklahoma Bill Would Make AP U.S. History History." CNN, February 19, 2015. http://www.cnn.com/2015/02/18/us/oklahoma-ap-history.

Cooper, Herbert, Jorgianne Civey Robinson, and Erica A. Patall. "Does Homework Improve Academic Achievement? A Synthesis of Research, 1987–2003." *Review of Educational Research* 76, no. 1. (2006): 1–62.

Cynkar, Peter, and Cynthia English. "Fewer Report Depression in Germany Than in U.S., UK." Gallup. November 23, 2011. http://www.gallup.com/poll/150944/fewer-report-depression-germany.aspx.

Daily Mail Reporter. "US Teens Worst in Western World for Binge-Drinking, Drugs, and Violent Deaths," *Daily Mail*, April 25, 2012. http://www.dailymail.co .uk/news/article-2135057/U-S-teens-worst-western-world-binge-drinking-drugs-violent-deaths.html#ixzz2aXNBSKAh%20.

Dearden, Lizzie. "German Police Forced to Ask Public to Stop Bringing Donations for Refugees Arriving by Train," *The Independent UK*, September 1, 2015. http://www. independent.co.uk/news/world/europe/german-police-forced-to-ask-public-to-stop-bringing-donations-for-refugees-arriving-by-train-10481522.html.

Der Spiegel. "Goldhagen—ein Quellentrickser?" *Der Spiegel* 33, August 8, 1997. http://www.spiegel.de/spiegel/print/d-8758240.html.

—"Three Killed in Explosion of World War II Bomb in Germany," *Spiegel Online*, June 2, 2010. http://www.spiegel.de/international/germany/routine-disposal-goes-wrong-three-killed-in explosion-of-world-war-ii-bomb-in-germany a-698245.html.

DeStatis Statistisches Bundesamt. "Bewolkerung." https://www.destatis.de/DE /ZahlenFakten/GesellschaftStaat/Bevoelkerung/Bevoelkerung.html.

—"Elterngeld regional: Höchste Väterbeteiligung in der thüringischen Stadt Jena." Pressemitteilung Nr. 357, October 6, 2016. https://www.destatis .de/DE/PresseService/Presse/Pressemitteilungen/2016/10/PD16_357_22922. html.

Deutsche Kinderhilfe. "Sicher zur Schule!" Accessed October 14, 2016. http://www. kindervertreter.de/downloads/DKH-Sicherer-Schulweg.pdf.

Deutsche Press Agentur. "Ausgehen—aber wie lange? Das sagt das Jugendschutzgesetz," on T-online, December 30, 2014. http://www.t-online.de/eltern/jugendliche

/id_18117010/jugendschutzgesetz-2014-so-lange-duerfen-jugendliche-ausgehen. html.

—"Sexualaufklärung: So sage ich es meinem Kind," on *Berlin.de,* February 6, 2014. http://www.berlin.de/special/familien/3292643-2864562-sexualaufklaerung-so-sage-ich-es-meinem-.html.

Deutsches Jugend Institute. "Kinderbetreuung," DJI Online, May 29, 2013. Updated January 20, 2016. http://www.dji.de/index.php?id=43414.

Doege, Paula and Heidi Keller. "Child-Rearing Goals and Conceptions of Early Childcare from Young Adults' Perspective in East and West Germany." *International Journal of Adolescence and Youth*, June 18, 2012.

The Economist. "German-Americans: The Silent Minority," February 7, 2015. http://www.economist.com/news/united-states/21642222-americas-largest-ethnic-group-has-assimilated-so-well-people-barely-notice-it.

European Commission. "European Youth: Participation in Democratic Life." Flash Eurobarometer 375, European Commission, May 2013. http://ec.europa.eu /youth/library/reports/flash375_en.pdf.

Eurosafe. "Injuries in the European Union: Summary of injury statistics from 2010–2012." Amsterdam: 2014. http://www.eurosafe.eu.com/uploads/inline-files /IDB_Report_2014_final%202010-2012.pdf.

Eurostat. "Share of Young Adults Aged 18–34 Living With Their Parents by Age and Sex—EU-SILC Survey." Last update October 16, 2016. http://appsso.eurostat. ec.europa.eu/nui/show.do?dataset=ilc_lvps08&lang=en.

Faiola, Anthony. "For Refugees, It's Destination Germany," *Washington Post*, September 5, 2015.

File, Thom. "Young-Adult Voting: An Analysis of Presidential Elections, 1964–2012." Current Population Survey Reports P20-572. Washington, DC: U.S. Census Bureau, 2013. https://www.census.gov/prod/2014pubs/p20-573.pdf.

Fry, Richard. "For First Time in Modern Era Living with Parents Edges Out Other Living arrangements for 18- to 34-year-olds." Pew Research Center. May 24, 2016. Accessed October 16, 2016. http://www.pewsocialtrends.org/2016/05/24 /for-first-time-in-modern-era-living-with-parents-edges-out-other-living-arrangements-for-18-to-34-year-olds.

Gensicke, Thomas, and Sabine Geiss. "Hauptbericht des Freiwilligensurveys 2009." *Zivilgesellschaft, soziales Kapital und freiwilliges Engagement in Deutschland 1999–2004.* Berlin: Bundesministerium für Familie, Senioren, Frauen, und Jugend, 2009.

German education server. "Primary Sector—Organisation and Structure." The German Institute for International Educational Research (DIPF). http://www.eduserver.de/zeigen_e.html?seite=558.

Gershoff, Elizabeth T., and Andrew Grogan-Kaylor. "Spanking and Child Outcomes: Old Controversies and New Meta-analyses." *Journal of Family Psychology,* 30(4), June 2016, 453–69.

Gibbons, Luz, Jose M. Belizan, Jeremy A. Lauer, Ana P. Betra, Mario Merialdi, and Fernando Althabe. "The Global Numbers and Costs of Additionally Needed and Unnecessary Caesarean Sections Performed per Year: Overuse as a Barrier to Universal Coverage." *World Health Report 2010.* World Health Organization. http://www.who.int/healthsystems/topics/financing/healthreport/30C-section costs.pdf.

Global Initiative to End Corporal Punishment for All Children. "Country Report for USA." July 2016. http://www.endcorporalpunishment.org/progress/country-reports/usa.html.

Glynn, Sarah Jane. "Fact Sheet: Child Care." Center for American Progress, August 16, 2012. https://www.americanprogress.org/issues/labor/news/2012/08/16/11978/fact-sheet-child-care.

Goldhagen, Daniel. *Hitler's Willing Executioners: Ordinary Germans and the Holocaust.* New York: Alfred A. Knopf, 1996.

Grass, Günter. *Two States—One Nation? Against the Unthinking Clamor for German Unification,* Translated and annotated by Krishna Winston with A.S. Wensinger. San Diego: Harcourt Brace Jovanovich, 1990.

Gray, Peter. "The Decline of Play and the Rise of Psychopathology," *American Journal of Play* 3, no. 4 (2011): 443–63.

—*Free to Learn.* New York: Basic Books, 2013.

Grossmann, Karin, Klaus Grossmann, Gottfried Spangler, Gerhard Suess, and Lothar Unzner. "Maternal Sensitivity and Newborns' Orientation Responses as Related to Quality of Attachment in Northern Germany," *Monographs of the*

Society for Research on Child Development 50, no. 1/2. Growing Points of Attachment Theory and Research (1985): 233–56.

The Harris Poll. "Four in Five Americans Believe Parents Spanking Their Children Is Sometimes Appropriate." September 26, 2013. http://www.theharrispoll.com/health-and-life/Four_in_Five_Americans_Believe_Parents_Spanking_Their_Children_is_Sometimes_Appropriate.html.

Hays, Sharon. *The Cultural Contradictions of Motherhood*. New Haven: Yale University Press, 1996.

Himmelrath, Armin. *Hausaufgaben? Nein Danke!* Bern: hep Verlag, 2015.

Hopkins, J. Roy. "The Enduring Influence of Jean Piaget," *The Observer*, December 11, 2011. http://www.psychologicalscience.org/index.php/publications/observer/2011/december-11/jean-piaget.html.

Huss M., H. Hölling, BM Kurth, and R. Schlack. "How Often Are German Children and Adolescents Diagnosed With ADHD?" *European Child Adolescent Psychiatry* 17, Supplement 1 (2008): 52–8. doi: 10.1007/s00787-008-1006-z.

Hyman, Mark. *Until It Hurts: America's Obsession With Youth Sports and How It Harms Our Kids*. Boston: Beacon Press, 2009.

Isensee, Laura. "How Textbooks Can Teach Different Versions of History," NPR, July 13, 2015. http://www.npr.org/sections/ed/2015/07/13/421744763/how-textbooks-can-teach-different-versions-of-history.

Juster, F. Thomas, Hiroi Ono, and Frank P. Stafford. "Changing Times of American Youth: 1981–2003." Institute for Social Research, University of Michigan, Ann Arbor, 2004. http://www.umich.edu/news/Releases/2004/Nov04/teen_time_report.pdf.

Katholische Nachrichten-Agentur. "Kirchensteuer einahmen der kirchen 2015 auf rekordniveau," *Der Tagesspiegel*, June 22, 2016. http://www.tagesspiegel.de/weltspiegel/kirchensteuer-einnahmen-der-kirchen-2015-auf-rekordniveau/13769240.html.

Kaye, K., K. Suellentrop, and C. Sloup. *The Fog Zone: How Misperceptions, Magical Thinking, and Ambivalence Put Young Adults at Risk for Unplanned Pregnancy*. Washington, D.C.: The National Campaign to Prevent Teen and Unplanned Pregnancy, 2009.

Konnikova, Maria. "Youngest Kid, Smartest Kid?" *The New Yorker,* September 19, 2013.

Konrad v. Germany. European Court of Human Rights (HUDOC) fifth section. App no. 35504/03 (2006). http://hudoc.echr.coe.int/eng?i=001-76925.

Landis, Jacquelyn. *The Germans.* San Francisco: Thomson Gale, 2006.

Largo, Remo. *Babyjahre.* Munich: Piper, 2003.

LeVine, Robert L. "Attachment Theory as Cultural Ideology," in *Different Faces of Attachment,* edited by Hiltrud Otto and Heidi Keller, 50–65. Cambridge: Cambridge University Press, 2014.

Lopez, Shane and Valerie J. Calderon. "U.S. Youth Say They Will Be Better Off Than Their Parents." Gallup. January 30, 2013. http://www.gallup.com/poll /160166/youth-say-better-off-parents.aspx.

Louv, Richard. *Last Child in the Woods.* Chapel Hill: Algonquin Books of Chapel Hill, 2008.

Lythcott-Haims, Julie. *How to Raise an Adult.* New York: Henry Holt and Co., 2015.

de Maizière, Thomas "Bundesinnenminister de Maizière gibt aktuelle Flüchtling- szahlen bekannt." September 30, 2016. http://www.bmi.bund.de/SharedDocs /Pressemitteilungen/DE/2016/09/asylsuchende-2015.html?nn=3315588.

McDonald, Noreen, Austin L. Brown, Lauren M. Marchetti, and Margo S. Pedroso. "U.S. School Travel, 2009: An Assessment of Trends." *American Journal of Preventative Medicine* 41, no. 2 (2011): 146–51.

Mehta, Sarah. "There's Only One Country That Hasn't Ratified the Convention on Children's Rights: US," American Civil Liberties Union, November 20, 2015. https://www.aclu.org/blog/speak-freely/theres-only-one-country-hasnt-ratified- convention-childrens-rights-us.

Merkel, Angela. "Sommerpressekonferenz von Bundeskanzlerin Merkel." August, 31, 2015. http://www.bundeskanzlerin.de/Content/DE/Mitschrift/Pressekon ferenzen/2015/08/2015-08-31-pk-merkel.html.

Michaels, Claudia. "Die Gründerin der Kinderläden," *Frankfurter Rundshau,*

May 2, 2014. http://www.fr-online.de/frankfurt/kinderlaeden-frankfurt-die-gruenderin-der-kinderlaeden,1472798,27014196.html.

Milhofer, Petra, and Andreas Gluszczynski. *"Sexualerziehung . . . die ankommt."* Köln: Bundeszentrale fur gesundheitliche Aufklarung (BZgA), 1999. https://www.berlin.de/sen/bildung/unterricht/faecher-rahmenlehrplaene/rahmen lehrplaene.

National Association of Scholars. "Letter Opposing the 2014 APUSH Framework." June 2, 2015. Archived at https://www.nas.org/images/documents/Historians _Statement.pdf.

National Center for Missing and Exploited Children. "Infant Abductions." Last updated September 2016. http://www.missingkids.com/InfantAbduction.

National Conference of State Legislators. "State Policies on Sex Education in Schools." February 16, 2016. http://www.ncsl.org/research/health/state-policies-on-sex-education-in-schools.aspx.

National Institute of Child Health and Development. "The NICHD Study of Early Child Care and Youth Development." National Institute of Health pub. no. 05-4318, 2006. https://www.nichd.nih.gov/publications/pubs/documents/seccyd _06.pdf.

National World War II Museum, New Orleans. "By the Numbers World-Wide Deaths." Accessed October 5, 2016. http://www.nationalww2museum.org/learn/education/for-students/ww2-history/ww2-by-the-numbers/world-wide-deaths.html.

Nattermann, Felix. "Gebt den Kindern die Verantwortung zurück," *Spiegel* Online, June 13, 2016. http://www.spiegel.de/lebenundlernen/schule/helikopter-eltern-gebt-den-kindern-mehr-verantwortung-a-1094841.html.

Organization for Economic Cooperation and Development (OECD). "Germany," in *Education at a Glance 2015*: OECD indicators. Paris: OECD Publishing. doi: 10.1787/eag-2015-57-en.

—"Country Note: United States." *Programme for International Student Assessment (PISA) Results From PISA 2012*. http://www.oecd.org/pisa/keyfindings/PISA-2012-results-US.pdf.

—"Country Note: Germany." *Programme for International Student Assessment*

(PISA) Results From PISA 2012. http://www.oecd.org/pisa/keyfindings/PISA-2012-results-germany.pdf.

— "Youth Not in Employment, Education, or Training (NEET)." 2016. doi: 10.1787/72d1033a-en.

Orosz, Marta. "Germans Opening Their Homes to Refugees," *EU Observer*, August 17, 2015. https://euobserver.com/beyond-brussels/129893.

Ottenschläger, Madlen. "Wie viel Krippe ist gut für unsere Kinder?" *Brigitte.* Accessed October 10, 2016. http://www.brigitte.de/liebe/beziehung/interview-mit-remo-largo—wie-viel-krippe-ist-gut-fuer-unsere-kinder—10129556.html.

Otto, Hiltrud, and Heidi Keller. "Is There Something Like German Parenting?" in *Contemporary Parenting: A Global Perspective*, edited by Guerda Nicolas, Anabel Bejarano, and Debbiesiu L. Lee, 81–94. New York: Routledge, 2015.

Otto, Jeanette. "Fundamentales Vertrauen," *Zeit* Online, June 14, 2012. http://www.zeit.de/2012/25/Fruehkindliche-Bindung/komplettansicht.

Ozment, Steven. *A Mighty Fortress: A New History of the German People.* New York: Harper Collins, New York, 2004.

ParentalRights.org. "20 Things You Need to Know About the U.N. Convention on the Rights of the Child." Accessed October 17, 2016. http://www.parental-rights.org/20_things.

PBS Frontline. "Innocence Lost the Plea." Accessed October 10, 2016. http://www.pbs.org/wgbh/pages/frontline/shows/innocence.

Pew Research Center. "Parents Say Kids Should Be at Least 10 to Be Alone at Home or in Public Without Adult Supervision." December 14, 2015. http://www.pewsocialtrends.org/2015/12/17/parenting-in-america/st_2015-12-17_parenting-44.

Pew Research Forum. "Faith in Flux." April 27, 2009. Revised February 2011. http://www.pewforum.org/2009/04/27/faith-in-flux.

Planned Parenthood. "Reducing Teenage Pregnancy." July 2013. https://www.plannedparenthood.org/files/6813/9611/7632/Reducing_Teen_Pregnancy.pdf.

Pondiscio, Robert. "Is Common Core Too Hard for Kindergarten?" Thomas Fordham Institute, February 11, 2015. https://edexcellence.net/articles/is-common-core-too-hard-for-kindergarten.

Preuschoff, Gisela. "Heimweh ist ganz normal," *Mobile-elternmagazine*. Accessed October 12, 2016. http://www.mobile-elternmagazin.de/kindergarten/kigazeit /details?k_onl_struktur=385561&k_beitrag=273338.

RBB/ARD. "Aktion Schulstunde zur ARD Themenwoche: Leben mit dem Tod." Accessed October 17, 2016. http://www.rbb-online.de/schulstunde-tod/fuer_leh-rer/fuer_lehrer.html.

—"Kinder vom Tod fernzuhalten ist, wie Kinder vom Leben fernzuhalten: *Interview mit Prof. Dr. Christoph Student*." *Accessed October 17, 2016*. http://www.rbb -online.de/schulstunde-tod/informationen_und/interview_mit_dr_dr_chris-toph_student.html.

Remes, O., C. Brayne, R. van der Linde, and L. Lafortune. "A Systematic Review of Reviews on the Prevalence of Anxiety Disorders in Adult Populations," *Brain and Behavior* 6, no.7 (2016). doi: 10.1002/brb3.497.

Ripley, Amanda. *The Smartest Kids in the World: And How They Got That Way*. New York: Simon & Schuster, 2013.

Robert Koch Institute. "Die Gesundheit von Kindern und Jugendlichen in Deutschland." KIGGS Studie. 2013. http://www.kiggs-studie.de/fileadmin/KiGGS-Dokumente/kiggs_tn_broschuere_web.pdf.

Robert Wood Johnson Foundation. "The State of Play: Gallup Survey of Principals on School Recess." February 1, 2010. http://www.rwjf.org/en/library/research/2010 /02/the-state-of-play.html.

Rosin, Hanna. "The Overprotected Kid," *The Atlantic*, April 2014.

Sandseter, Ellen Beate Hansen and Leif Edward Ottesen Kennair. "Children's Risky Play From an Evolutionary Perspective: The Anti-Phobic Effects of Thrilling Experiences." *Evolutionary Psychology* 9, no 2 (2011): 257–84. http://evp.sagepub. com/content/9/2/147470491100900212.full.pdf+html.

Schulze, Hagen. *Germany A New History*. Translated by Deborah Lucas Schnei-der. Cambridge, MA: Harvard University, 1998.

Schuman, Rebecca. "There's Nothing Wrong With Young Adults Living With Their Parents," Slate, June 7, 2016. http://www.slate.com/articles/life/family/ 2016/06/there_s_nothing_wrong_with_young_adults_living_with_their_par-ents.html.

Sears, William and Martha. *The Baby Book*. New York: Little, Brown and Company, 1993.

Senatsverwaltung für Bildung, Jugend und Wissenschaft, Berlin. "Rahmenlehrpläne kompakt: Themen und Inhalte des Berliner Unterrichts in der Grundschule." Accessed October 12, 2016. http://www.berlin.de/imperia/md/content/sen-bildung/unterricht/lehrplaene/rlp_kompakt_gs.pdf?start&ts=1450262874&file=rlp_kompakt_gs.pdf.

Shannon, Don. "Reagan Defends Cemetery Visit: Says German Dead Are Also Victims of Nazis," *LA Times,* April 19, 1985. http://articles.latimes.com/1985-04-19/news/mn-14900_1_concentration-camp.

Shaw Ben, Martha Bicket, Bridget Elliott, Ben Fagan-Watson, and Elisabetta Mocca. *Children's Independent Mobility: An International Comparison and Recommendations for Action*. London: Policy Studies Institute, 2015.

Shaw, Ben, B. Watson, B. Frauendienst, A. Redecker, T. Jones, with M. Hillman. *Children's Independent Mobility: A Comparative Study in England and Germany (1971–2010)*. London: Policy Studies Institute, 2013.

Skenazy, Leonore. *Free Range Kids*. San Francisco: Jossey-Bass, 2010.

Spallek, Jacob, Jessica Lehnhardt, Anna Reeske, Oliver Razum, and Matthias David. "Perinatal Outcomes of Immigrant Women of Turkish, Middle Eastern and North African Origin in Berlin, Germany: A Comparison of Two Time Periods." *Archives of Gynecology and Obstetrics* 289, no 3 (2014): 505–12.

Spanhel, Dieter. "Erziehung zur Selbständigkeit in der Familie." *Familienhandbuch,* May 30, 2001. Updated *June 24, 2014.* http://www.familienhandbuch.de/babys-kinder/bildungsbereiche/selbststaendigkeit/ErziehungzurSelbstaendigkeitinderFamilie.php.

Stop It Now! "Safety in Daycare and Education Settings." Accessed October 10, 2016. http://www.stopitnow.org/ohc-content/tip-sheet-2.

Strasser, Todd. *The Wave: The Classroom Experiment That Went Too Far*. New York: Dell-Laurel Leaf, 1981.

Suggate, Sebastian, Elizabeth A. Schaughency, and Elaine Reese. "The Contribution of Age and Reading Instruction to Oral Narrative and Pre-reading Skills," *First Language* 31, no.4 (2011): 379–403.

Taylor, Andrea Faber and Frances E. (Ming) Kuo. "Could Exposure to Everyday Green Spaces Help Treat ADHD?" *Applied Psychology Health and Well-Being* 3, no. 3 (2011): 281–303. doi: 10.1111/j.1758-0854.2011.01052.x.

Tough, Paul. *How Children Succeed.* New York: Houghton Mifflin Harcourt, 2012.

United Nations. "Convention on the Rights of the Child (CRC)." Entry into force September 2, 1990. UN Office of the High Commissioner. http://www.ohchr.org /en/professionalinterest/pages/crc.aspx.

U.S. Census Bureau. "People Reporting Ancestry." 2015 American Community Survey, one-year estimates http://factfinder.census.gov/faces/tableservices/jsf/pages /productview.xhtml.

—"School Enrollment: CPS October 2013—Detailed Tables." 2013. https://www .census.gov/hhes/school/data/cps/2013/tables.html.

U.S. Congress. "Every Student Succeeds Act" S.1177. 114th Congress (2015–2016). https://www.congress.gov/bill/114th-congress/senate-bill/1177/text.

Valentin, Stephan R. "Commentary: Sleep in German Infants—The 'Cult' of Independence," *Pediatrics* 115, Issue Supplement 1 (January 2005).

Vasagar, Jeevan. "Germany and Its Nazi Past: Forever Seeking Closure," *The Telegraph*, September 4, 2013. http://www.telegraph.co.uk/comment/10286606 /Germany-and-its-Nazi-past-forever-seeking-closure.html.

Vasilogambros, Matt. "Teaching Kids About Genocide," *The Atlantic*, June 14, 2016. http://www.theatlantic.com/news/archive/2016/06/teaching-kids-about-genocide/487088.

Warner, Judith. *A Perfect Madness: Motherhood in an Age of Anxiety.* New York: Riverhead Books, 2005.

Wolak, Janis, David Finkelhor, and Andrea J. Sedlak. "Child Victims of Stereo-typical Kidnappings Known to Law Enforcement in 2011," in *Juvenile Justice Bulletin,* U.S. Department of Justice, June 2016. http://www.ojjdp.gov/pubs /249249.pdf.

World Fact Book. "Infant Mortality Rates." Washington, D.C.: Central Intelligence Agency, 2016. Accessed October 6, 2016. https://www.cia.gov/library/publications /the-world-factbook/rankorder/2091rank.html.

World Health Organization. "Caesarean Sections Should Only Be Performed

When Medically Necessary." April 10, 2016. http://www.who.int/mediacentre /news/releases/2015/caesarean-sections/en/.

— "Maternal Mortality 1990–2015: Germany." http://www.who.int/gho/maternal_health/countries/deu.pdf?ua=1.

—"Suicide Rates (per 100,000 Population)," Global Health Observatory Data, 2012. http://www.who.int/gho/mental_health/suicide_rates/en.

Zensus 2011. "Personen nach Migrationshintergrund." https://ergebnisse.zensus 2011.de/#dynTable:statUnit=PERSON;absRel=ANZAHL;ags=00,02,01,13,03,05,0 9,14,16,08,15,12,11,10,07,06,04;agsAxis=X;yAxis— HGLAND_HLND.

Acknowledgments

Danke Schön Deutschland! It may seem odd to thank an entire country, but if Germany as a whole had not embraced a *willkommenskultur* ("welcome culture") that included my little *Ami* family, I would have learned nothing.

Specifically, I would like to thank the many people who informed this book—the experts, teachers, colleagues, parents, and friends who appear on these pages. They made the final manuscript so much richer than if it were one family's story alone. I want to be sure to express special gratitude to a few Berlin families: the Harnischfegers, the Hassmanns, the Schulers, and the Wibawas, whose friendship made Berlin an even brighter place. I had great support from members of my Berlin writers' group, in particular two fantastic and generous writers: Madhvi Ramani and Marian Ryan. I also want to acknowledge translator Jaime McGill who helped make my German-to-English translations more accurate.

Thanks to Belinda Luscombe, an editor at Time.com, for taking a chance on a new parenting writer, which resulted in the initial, wildly popular article on this topic. My friend and fellow expat Chiquira Wagner was the first to tell me I should write a book about German parenting. And *Veilen Dank* to Stefanie Chalberg, a German living in the United States— at the time a stranger to me—for picking up my article and sending it to her sister-in-law in New York City, who ultimately became my agent. She also took the time to read through the draft manuscript and give me her valuable perspective on the text as a native German.

I feel very fortunate to have Terra Chalberg as my agent. Her patience and insightful editing helped get the book proposal off the ground. I'm also grateful to my editor, Anna deVries, along with the fantastic team at Picador USA, for bringing this book to life.

Of course, none of this would have ever happened if not for my husband, Zac, who brought us to Germany in the first place, and for my two children, Sophia and Ozzie, who teach me lessons daily about the adventure of life. I love you all *unendlich*.

Index